PCWEEK
How to Implement Microsoft Windows NT Server 4

PCWEEK
How to Implement Microsoft Windows NT Server 4

John W. Taschek
Michael R. Surkan
Mark Stanczak

Ziff-Davis Press
An imprint of Macmillan Computer Publishing USA
Emeryville, California

Acquisitions Editor	Brett Bartow
Copy Editor	Candace Crane
Technical Reviewer	John Holman
Proofreader	Pamela Vevea
Cover Illustration	Regan Honda
Cover Design	Megan Gandt
Book Design	Megan Gandt
Technical Illustration	Sarah Ishida
Page Layout	M.D. Barrera
Indexer	Valerie Robbins

Ziff-Davis Press imprint books are produced on a Macintosh computer system with the following applications: FrameMaker®, Microsoft® Word, QuarkXPress®, Adobe Illustrator®, Adobe Photoshop®, Adobe Streamline™, MacLink®Plus, Aldus® FreeHand™, Collage Plus™.

Ziff-Davis Press, an imprint of
Macmillan Computer Publishing USA
5903 Christie Avenue
Emeryville, CA 94608

ISBN 1-56276-476-4

Manufactured in the United States of America
10 9 8 7 6 5 4 3 2

■ Contents at a Glance

■ Table of Contents

■ Acknowledgments

The challenge of putting this book together in two months has been an intense, grueling, sometimes maddening, but ultimately satisfying process. Our friends, family, and colleagues have had to deal with our surly attitudes and lack of time for them as we hunkered down to concentrate on writing the book, while still trying to do our regular reviews for the weekly publication of *PC Week*. Without the understanding and assistance from these people, this book could never have happened.

Specifically, Lynda Taschek managed to put up with John's late hours, crankiness, and neglect of their home. Perhaps Mark Stanczak's children will finally realize they have a dad, now that he's able to take them to hockey games.

A significant contribution to the book was also made by Michelle Campanale, whose work in generating screen images and other illustrations helped immensely.

Of course, the entire team at ZD Press deserves plaudits and recognition for their long suffering attitudes with such haughty prima donnas as ourselves. Brett Bartow took our writing delays in stride, calmly rescheduling the book without ripping our faces off each time we missed yet another deadline.

The ZD Press production staff put in a stellar performance, by dealing with the torrents of text we eventually delivered in record time. Many thanks to Carol Burbo, Valerie Perry, and Madhu Prasher. Also, special thanks goes to Candace Crane, who helped pull this whole project together and make sense of it during editing. It takes an extraordinary person to meld the work of three separate authors into one cohesive whole.

■ Preface

The advent of Windows NT has changed how network operating systems are used in many organizations. Small companies that once relied on the so-called sneaker-net to exchange files among computers now want e-mail capabilities, Internet access, and even Web publishing engines. The problem that comes to mind is one of facility: who will manage these great new projects? For the most part, Windows NT is easy enough that power users can handle many of these tasks.

But nothing can replace careful planning and execution. Companies can't afford to toy or experiment via trial and error with their mission-critical applications, and an operating system certainly falls into this class. That's where *How to Implement Microsoft Windows NT Server 4* comes in. This book logically walks those new to Windows NT through the steps of setting up and administering Windows NT Server 4. Because we can't be everything to all people, we've aimed our approach to help new administrators in small organizations.

Our book may also appeal to administrators in companies with small but autonomous departments that are just now setting up Windows NT 4 or plan on doing so in the near future. This book will give these administrators a jump-start to get their work done quickly and efficiently.

When it comes to the age of the Internet, there's no time for delays. We hope the logical organization of this book, our frequent use of notes, tips, and cautions, and our problem/solution approach to writing helps all new Windows NT administrators work better regardless of the size of their company. In fact, we're open to suggestions to make the next edition of this book even better. Our e-mail addresses appear below; feel free to contact us at any time. We wish you the best in your upcoming adventures with Windows NT.

John Taschek: john_taschek@zd.com

Mark Stanczak: mark_stanczak@zd.com

Michael Surkan: michael_surkan@zd.com

1

Introduction

- *The Legacy of Windows NT*

- *First Release*

- *The State of the NOS*

- *Our Experience with Windows NT*

1

What Is Windows NT?

In the simplest of terms, Microsoft Corporation's Windows NT Server 4 is an operating system that can function as the heart of a computing infrastructure. Like other network operating systems, Windows NT is software that controls the communication among the clients connected to it and manages a central storage repository for files and applications. The infrastructure may consist of a few connected PCs at a small company, or it may be comprised of several hundred Windows NT servers with thousands of computers connected to them. Windows NT can work in organizations of any size, as well as those that use other network operating systems and those that rely on a more centralized processing center, such as a mainframe. That's because Windows NT was created to be flexible as well as powerful.

Windows NT features fall into two key categories: those that serve users' needs for file and printer sharing, and those that run network applications. Windows NT is particularly adept in these areas, making it one of the most powerful network operating systems available. This is quite an accomplishment considering it was first released in September 1993.

Since then, the role of the network operating system has changed from one in which file and printer sharing was the main purpose to one in which the operating system is used as an application server to run high-powered network programs, such as databases. Additionally, as local area networks (LANs) have grown, demands on them have increased logarithmically. This situation highlights one of the key weaknesses of Windows NT: it does its job much better when the scale of implementation is kept in check.

■ The Legacy of Windows NT

Windows NT has a mixed history, which we've summarized in Figure 1.1, and it's helpful to review the past to better understand the product. Development of Windows NT began in 1988, only two years after Microsoft became a publicly traded company and back when MS-DOS was the most commonly used operating system for personal computers. At the time, Novell Corporation's NetWare was the most popular network operating system. To a large degree, it remains that way today.

Figure 1.1

Timeline outlining development of Windows NT

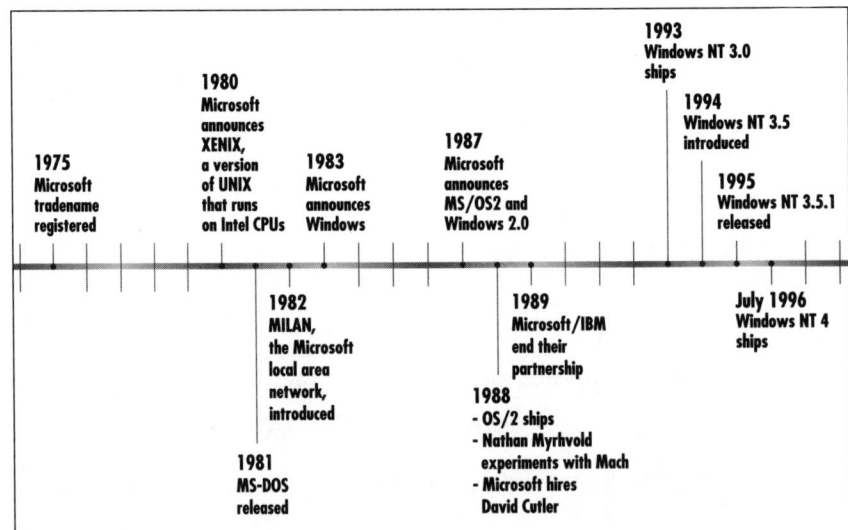

Prior to 1988, Microsoft and IBM Corporation had been working on OS/2, touted to become a DOS successor. OS/2 had many advantages over DOS; most notably it had a graphical operating system, and it used a flat memory model, which was far superior to the 640K limitation of DOS. However, because of its increased hardware requirements and lack of native applications, OS/2 did not sell well initially. A well-publicized rift between the two companies resulted in IBM taking over the marketing and development of OS/2, while Microsoft was able to keep some of the technology it developed for use in its own products.

One of the first applications for OS/2 was LAN Manager, a product developed mainly by Microsoft, with key technologies developed by 3Com Corporation and IBM, both of which became product licensees. (3Com relinquished rights to Microsoft in 1990-1991). Though LAN Manager never rose to the level of success of NetWare, which was installed from the ubiquitous DOS, LAN Manager gave Microsoft key expertise in local area networks. In fact, key parts of LAN Manager still exist in Windows NT. IBM took over most of LAN Manager development and later incorporated some of its technology into the newest versions of OS/2 and its Warp offshoot.

While this was happening, Microsoft was busy developing Windows NT, which was to be a successor to OS/2. Initially, the project was under the hand of Nathan Myhrvold, then the director of special projects, who wanted to develop an operating system that ran on a variety of processors, including Intel- and RISC-based systems. Myhrvold, who now is now a vice-president of applications and content at Microsoft, experimented with Mach, a version of the UNIX kernel that would be able to run on different processors.

Shortly afterward, Microsoft hired David Cutler, an architect of VMS, the operating system for Digital Equipment Corporation's VAX minicomputers. Prior to arriving at Microsoft, Cutler was working for Digital on an operating system to run on RISC computers, a project that Digital pulled the plug on in 1989. Ironically, Cutler was proported to be anti-UNIX; however, he and Microsoft built many of the features of UNIX into Windows NT. Cutler became the driving force behind NT, a fact that is apparent in the NT name. If you take the letters VMS and increase each letter by one, you get WNT, or Windows NT, which is rumored to be the origin of the NT name. Others say NT simply means New Technology.

■ First Release

The first version of Windows NT was released in 1993, five years after it was begun. This first product, called Windows NT 3.0 to match the version number of the desktop Windows then in use, met with lukewarm reception. Ironically, the product ran into many of the problems that plagued OS/2 when it was released.

For example, NT was considered to be resource intensive, and few applications were written for it. The product sold fewer than one-third of the 1 million copies Microsoft expected it to sell in its first year. The core components of Windows NT were intact, however, and one of the most influential operating systems had arrived. Windows NT was a 32-bit operating system designed to take advantage of the full bandwidth of the currently available processors, including those from Intel and RISC vendors. It also was multi-threaded, which means that it separated various applications and processes of individual applications into threads. These threads ran simultaneously on their own virtual machines, so that if one crashed, it only stopped the thread and not the entire operating system.

The next versions of Windows NT came rapidly: version 3.5 appeared in 1994 and version 3.51 in 1995. These versions were slimmer and faster than the original and fixed many of the problems in the first release. Version 3.5 sold more than 700,000 units, and Windows NT was off and running. In comparison, Microsoft Windows sold more than 40 million copies, but considering the number of clients connected to NT servers, the sales of NT units were remarkable.

Perhaps one of the most important features of Windows NT was the way it looked. Rather than the bleak and Spartan interfaces of the various flavors of UNIX or the blue screens of NetWare, Windows NT had a splendid user interface that looked almost exactly like the one in front of Windows 3.0. This interface allowed network administrators to manage their networks more easily than ever before.

Microsoft also decided to split Windows NT into two product lines—one geared to run networks and one to be used on a workstation. Both operating systems have significant overlap with the server version, including more advanced networking and security features. Though Windows NT Workstation can act as a work group server and even a small-scale World Wide Web (WWW) Internet server, it's mainly designed to act as a network client, and it lacks the features that raise it to the class of a Windows NT server. For one thing, Microsoft has limited its license description so no more than ten users may be attached to it at one time. In addition, the network applications that can run on a Windows NT server will not run on the workstation edition.

■ The State of the NOS

So where does this leave NT? Right now, Windows NT is platform independent and runs on Intel, millions of instructions per section (MIPS), PowerPC, and Digital Equipment's Alpha processors.

No other single operating system has this flexibility, as you can see from Figure 1.2. Applications developed for NT on a particular platform can also be ported to another platform, often with a simple recompile. Tools in NT even let developers know where to make changes in their code to allow for easier porting. This gives developers a chance to write applications for Windows NT without worrying about the internals of the hardware devices.

Figure 1.2

Flexibility and power make Windows NT a good fit into any organization.

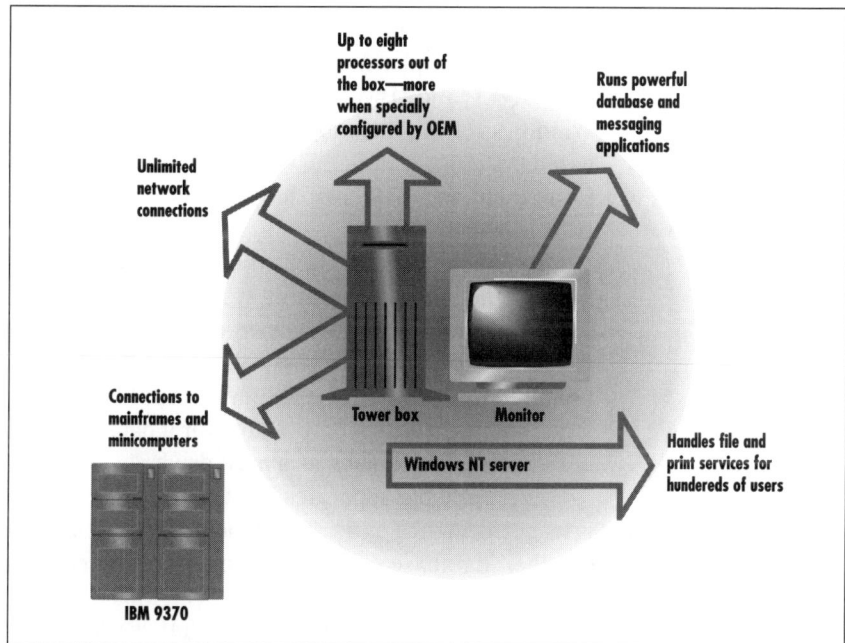

Up to eight
processors out of
the box—more
when specially
configured by OEM

Runs powerful
database and
messaging
applications

Unlimited
network
connections

Connections to
mainframes and
minicomputers

Tower box   Monitor

Windows NT server

Handles file and
print services for
hundreds of users

IBM 9370

Windows NT is also POSIX-compliant. POSIX is the only U.S. government standard specification for how applications should be compiled on different operating systems. POSIX runs at the subsystem level; thus, POSIX applications most likely will be sparse and not graphical. However, programs written to the POSIX specification on other operating systems, including those written for the mainframe, can be easily ported to NT, bringing powerful centralized applications to the newer client/server paradigm.

As mentioned before, Windows NT is an advanced file and print server capable of supporting hundreds of networked printers and thousands of gigabytes of disk storage. It is also scalable, meaning that it will generally provide better performance when used with faster hardware, especially systems that take advantage of multiprocessor architecture. In fact, out of the box, with no administrative changes to the operating system, Windows NT will scale to systems running up to eight processors.

Why is this important? It means that Windows NT can grow with companies that are growing. When a single Windows NT system hits a tableau, administrators can add new Windows NT servers to handle more users. While this introduces administrative headaches that we'll cover in this book, it also means that Windows NT can work in an organization of any size and is not limited by a theoretical maximum number of users.

Since Windows NT is designed for flexibility in the organization, it works with dozens of different client platforms over a variety of networking transports. For example, Windows NT works with Macintoshes; RISC systems running UNIX; and IBM PCs running DOS, Windows 3.1, Windows 95, or Windows NT Workstation. Likewise, it's able to communicate with host-based systems, including VAX and AS/400 minicomputers from Digital Equipment and IBM, respectively; and mainframes, such as the heavy-iron IBM 3090.

To handle the communication among the thousands of potential users running the various operating systems, Windows NT requires a powerful internal security system. The operating system supports mandatory logon and includes discretionary access control, memory protection, and auditing. Additionally, Windows NT does not allow applications to access hardware devices, making it nearly impossible for a hacker to corrupt an essential networking device, such as a hard drive.

Perhaps what separates Windows NT most from other operating systems is its performance as an application server. Companies can install and manage their database servers, their messaging servers, and most network-ready application servers from Windows NT. This means they don't have to learn two operating systems to accomplish these common network functions. Of course, this would mean nothing if Windows NT was a dog or if no applications ran on the operating system.

Quite the opposite is true. Windows NT offers performance competitive to UNIX and NetWare systems, often for a lower cost. Microsoft also has rallied developers to write new applications for Windows NT so they're often developed first for the Microsoft operating system. This makes Windows NT even more attractive.

One of the most popular applications for Windows NT Server is Microsoft BackOffice, a set of applications that actually contains a copy of Windows NT server. BackOffice consists of a computer running Microsoft Exchange Server, Microsoft SQL Server 6.5 database, and Microsoft server management software. These applications are powerful enough to get a small company up and running on Windows NT fairly easily. Companies are not limited to running these applications, however. If a company has expertise in another database server, they can find solutions from Oracle, IBM, Informix, and Sybase. Likewise, most mail servers and server management packages run on NT as well.

■ Our Experience with Windows NT

The authors of this book—Michael Surkan, Mark Stanczak, and John Taschek—have all used Windows NT since it's been available. As part of our jobs in *PC Week* Labs, we've each installed the operating system hundreds of times and set up everything from stand-alone servers to modestly sized networks with hundreds of clients attached to it. We've also been beta testers of Windows NT and have installed it on all the major computer systems from RISC boxes to Intel-based Compaq multiprocessing systems.

Still, we don't stake our careers solely on covering Windows NT. Though we work with it every day and know the ins and outs of the entire Microsoft BackOffice product line, we also cover competing operating systems. We feel this experience gives us a unique perspective on Windows NT, which we hope to convey in this book.

We'll use our knowledge of the product to cut through the chase on setting up and administering Windows NT. We're not going to sugar-coat bugs and glance over glitches we find in the product. We feel it's our duty to report to you exactly what to expect from Windows NT. We do it as part of our job at *PC Week*, and we'll do it in this book.

- *The Shell Game*
- *Easier to Use Administrative Tools*
- *Diagnostics and Monitoring*
- *Faster than Ever*
- *Internet in a Box*
- *Communications and Integration Features*

2

What's New in Version 4

W INDOWS NT 4 IS KNOWN AS THE SHELL UPDATE. BY THIS MICROSOFT means that it has totally revamped the look and feel of the product by integrating the Windows 95 graphical user interface. If you've used previous editions of Windows NT Server or Workstation, you'll be pleasantly surprised by the operating system's new interface, shown in Figure 2.1. The interface makes the server easier to manage and administer.

Figure 2.1

Windows NT now features
the Windows 95 user
interface, making it
easier to manage the and
monitor the network.

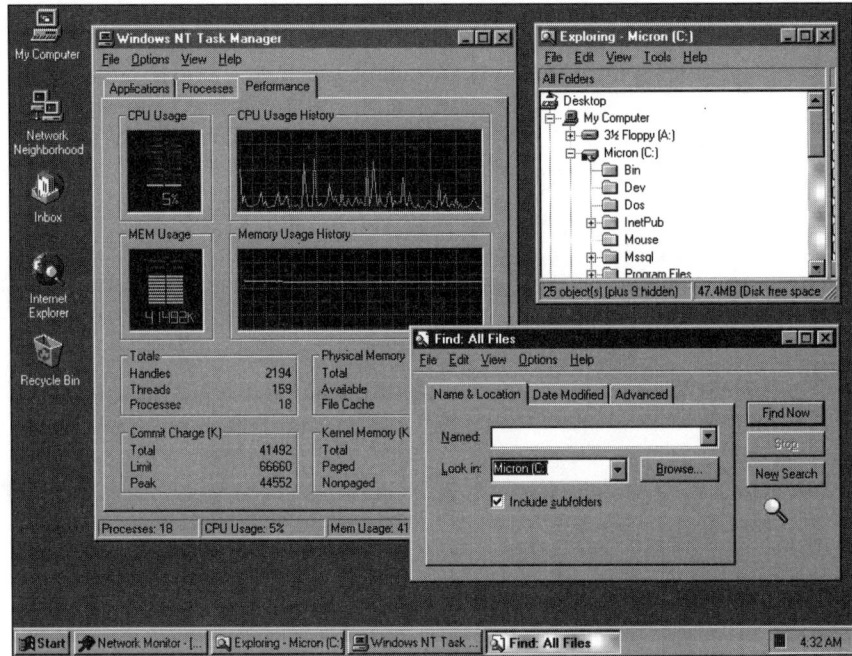

Though the appearance of Windows NT is the most apparent change in the operating system, it's not the most important. Besides superficial changes, Windows NT has gained more power, better networking integration, and it has some new Internet software that makes it easier than ever for a company to create and manage an Internet or intranet site. This chapter outlines the new features of Windows NT Server 4. In-depth information on how to use these new features is found further inside the book. So, if you're already familiar with the new features, jump ahead to the appropriate chapters. Otherwise, read on. We've broken down our coverage of what's new by topics, starting with the user interface and progressing to the new and improved features of the internal Windows NT Server architecture.

■ The Shell Game

Along with the integration of the Windows 95 interface, Windows NT Server 4 also inherits many of the accessory programs from Windows 95. The most important of these tools is Windows Explorer, an update to File Manager that makes it easier to manage the files on multiple local and network drives. Unlike File Manager, Windows Explorer shows all available drives and directories by default, making it easier to copy and move files among the directories. Subdirectories, incidentally, are now called folders, and they're designated by the folder icon. Of course, if you don't like the new Explorer or if you need a longer adjustment period, Windows NT Server still supports File Manager. Just run WinFile.

Windows NT also inherits the Windows 95 Briefcase and multimedia accessories, file-finding tools, and the Microsoft Exchange mail client. Microsoft Exchange is more flexible than the old MS-Mail; however, the Windows NT Server still supports MS-Mail, and it can be used with Internet mail as well as internal mail using MS-Mail or Microsoft Exchange servers. While we're not going to focus on the Windows NT Server's accessories (there are more important things to cover!) you can get a quick idea of what's new from Table 2.1.

Table 2.1

Windows NT Server accessory replacements

OLD ACCESSORY	WINDOWS NT 4 REPLACEMENT	COMMENT
Terminal	HyperTerminal	A modest update to the original program
*	CD Player	Plays audio CDs on systems equipped with CD-ROMs
*	Media Player	Plays CD Audio and Video for Windows files
Calculator	Calculator	Incremental update
*	Dial-Up Networking	Supports remote dial-up sessions via PPP and SLIP (for Internet access)
Paintbrush	Paint	Easier to use, but now can only save into BMP format
MS-Mail	MS-Mail	No changes, but Windows NT Server 4 also includes the Microsoft Exchange client for improved messaging
*	Internet Explorer	Version 2.0 of Microsoft World Wide Web browser
Help and Books Online	Help and Books Online	These products are vastly improved over the earlier versions
File Manager	Windows Explorer	Easier management of multiple local and network drives
*	Recycle Bin	Windows NT Server 4 now supports the Undelete command

**Table 2.1
(Continued)**

Windows NT Server
accessory replacements

OLD ACCESSORY	WINDOWS NT 4 REPLACEMENT	COMMENT
*	Briefcase	Allows easier synchronization of files between two or more systems (better run on the Windows 95 or Windows NT Workstation)

* Does not exist in this version of Windows NT Server

■ Easier to Use Administrative Tools

We've said that Windows NT Server is easier to manage than previous versions. Some of the new tools that make this so are wizards that simplify most administrative tasks. For example, Windows NT Server has a wizard that walks you through the steps to create and manage users and groups. Because these wizards are grouped in a single place, you don't have to grope to find the appropriate tool and the chance of error is minimized.

Version 4 also has a wizard for adding printers. In previous versions, administrators had to pick a printer from a list and then assign it a network queue. These steps have been combined into one. The wizard automatically installs printer drivers on the server so administrators don't have to worry about installing each printer driver on each client desktop.

Speaking of clients, the Windows NT Server now has a client administrative wizard that creates client installation disks by clicking on a button. Likewise, there's a wizard for managing clients' permissions to access Windows NT Server files and folders, a tool that allows administrators to make sure that a company is adhering to the Microsoft license policy, and a wizard that automatically sets up modems attached to a computer.

One of the more powerful improvements in Windows NT Server 4 is the System Policy Editor. The policies available in this editor help administrators create a desktop and security standard for all users that log on to the network. For example, you can remove programs, add wallpaper, or disable the Shut Down command for all users by defining a single policy. All of this is accomplished though an easy-to-use editor, in which you merely check the items you want enabled or disabled.

An improved tool that works in conjunction with the System Policy Editor is the User Profile Editor, which allows you to set up and assign a work environment to each user's logon ID. This means users will get the same desktop settings, even if they log on to a different physical computer system.

■ Diagnostics and Monitoring

Windows NT Server brings several new tools to the plate to allow you to document performance problems or to reveal potential problems before they begin causing the network to crash. One tool most organizations will appreciate is the Network Monitor, which can capture network traffic at the packet level. This allows you to analyze network throughput and use in real time or by looking at snapshots taken throughout the day. Though Network Monitor does not feature any scheduling capabilities, it allows you to peek at the frames and broadcasts of any network running on Windows NT Server. This way, you can probe all of your networks from a single Windows NT Workstation.

The Network Monitor is a new tool that can work in conjunction with Performance Monitor, which existed in previous versions of Windows NT Server. Performance Monitor, which provides a view of performance from a high level, is largely unchanged in this version, but it can be launched from within Network Monitor for a complete overview of a network. See Figure 2.2 to get an idea of how Network Monitor operates.

Figure 2.2

Network Monitor allows administrators to peer into the frames and packets of their networks and diagnose problems quickly.

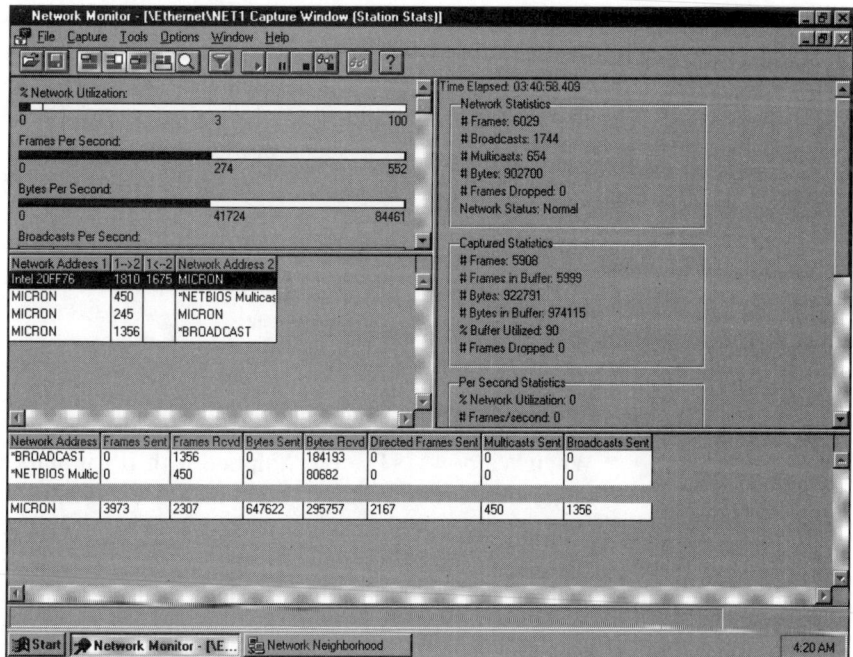

Another utility for performance monitoring is actually a totally re-vamped version of an old standby. The new Task Manager is souped up from previous versions of Windows NT Server. The new Task Manager lets you view and kill running processes (executables and dynamic-link libraries, for example) and see how much memory each process is tying up.

The Task Manager also displays graphs showing the histories of CPU and memory usage. The previous version only showed how much physical and total RAM was used and available. Of course, like the previous version of Task Manager, the new one allows you to end applications that have stopped running.

■ Faster than Ever

We'll go into this quite a bit more in Part 8, "Tuning Windows NT for Perfor-mance," but Windows NT Server 4 has some significant performance en-hancements. First, it's more scalable than previous versions, especially when run on systems with more than four processors. Thus, it will offer faster file and print services and will run network applications faster than previous ver-sions. Our tests show that Microsoft may be on to something.

Microsoft also claims that Windows NT Server performs better on 100Mbps Fast Ethernet. This is most likely due to improved drivers and pro-tocol stacks, and in later chapters we'll include some of our performance data on fast networking.

Regardless of the speed of the network, adding Internet Information Server (IIS) 2 to Windows NT Server should boost the product's perfor-mance as a Web server as well. IIS is a World Wide Web server that allows companies to easily publish information on the Web to anyone with a Web browser, such as Microsoft's Internet Explorer (also included) or Netscape Navigator.

■ Internet in a Box

When Windows NT Server shipped with IIS, it marked the first time that a major network operating system included a built-in Web server (Novell has just announced that it will bundle a Web server called IntranetWare with a special version of NetWare). Version 2 of IIS includes better administrative tools, improved connectivity to databases via the optional Microsoft Internet database connector (IDC), and improved programmability through the Mi-crosoft Internet services application programming interface (ISAPI).

However, a Web server alone isn't enough to get a company up and run-ning on the Web. Microsoft also bundles FrontPage, a powerful hypertext markup language (HTML) editing package that allows designers to create spiffy-looking Web pages with a graphical user interface. Though FrontPage isn't a best-of-breed package, it's good, and it's included with Windows NT Server 4.

An optional product that's a free download from the Microsoft Web site (http://www.microsoft.com) is the Microsoft Index Server, which allows users to query entire sets of documents of various types that are stored on IIS.

Further under the hood is a new version of Microsoft Domain Name System (DNS) Server. The DNS Server, which maps easy-to-understand names to Internet Protocol (IP) addresses, now includes a graphical utility that makes it easier to administer. DNS Server also now works with the Windows Internet Naming Service (WINS), which does the same job as the DNS Server but works only on Windows.

■ Communications and Integration Features

Several new features step up the product's already good communication services. For example, Windows NT Server 4 now supports multilink channel aggregation, which can increase the bandwidth of a remote connection. This is possible by combining the throughput of any two or more modems and integrated digital network services (ISDN) terminal adapters into a single aggregate channel. This makes Windows NT Server 4 more easily managed from a remote connection.

Another feature that works with remote access services (RAS) is the Windows NT Server 4 Point-to-Point Tunneling Protocol (PPTP), which makes it possible for companies to create secure private networks over phone lines or network connections. Though PPTP is not a standard part of the mix, Microsoft is promoting it heavily, and third-party products that work with it should be available by now.

As if we haven't already introduced enough acronyms, Windows NT Server 4 now can work as a Multiprotocol Router (MPR). This technology allows small companies to use the server to connect separate LANs. This saves money because the companies don't need to purchase a dedicated router. However, the product is not intended to replace routers in larger companies.

Those who know the usual Microsoft game plan know about the Component Object Model (COM), which is the Microsoft standard for building component-based applications. Microsoft has added some new capabilities to COM in the Windows NT Server to allow components to interoperate across networks. Now called DCOM (the D stands for "distributed"), the framework builds on COM, and developers who know COM won't lose their training investment.

The last new feature, but certainly not the least, especially to companies that also use NetWare, is the improved connectivity to the Novell network operating system. Windows NT Server 4 now allows administrators to browse Novell's NetWare Directory Service (NDS) resources. Though it would be better if NDS could register and manage Windows NT servers without a hitch, it's a step in the right direction.

- *Where to Get Started*
- *Configuring the Windows NT Server 4*
- *Users, Domains, and Security*
- *Interoperability with Other Operating Systems*
- *Remote Computing*
- *The Internet*
- *Getting the Most Bang for the Buck*

- *The Last Word*

3

What's Covered in This Book

THIS BOOK IS AIMED AT COMPUTER PROFESSIONALS WHO ARE installing and setting up the Windows NT Server 4 for the first time. If that's you, you may be new to the Windows NT Server or you may already be familiar with previous versions of the product. You may be familiar with other networking operating systems, or you may be altogether new to networking. The flexibility of the Windows NT Server lends itself to diversity among its users.

Because of its broad scope, we organized this book so that we start where a typical administrator would—right at the beginning, with a chapter on planning a Windows NT Server 4 installation. We then progress more or less though the same steps that administrators might follow in setting up their own networks. We've set up the Windows NT Server 4 ourselves following these steps, so they're tried and true. We also divide our book into clearly defined parts and chapters, so you can go where you need to whenever you need to.

■ Where to Get Started

After the introductory part, of which this chapter is a section, we cut to the chase. In Part 2: "Setting Up a Windows NT Server 4," we'll discuss the steps that companies should take *before* inserting the Windows NT Server 4 CD-ROM into the computer. This is one of the most important sections in the book, and we think it's required reading for anyone new to the Windows NT Server. In this section, we'll review hardware requirements and give an overview on domains—a concept critical to a Windows NT Server installation.

We'll also review the different file systems the Windows NT Server 4 supports and give pointers on which one is best for your particular needs. Then we'll cover how to set up the network protocols. These include the Transmission Control Protocol/Internet Protocol (TCP/IP), the Internet Packet Exchange (IPX), and Net-Bios Extended User Interface (NetBEUI). Finally, we'll provide an overview of the services needed to set up the Windows NT Server as an Internet server platform.

No matter what subject we're talking about in this section, we'll make sure to let you know about performance issues and the impact of using any of the Windows NT Server 4 services we discuss.

■ Configuring the Windows NT Server 4

Part 3, "Configuring the Windows NT Server 4," builds on the previous section but gets more into the nitty gritty of the server once it has been set up. You'll find chapters on formatting disk drives, setting up the server for a redundant array of inexpensive disks (RAID), and creating the necessary but too often overlooked emergency disks. Chapter 13, "How to Create Shared File Volumes" explains in detail how to make a Windows NT Server accessible to the clients connected to it. We'll conclude the section with a chapter on backup and recovery, which help protect the hours of investment you've already put into your installation.

■ Users, Domains, and Security

In Part 4, "Setting Up Users," we discuss user administration and security in detail. Because of the complexity of this topic, this is the longest section of the book and one of the most important to read. Here we'll cover the concept of the Windows NT Server domain in far more detail than we covered in Part 2. For example, we'll discuss the different types of domains and the multiple domains that can be set up. We then provide step-by-step details on how to create users and groups, and we'll describe the relationships between them and domains. Of course, we'll provide several diagrams and screen shots that will make it easier to understand all of these concepts.

In Chapters 23 through 26, we discuss Profiles, the Windows NT Server 4 way of making mass user management a bit easier. We also cover the problems of and solutions to managing multiple profiles on different domains with a variety of different clients. Finally, we discuss setting up clients, including DOS, Windows, Unix, and Macintosh clients, each of which has totally different requirements.

■ Interoperability with Other Operating Systems

Part 5 marks the halfway point of the book, and here we'll switch gears from covering Windows NT Server as the primary network operating system to one in which it's only a part of an organization's network. For example, we'll discuss how the Windows NT Server 4 works with NetWare and how to make the two competing operating systems coexist in a single environment. Some of the things we'll cover are Gateway Services and Directory Service Manager for NetWare, which provides Windows NT Server with access to NetWare's shared disk volumes and resources. We'll also discuss, in Chapter 28, integrating UNIX workstations and servers into a Windows NT Server environment.

■ Remote Computing

Connecting to a network without a high-speed network connection is essential, because it allows administrators to manage networks without being tied to the office. It also allows clients to dial into their networks from the road, an increasingly important part of computing in the mobile world. Part 6 covers all aspects of setting up the Windows NT Server 4 remote access services (RAS), and we include a chapter that details how to optimize the RAS connections.

We'll also cover some of the new technologies in the Windows NT Server 4, including Multi-Link Channel Aggregation and the Point-to-Point

Tunneling Protocol (PPTP), both of which can help companies make the most out of remote computing.

■ The Internet

Windows NT Server 4 marks the first time complete Internet services have been included in a network operating system. We'll cover the ins and outs of setting up a Windows NT Server 4 for the Web and setting up Gopher and File Transfer Protocol (FTP) services. We'll also cover creating and designing Web pages with Microsoft FrontPage, a Hypertext Markup Language (HTML) editor included free with your Windows NT Server 4. Additionally, we'll discuss the Microsoft Index Server, a text indexing engine that can be downloaded from the Microsoft Web site.

■ Getting the Most Bang for the Buck

After setting up your Windows NT Server and making sure that all the connections are working properly, you'll probably want to turn to Part 8, "Tuning Windows NT for Performance." This section contains information on how to boost the speed of your Windows NT Server. We'll discuss the server's many performance monitoring utilities, including some of the hidden programs that can be used to tweak a few more processing cycles out of your hardware.

We'll make sure to concentrate in this section on the different tuning parameters and how setting one for a certain situation may slow down another process later on. We'll even include performance results of the tests we've run at *PC Week* Labs and give you an overview of tuning the Windows NT Server 4 for database performance.

■ The Last Word

The appendices may be your favorite section, because they provide a quick reference to important information. We realize this and tried to make our appendices comprehensive but concise.

- *Sidebars*
- *Tips*
- *Notes*
- *Cautions*

4

How to Read This Book

Y OU'RE PROBABLY WONDERING WHY WE HAVE SUCH A CHAPTER. If you've reached this point, we have no doubt that you're well on your way to finishing this book. The problem, however, is that few people read "how to" books, such as this one, from cover to cover. Instead, people skip around, perusing chapter headings and scanning the indexes, glossaries, or appendices for some key piece of information they can't seem to find anywhere else.

Our goal is to make sure that you don't have to change your reading style in order to make this book worthwhile. We don't want you to feel as if you've "been there, done that" just because we've covered something you already know. So to save you time, we've prepared Table 4.1, which can serve as a kind of supplementary Table of Contents.

Table 4.1

How to find the information you're looking for

IF YOU ARE PLANNING TO...	THEN JUMP TO...	PAY CLOSE ATTENTION TO:	AND ALSO CHECK OUT...
Set up Windows NT Server for the first time	Chapter 5, "Planning for Windows NT Server Installations"	Planning domain options	1. Chapter 6, "Installing Windows NT Server" 2. Chapter 7, "How to Configure Network Options"
Prepare Windows NT as a public Internet server	Chapter 7, "How to Configure Network Options"	1. Setting up network protocols 2. Configuring DNS, WINS, and Dynamic Host Configuration Protocol (DHCP) services	1. Part 7, "Setting Up Windows NT for the Internet" 2. Chapter 33, "Installing the Internet Information Server" 3. Chapter 34, "Building a Web Site with FrontPage"
Set up a redundant array of inexpensive disks (RAID)	Chapter 11, "How to Use Disk Administrator"	Setting up redundant array of inexpensive disks (RAID)	1. Chapter 8, "How to Choose a Disk File Subsystem" 2. Chapter 17, "Backup and Disaster Recovery"
Set up a Windows NT Server as a Domain Controller	Chapter 18, "Introduction to Domain Security"	NT domain concepts	1. Chapter 5, "Planning for Windows NT Server Installations" 2. Chapter 7, "How to Configure Network Options"
Configure Windows NT Server to work with multiple domains	Chapter 22, "Configuring Directory Replication"	Configuring trust relationships	1. Chapter 20, "How to Use Server Manager" 2. Chapter 19, "How to Use the User Manager" 3. Chapter 21, "Synchronizing Domain Controllers"
Set up large numbers of users	Chapter 23, "How to Configure Windows NT Profiles"	Maintaining multiple profiles on all primary and backup domain controllers (PDCs and BDCs) Managing Windows 95 profiles	1. Chapter 19, "How to Use the User Manager" 2. Chapter 20, "How to Use Server Manager"

**Table 4.1
(Continued)**

How to find the
information you're
looking for

IF YOU ARE PLANNING TO...	THEN JUMP TO...	PAY CLOSE ATTENTION TO:	AND ALSO CHECK OUT...
Debug a faulty installation	Chapter 14, "How to Use the Event Viewer"	Chapter 17, "Backup and Disaster Recovery"	1. Appendix C, "Certified Backup Software"
Integrate Windows NT Server into a pre-existing local area network (LAN) environment	Part 5, "Integration with Other Networks"	Chapter 26, "Cohabitation with Other Networks "	1. Chapter 24, "How to Set Up Windows NT Clients"
Implement remote access	Chapter 30, "Setting Up Remote Access Services"	Overview of capabilities, limitations	1. Chapter 30, "Setting Up Remote Access Services" 2. Chapter 7, "How to Configure Network Options"
Optimize Performance	Chapter 37, "How to Monitor Server Performance"	Setting up performance monitor charts	1. Chapter 38, "How to Set Thread and Processor Priorities" 2. Appendix B, "More Performance Monitoring Tools"

We've tried to organize this book logically, tracing the steps that an administrator with a Windows NT 4 installation CD-ROM in hand would take when setting up a network from scratch.

Of course, not everyone has the luxury of starting a network from scratch, and we've added a few diversions along the way to take into account the obstacles and considerations companies face when setting up a new network. To help you sort through these, and to make your installation go as smoothly as possible, we've included tips, sidebars, notes, and cautions.

■ Sidebars

Occasionally, we'd like to cover a topic that's only tangentially related to our subject matter at hand. We'll cover these topics in sidebars, which you'll find set apart from the main text of the chapter. Sidebars most often contain important information that you need to keep in mind when implementing a procedure outlined in a chapter. Sidebars also may include some information that *PC Week* uncovered during testing of Windows NT Server.

■ Tips

A tip is a sentence or two that may just make your life a little easier. As everyone works with a product, they become more familiar with it and find their own shortcuts. The tips in this book have saved us time in our testing, and we wanted to pass them on to you.

■ Notes

Sometimes our tips get too long or complicated to be expressed in a pithy manner. When we need to provide background or supporting information to a tip, we call it a note. Notes also include comments, explanations, and additional advice on setting up a package. If you're already knowledgeable about a chapter's subject, you can probably get by just reading these notes.

■ Cautions

Danger! No matter how good or easy to use Windows NT Server is, it's a complex operating system, at the least, and perhaps even a new paradigm in setting up information technology infrastructures. When dealing with something this important, tread as cautiously as possible, for failure to do so may destroy a company's second most valuable asset—its data. (At *PC Week*, we still think people rate the highest.) These cautions are items we've dug up or discovered ourselves through trial and error. If one of our cautions saves a piece of critical data in your installation, we consider this book a success.

2

Setting Up a Windows NT Server 4

- *What Hardware Works Best?*
- *Network Topography*

5

Planning for Windows NT Server Installations

Even before selecting the hardware to run the NT Server, it's important to have an understanding of the network the new server will become a part of. If the Windows NT Server is the first server, or host, on the network, it will need to be configured as a domain controller; for installations in existing networks, basic information about the current environment is necessary.

The NT installation process asks many questions ranging from the protocols, or languages, on the network, to what its name should be (all networked servers, or hosts, require a unique name).

Luckily, the Windows NT domain network design is rather flexible, leaving the option to make alterations to its configuration even after installation. Unfortunately, there are still a few changes to the NT system that can only be made by a total re-installation of the operating system. A stand-alone installation of Windows NT Server, for example, cannot become a domain controller without a re-installation of the operating system.

■ What Hardware Works Best?

The purpose of the new NT Server and the type of network it is going to work in will have effects on the computing equipment used. An NT Server that is to be a domain controller of a large network of hundreds, or thousands of users, needs to be fairly powerful just to handle user authentication. On the other hand, a stand-alone installation of Windows NT Server that simply holds some shared data for 20 accounting users and manages a print queue does not need as much memory, CPU power, or disk space.

Obviously, the type of hardware needed is highly dependent on what the networked users do with it. Storing spreadsheets requires far less server space than desktop publishing files with full color images that take hundreds of megabytes.

In many cases, the various peripheral components of a server may have greater significance in overall system performance than the speed of CPU. Today's Pentium class CPUs, not to mention the reduced instruction set computing (RISC) offerings, have reached such performance capacities that they are held back by the available random access memory (RAM) and disk drives. Increasing the speed of a central processing unit (CPU) in a system where the disk systems are already overtaxed will not help. Likewise, if the Windows NT Server operating system is constantly having to use the hard disk as virtual memory for lack of RAM, a faster CPU will help little in this case. Faster disks would help a bit, but not significantly.

Helpful Tip

The Windows NT Hardware Compatibility List, available at the Microsoft Web site (http://www.microsoft.com/ntserver/hcl/hclintro.htm) can be a useful starting place to discover known supported hardware. A wide list of computers, disk controllers, network interfaces, and printers, have been tested with Windows NT Server 4. The compatibility list is also available on the Windows NT Server 4 CD-ROM inside the "/support" directory.

Windows NT Server's Minimum Requirements

Although Microsoft claims Windows NT Server 4 can run on relatively small hardware platforms, we strongly recommend that some of these suggestions be exceeded to avoid extreme frustration with performance.

In particular, the minimum recommended 16MB of RAM is far too low. Windows NT Server 4 will perform pretty much like molasses without at least 32MB of RAM. If a server is acting as a Primary or Backup Domain Controller, as well as running several other network services, such as the Web server or NetWare gateways, it may be well worth the money to jump to 64MB RAM. In many cases, increasing the amount of system memory brings a far greater performance gain than upgrading the CPU.

Unlike the previous versions of Windows NT Server, Windows NT Server 4 no longer works with Intel 80386 microprocessors. Any other x86-based processor will work, but Pentium chips are preferable. Windows NT Server also supports several other reduced instruction set computing (RISC) CPU types from Digital Equipment Corporation, MIPS Computer Systems, and Motorola Inc. However, the Intel platform is still the best supported, since little third-party hardware—including network cards and Small Computer System Interface (SCSI) controllers—have the necessary drivers for RISC systems.

Screen real estate is another hardware resource that Windows NT Server 4 eats voraciously.

Large monitors and high resolution video cards can make the administration of Windows NT Server 4 considerably easier, allowing various administration tools to be expanded and placed beside one another. Of course, if server administration is carried out remotely, from other workstations on the network, a Windows NT Server 4 can function quite well with merely a VGA display. See Table 5.1 for the minimum requirements as we see them.

Application Servers vs. File Servers

On desktop computers the speed of the CPU can be very important; it can mean the difference between a spreadsheet being calculated in 30 seconds or ten minutes. CPU speed in a server, however, may be secondary if the machine is to be used primarily as a basic file server, allowing users to store data files over the network instead of on their local disk drives. Servers intended

Table 5.1

Minimum hardware
requirements for
Windows NT Server 4

CATEGORY	REQUIREMENT
CPU	Intel x86-based microprocessors 486, Pentium, and better; RISC-based processors such as the MIPS R4x00, DEC Alpha, or Motorola PowerPC
VIDEO	VGA or better
MEMORY	32MB RAM or better
DISK	Core operating system needs 124MB free space for Intel-based machines and 158MB in RISC systems; CD-ROM is essential for Windows NT Server installation and configuration
NETWORK	Windows NT Server 4 can run without any network support, but it rather defeats the purpose
MISCELLANEOUS	Mouse, keyboard

for use as file servers could benefit far more from the sophisticated disk subsystems called redundant array of inexpensive disks (RAID) than faster processors could.

Application servers have somewhat different system demands than traditional file servers. Rather than acting as dumb repositories of end-user data that's processed on local PCs, application servers provide answers to complex user requests for analyses. This allows end-user PCs to have less processing power, since the thinking is done by the server. However, the servers need to be designed with powerful enough CPUs and working space (RAM) to handle the loads. Database servers, such as Microsoft SQL Server, can suggest configurations with up to 1MB per simultaneous user. In an organization of one thousand users, where 150 people could be running a database at the same time, a Windows NT Server 4 running a SQL Server may need to have upwards of 200MB RAM. This seems expensive, but think about how much it would cost to equip everyone with the top-of-the line PCs.

Domain Controllers vs. Stand-alone Servers

To manage the network security for user authentication and access privileges across multiple Windows NT Servers, at least one Windows NT Server must act as a controller.

If an NT Server is to be configured as either a primary or backup domain controller (PDC or BDC), somewhat more overhead will be required to run the services necessary for user authentication. On networks with more than 200 users in a domain, it may even be wise to dedicate a server exclusively to domain control. In extremely large network environments, the domain user data base, which is replicated between all primary and backup domain controllers, may be great enough to require large hard drives.

For small local area networks (LANs), however, a single NT Server 4 can perform well as both a domain controller and file server.

If domain controllers already exist on the network, the NT Server 4 installation provides the option of stand-alone operation. Stand-alone NT servers can still join domains, using the security information, but they don't take on the overhead of authenticating users or storing network security data.

Choosing Disk Subsystems

Multiple hard disk drives can be used in the NT Server 4 to provide both fault tolerance as well as improved performance. Using built-in RAID, Windows NT Server 4 can span a partition across multiple disks so they behave as one. This is a process called striping. (Disk mirroring, in which two drives act as duplicates for protection in case of failure, is also supported.)

Striping can significantly improve throughput and overall system performance by allowing read/write requests to be handled simultaneously across many disks. Individually, disk drives work in a serial fashion, with only one active head to process requests in the order they were received. Some drives are faster than others, but there's a limit to how fast they can be without the ability to perform simultaneous read/write requests.

Redundancy can also be achieved with striping options that dedicate a certain portion of each drive in the stripe set to parity, or reconstructive index.

If any one disk should fail, its data would be automatically rebuilt from parity indexes when a new drive is attached to the system.

Standard integrated development environment (IDE) hard drives work well with the Windows NT Server 4, but when using more than two hard drives with RAID options, we strongly suggest that SCSI hard drives be used, which require special controllers. The SCSI architecture can allow up to seven hard drives to be added to a system easily.

Although Windows NT Server 4 supports RAID on the software level, you also have the option to use dedicated RAID systems that have the RAID logic embedded in the controllers. This can sometimes create fewer hassles than software RAID, particularly when it comes to being able to pull disk units out of the chassis for replacement while the operating system keeps running. Although the data of defective hard drives can be easily rebuilt by NT Server 4 software RAID, the system must be brought down first. Network managers usually have better things to do with their time than come in at strange hours to swap hard drives. The biggest drawback with hardware RAID solutions is their high cost.

■ Network Topography

The choice of which network type to use is often a moot point in existing LANs, and you only need to find an appropriate interface card that NT 4 Server supports. More subtly, however, the capacity of various LAN media can help determine other hardware choices. There may be little point in having a high-capacity multi-disk RAID setup when the network is limited to standard 10 megabits per second (Mbps) Ethernet. Conversely, it would be silly to invest in 100Mbps fast Ethernet hubs and network cards when the NT Server 4 is equipped with only 32MB RAM and two hard drives; the server would never be able to use a fraction of the bandwidth.

When designing a network it's important to take these needs into account. In large LANs, it may be a good idea to have a fast Ethernet or Fiber Distributed Data Interface (FDDI) segment at 100Mbps. A few file servers, with client PCs attached to the LAN, can attach to this FDDI via the less expensive 10Mbps Ethernet.

Windows NT Server can run on virtually any network infrastructure in existence, whether it's Token Ring, Local Talk, asynchronous transfer mode, fast Ethernet, or even the ubiquitous Ethernet that comprises most LANs today. Functionally, Windows NT Server works the same on any of these topographies, as long as you have a good network adapter and driver. Even wide area network (WAN) connections using analog modems or ISDN behave as fully functional network links.

- *Starting Setup*

- *The Setup Process*

- *Entering Personal Information*

6

Installing Windows NT Server

THE SETUP PROGRAM FOR WINDOWS NT SERVER 4 REDUCES MUCH of the pain in traditional network operating system installations. However, the method of running the Setup routine can vary depending on the hardware used and the administrator's preference.

■ Starting Setup

The Setup routine requires twice the amount of disk space the installation files take. This is because Setup creates a duplicate image of the NT installation files (in non-compressed format) on the hard drive to speed up the installation process. The image is automatically erased at the end of the installation. Therefore, the minimum amount required for the installation is 248MB of free disk space.

Setup from Boot Floppies

Windows NT Server 4 comes with three boot floppies that contain the initial Setup program functions. First, make sure the Windows NT Server 4 CD is inserted in the CD-ROM drive. Then start Setup by booting the computer with the disk labeled *Windows NT Setup Boot Disk* in drive A.

Helpful Tip

> *Don't fret if the Windows NT Server 4 installation floppy disks are corrupted or—heaven forbid—missing. You can easily create new diskettes from the CD.*

Find a PC running DOS or Windows 95 and equipped with a CD-ROM. Insert the Windows NT Server 4 CD. Execute the WINNT program on DOS or Windows 95 machines, and the WINNT32 program from Windows NT computers. Be sure to use the /OX parameter. This will create boot diskettes with CD-ROM support. For example, from DOS or Windows 95, you would enter

    D:\i386\winnt /ox

From another Windows NT machine, enter

    D:\i386\winnt32 /ox

Setup from Auto-Boot CD-ROM

Unlike earlier versions of the server, the Windows NT Server 4 has bootable CD-ROMs. If your system's basic input/output system (BIOS) supports the El Torito Bootable CD-ROM format, it should be possible to boot a Windows NT Server 4 CD and bypass the diskettes altogether.

However, not all system BIOSs that support bootable CDs will work properly, and it may still be necessary to use either the floppy disk or the direct copy install method, which we'll explain later.

Setup by Copying CD-ROM to Hard Drive

Although the Windows NT 4 boot floppies do an admirable job of detecting system devices to perform the install, the process still fails on a few machines. If you're having problems getting Windows NT to detect your CD-ROM drive or disk controllers, or if you're experiencing system hangs when the Setup routine restarts your server, we suggest a fail-safe method of installation.

This fail-safe method is, in a nutshell: format the system hard drive with DOS and copy the contents of the Windows NT 4 CD-ROM system files to the hard drive. Run Setup directly from the hard disk. You will, of course, need to have the DOS drivers for your CD-ROM drive installed on your hard disk. This will take approximately 107MB of extra disk space.

The entire Windows NT Server 4 CD does not need to be copied to the local hard drive; you just need the contents of the I386 directory. Use the XCOPY command, instead of COPY, since there are subdirectories inside the I386 directory that must be copied as well. Be sure to create a local directory for the I386 files before running XCOPY. Otherwise, all the data will go directly into the root. For example,

c:\md \i386

c:\xcopy d:\i386 c: /e

(The /e also copies the subdirectories.) Be prepared to take a coffee break once the copying starts; it can take a while.

After the CD has been copied, start the WINNT Setup program from inside the new I386 directory. We suggest using the WINNT /B parameter for installation without floppies. If you want them, be sure to have three formatted 1.44MB 3.5-inch floppy diskettes available for Setup to generate the install disks.

Setup Over a Network

If the Windows NT Server 4 CD has been placed on an existing file server for sharing over the LAN, the Setup can be run remotely. All you need to do is run the network drivers from either a floppy diskette or a hard drive to gain network access to the Windows NT Server 4 CD.

Windows NT 4 network installation procedures are basically the same as those used after copying the CD to the local hard drive. Use the WINNT command with the /B parameter for installation without floppies.

If the network is being accessed from an older version of Windows NT Server, use the WINNT32 executable instead of WINNT. (We still recommend using the /B parameter.)

Setup on a RISC-based System

Unfortunately, the Windows NT Server 4 boot diskettes do not work on RISC systems. Installations are accomplished through the attached resources computing (ARC) screen in the system BIOS.

At the prompt on the RISC BIOS Setup screen, type cd:\system\Setupldr. For the word "system," substitute the correct directory on the Windows NT Server CD. Your choices are: ALPHA, MIPS, and PPC for the PowerPC. Because the installation can vary in RISC systems, we advise you to refer to your system documentation. After starting Setup, however, the installation is the same as for Intel machines.

■ The Setup Process

Once Setup has started, the installation steps are the same for all systems, be they RISC or Intel-based. The initial Setup of disk controllers and basic hardware is done from text screens, as shown in Figure 6.1. The system reboots and enters the graphical mode shown in Figure 6.2 to continue asking questions about system names, network options, and optional features.

Figure 6.1

Users have the choice of aborting Setup, repairing an existing NT system, or performing a fresh installation.

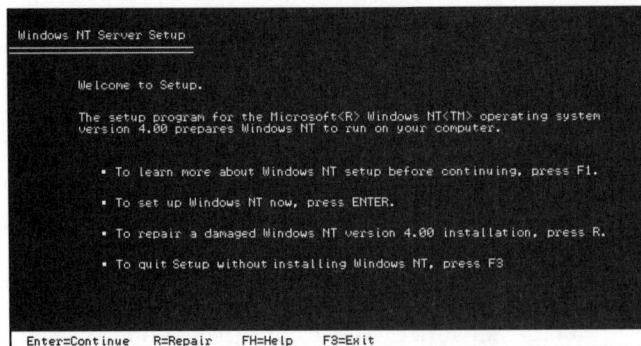

```
Windows NT Server Setup

      Welcome to Setup.

      The setup program for the Microsoft<R> Windows NT<TM> operating system
      version 4.00 prepares Windows NT to run on your computer.

        • To learn more about Windows NT setup before continuing, press F1.

        • To set up Windows NT now, press ENTER.

        • To repair a damaged Windows NT version 4.00 installation, press R.

        • To quit Setup without installing Windows NT, press F3

   Enter=Continue    R=Repair    FH=Help    F3=Exit
```

Configuring a Disk Controller

The Windows NT Server 4 installation program is able to auto-detect a wide variety of disk controllers and presents a text screen, shown in Figure 6.3, showing the devices it has found.

As long as Setup has found the primary controller running the drive that the server is to be installed on, you can continue to the next step. You can select additional disk controllers after installation using the Windows NT Server 4 Control Panel.

Figure 6.2

The second, graphical part of installation requests information about the new NT system and configures networking.

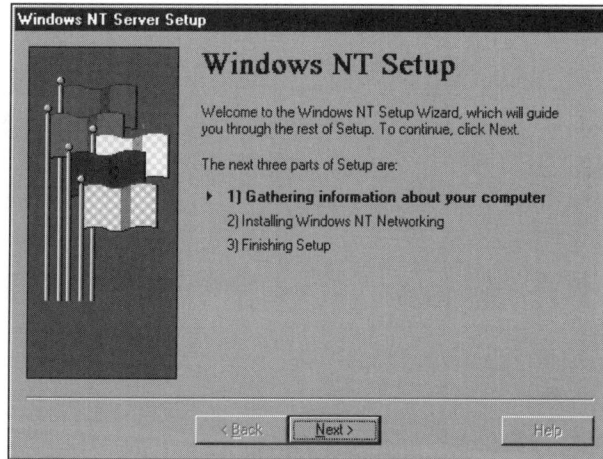

Figure 6.3

Device drivers for hard drives and a CD-ROM device must be specified.

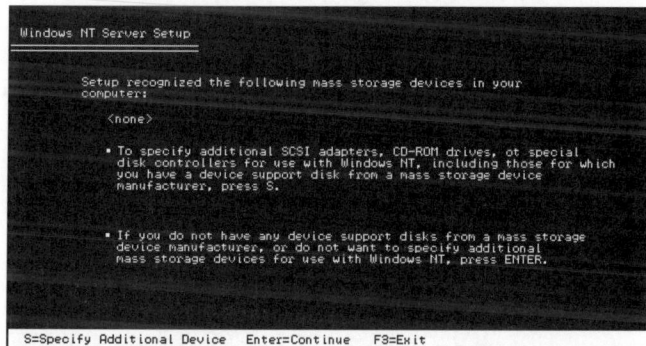

If Setup doesn't find any controllers automatically, you may need to press the option at the bottom of the screen, S=Specify Additional Device. This option displays a lengthy list of controllers, but in some cases you may need device drivers on a floppy from the manufacturer. These device drivers would be provided to you by the manufacturer and are located on a diskette accompanying the controller.

With the controller drivers successfully loaded, Setup proceeds to a screen asking for confirmation of the standard system settings shown in Figure 6.4.

Figure 6.4

Setup asks for confirmation of detected components.

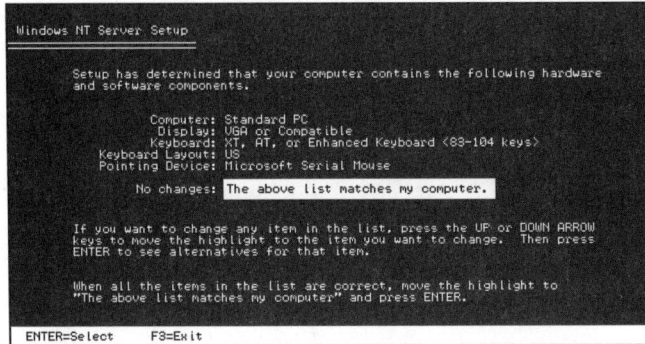

```
Windows NT Server Setup

        Setup has determined that your computer contains the following hardware
        and software components.

                  Computer: Standard PC
                   Display: VGA or Compatible
                  Keyboard: XT, AT, or Enhanced Keyboard (83-104 keys)
          Keyboard Layout: US
          Pointing Device: Microsoft Serial Mouse

              No changes: The above list matches my computer.

        If you want to change any item in the list, press the UP or DOWN ARROW
        keys to move the highlight to the item you want to change.  Then press
        ENTER to see alternatives for that item.

        When all the items in the list are correct, move the highlight to
        "The above list matches my computer" and press ENTER.


    ENTER=Select      F3=Exit
```

Helpful Tip

If Setup asks for the NT 4 Server CD-ROM to be inserted, it has likely failed to load the proper drivers for the CD-ROM controller (assuming the CD is in the drive, of course). This could be the result of using manually created boot floppies without the WINNT /OX option, or you may need to select a different controller from the driver list. If the problem persists, refer to our fail-safe installation method outlined earlier in "Setup by Copying CD-ROM Drive to the Hard Disk."

Configuring Disk Partitions

During Setup you must specify the disk drive and the partition where the Windows NT Server 4 is to be installed. Existing partitions, or logical hard drive definitions, may be used, but Setup can also change the setting, allowing current partitions to be deleted and new ones created. (See Figure 6.5.)

Figure 6.5

The drive and partition for the NT system files must be specified during Setup.

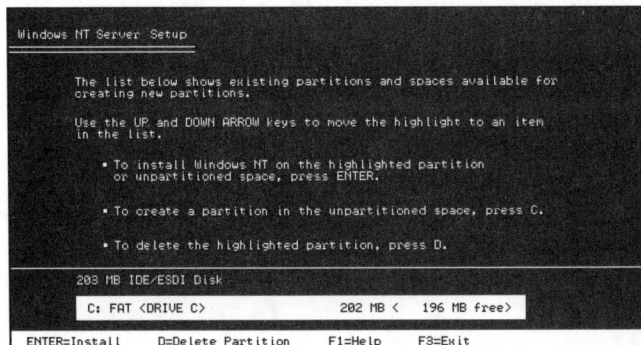

```
Windows NT Server Setup

        The list below shows existing partitions and spaces available for
        creating new partitions.

        Use the UP and DOWN ARROW keys to move the highlight to an item
        in the list.

              • To install Windows NT on the highlighted partition
                or unpartitioned space, press ENTER.

              • To create a partition in the unpartitioned space, press C.

              • To delete the highlighted partition, press D.

        203 MB IDE/ESDI Disk

          C: FAT <DRIVE C>                    202 MB <   196 MB free>

    ENTER=Install      D=Delete Partition    F1=Help      F3=Exit
```

For new installations we advise creating one big partition and configuring it for the NT file system (NTFS). Windows NT Server 4 can be installed on hard drives partitioned for either this disk structure, which is preferred because it offers improved reliability and security, or, as shown in Figure 6.6, it can be installed on a file allocation table (FAT) partition used by DOS and Windows 95. See Table 6.1 for a comparison of these two systems.

Figure 6.6

Drives can be formatted with either FAT or NTFS.

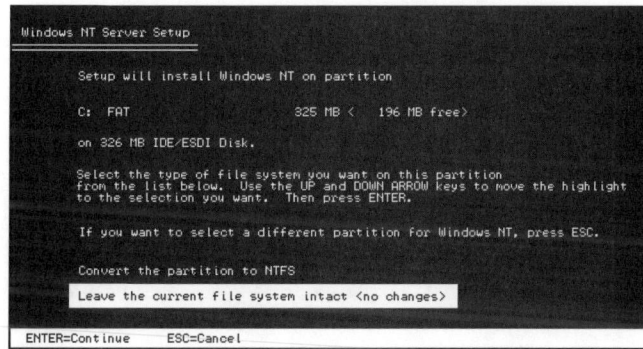

```
Windows NT Server Setup

    Setup will install Windows NT on partition

    C:  FAT                    325 MB <   196 MB free>

    on 326 MB IDE/ESDI Disk.

    Select the type of file system you want on this partition
    from the list below. Use the UP and DOWN ARROW keys to move the highlight
    to the selection you want.  Then press ENTER.

    If you want to select a different partition for Windows NT, press ESC.

    Convert the partition to NTFS
    Leave the current file system intact <no changes>

ENTER=Continue     ESC=Cancel
```

Table 6.1

Windows NT file system comparison

PARAMETER	NTFS	DOS
Security	Supports security access privileges down to file and directory level	No user security possible on file or directory levels
Activity logs	Keeps a history of disk events that can be used to recover data in case of crash	No histories kept
File sizes	Supports up to 64GB disks	Maximum file size is 4GB
File compression	Compression is supported on a per-file basis	Special compressed volumes can be created under DOS
Compatibility	Only Windows NT is able to recognize NTFS. DOS boot floppies will think NTFS partitions are empty.	Most operating systems are able to read FAT; including OS/2, DOS, Windows 95, and Windows NT

In particular, NTFS is essential to support long file names and maintain user access rights on files. It is simply not possible to specify privileges on specific directories or files on FAT partitions. The Windows NT Server RAID support for disk striping and mirroring works exclusively with NTFS partitions.

The only reason for installing Windows NT Server 4 on a FAT partition is for dual boot functionality, allowing another operating system like Windows 95, DOS, or OS/2 to coexist on the same system with Windows NT Server 4.

Even when a new partition is specified as NTFS during Setup, it is actually formatted as FAT and then converted to NTFS when the system reboots after running Setup.

Helpful Tip

Windows NT Server 4 will not be able to recognize any compressed file systems other than those created with Windows NT Server 3.51. Also, unlike previous versions of Windows NT Server, version 4 no longer recognizes the High Performance File System (HPFS) used by OS/2.

Helpful Tip

To work in dual-boot situations, allowing an operating system other than Windows NT Server to be selected by the boot manager at startup, you must install the other operating system before Windows NT Server 4. Be sure that the primary partition remains FAT.

Choosing a Directory for Installation

If Windows NT Server 4 is being installed on a new computer, the directory name you choose makes little difference. If, however, Windows NT Server 4 notices another Windows operating system on the hard drive, it will suggest upgrading the current system. For further information on this topic, see our sidebar, "Upgrading Existing Systems."

By specifying a new directory, the computer will automatically be configured in a dual-boot mode, allowing you to select from a menu at boot the operating system you desire.

Helpful Tip

Microsoft provides tools to help you migrate from NetWare bindery servers, but these are designed to transfer data from one existing NetWare server to an already configured Windows NT Server 4. There is no way to upgrade an entire NetWare 3.x file server to a Windows NT Server 4 in place, as it were.

Upgrading Existing Systems

When you see the screen shown in Figure 6.7, it's time to make a choice to upgrade. Although it's possible to upgrade a system running on Windows 3.1 to one that runs on Windows NT Server 4, we recommend a scratch installation in a separate directory. Unfortunately, there's no way to convert a Windows 95 PC to one that runs on Windows NT Server 4. However, the more typical upgrades to Windows NT Server 4 from previous versions of the product—3.1, 3.5, and 3.51—work well.

The Windows NT Server 4 installation will search for a previous version of Windows NT and ask if it should be upgraded. At this point it's possible to specify a new location for Windows NT Server 4, allowing multiple versions of Windows NT to exist on the same machine. Henceforth, the system startup will contain options for the different versions of Windows NT Server.

If you choose to upgrade an old version of Windows NT Server, the installation program will convert all the old drivers and registry settings in a relatively seamless process, asking few questions. Unfortunately, the Windows NT Server 4 installation does not automatically update all the system drivers, keeping the old ones. This usually doesn't prevent the new system from functioning, but it could lead to anomalous behavior and decreased system performance.

In some cases the installation warns that newer versions may be available (as with video cards and network adapters). These warnings are not always given, however, such as when the Windows NT Server 4 upgrade doesn't inform users about the need to update installed modems to the new unimodem .INF files for better performance. Upgraded Windows NT Server systems should be checked to ensure that the latest versions of the peripheral drivers are being used.

■ Entering Personal Information

After rebooting the system, Setup enters a graphical mode, shown in Figure 6.8, and asks for information on the system owner, licensing, and designated server name.

Name and Organization can be set to anything; they're merely a way to ingrain the server's owner information so that the name always shows up in help screens. Typically, many servers are set up with the department or group

Figure 6.7

The directory for Windows NT Server 4 installation can be chosen during Setup.

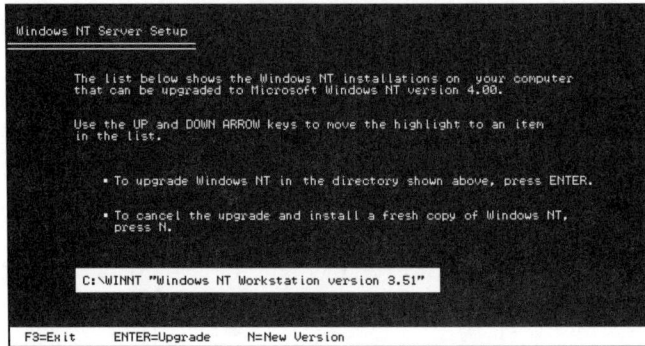

Figure 6.8

The NT Server 4 name licensing options are set during installation.

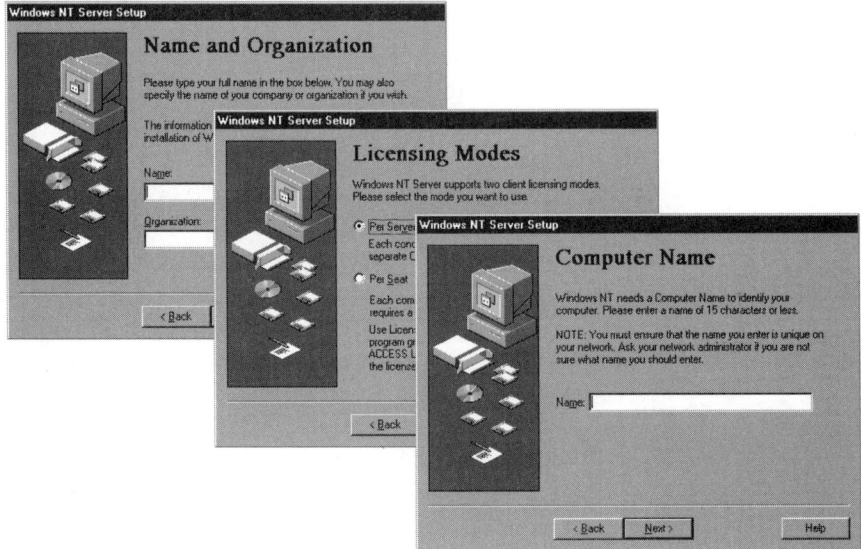

name, such as Finance Department, in the Name field and the corporation name in the Organization field.

Setup Options

Several default Setup options are provided to simplify installations on standard systems, shown in the Setup Options screen of Figure 6.9, but there isn't really a lot of difference between them. A Typical installation choice will automatically load all the optional Windows NT Server 4 components, and Compact will install everything except the options. The Custom option will give you the choice of which components you want.

Figure 6.9

Pre-defined Setup
configurations optimize
NT Server 4 for the
machine it will run on.

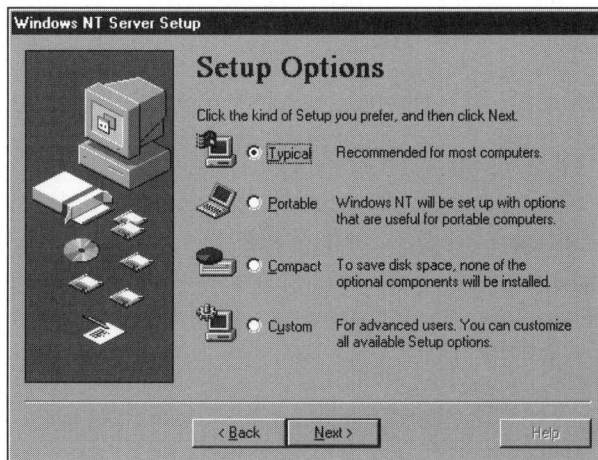

Helpful Tip

With Windows NT Server 4, you can undo mistakes. The installation wizard allows you to bring up previous configuration screens by clicking Back on any of Setup's three user information screens. Unfortunately, because Setup has been written in modules it can be impossible to go back and change some settings from within Setup. Luckily, however, rebooting the system will automatically bring back the first page of the NT 4 Setup Wizard.

Licensing Modules

Licensing options have been included in Windows NT Server since version 3.51 to help administrators ensure that violations to the license agreement do not occur through over-usage. The Per Server option makes it possible to specify how many users can access the file server simultaneously. The Per Seat option offers greater flexibility by allowing as many users as the hardware can handle to have access.

However, Per Seat licensing should be used with caution, since it can inadvertently lead to breaking the law when more people use the system than have been licensed. This issue of paying for slips of paper to legally support more users may seem silly, but it's no laughing matter when auditors show up to ensure that your organization isn't pilfering software.

Luckily, you can change these licensing options through the Control Panel after installation, so the decisions you make during Setup aren't cast in stone.

Product Identification Number

You must enter a proper ID number during the installation. You'll find this number on the Windows NT Server 4 CD, as well as on the inside back cover of the installation manual. The ID number is also printed on the registration card. This ID is useful for support purposes, when Microsoft engineers ask for product verification. After installation, you can place it under the System icon in the Control Panel so it's handy.

Defining a Computer Name

The name you give to your NT Server must be entirely unique in the domain. Even multiple versions of Windows NT on the same machine must have different names, in spite of the fact that only one system is run at a time.

If a previous Windows NT computer no longer exists in a domain, you can reuse its name, but an administrator must first eliminate it from the domain security data base. This is done via the Server Management tool.

Selecting a Server Type

The Windows NT Server Type screen shown in Figure 6.10 allows you to set up domain controllers. Windows NT domains need domain controllers to manage user authentication and security across groups of servers. Only one NT server in a given domain can be a primary domain controller (PDC); the other domain controllers must be backup domain controllers (BDC). The first server on an NT network should be configured as a PDC; BDCs are added as the user load becomes too heavy for one machine to handle authentication tasks alone. BDCs also offer redundancy in user authentication, in case the PDC crashes.

Windows NT Server 4s intended to be used merely as application or file servers will function best as stand-alone servers.

Helpful Tip

> *You can't make stand-alone servers into primary or backup domain controllers without re-installing the entire Windows NT Server 4. If you think you may want to use the server as a PDC or BDC, you should configure it as such in the first place.*

Configuring the Administrator Account

Every Windows NT Server 4 has a local user account, the Administrator Account shown in Figure 6.11. It can't be removed. During installation the password is set for this account. Remember it! (This password is not to be confused with the domain administrator account.)

Figure 6.10

Windows NT Server 4 can be configured as a domain controller or stand-alone server.

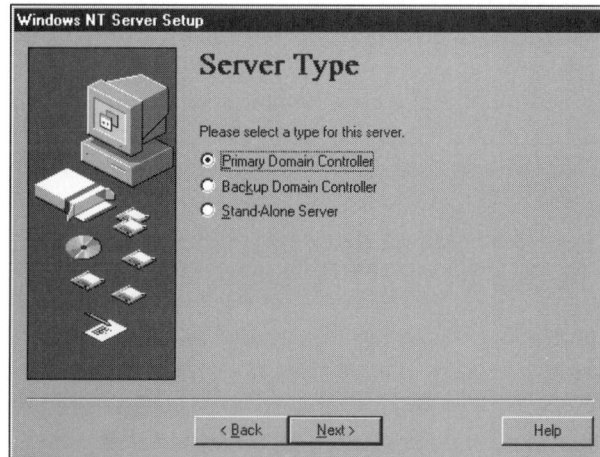

Figure 6.11

An administrator password must be defined at Setup.

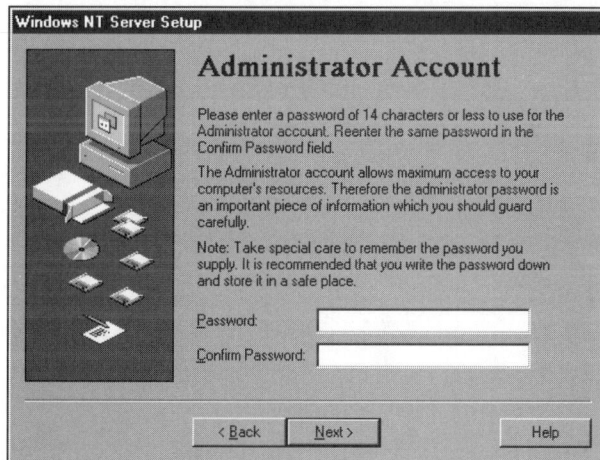

Helpful Tip

Windows NT 4 automatically detects the math co-processor flaw in first-generation Pentium chips and offers an option to compensate for this error. Although this bug may be important to engineers running Windows NT Workstation, it's of little importance to File Server. Selecting the work-around may even harm system performance.

Creating the Emergency Repair Disk

One of the final steps of your Setup, shown in Figure 6.12, is to create an emergency repair disk, using a blank, formatted 1.44MB 3.5-inch diskette. This disk can prove invaluable in helping you recover from system crashes. You can skip this step, but make sure to run the RDISK utility from the Administrative Tools menu as soon as the installation is complete. This menu appears with the rest of the NT Server administrative icons under the Programs group.

The emergency disk needs to be updated any time you make changes to the disks, such as formatting, partitions, and RAID configurations. Also, remember to keep the boot floppies close at hand, since they're an essential part of the emergency disk restore process.

Figure 6.12

During Setup, you can create an emergency repair disk.

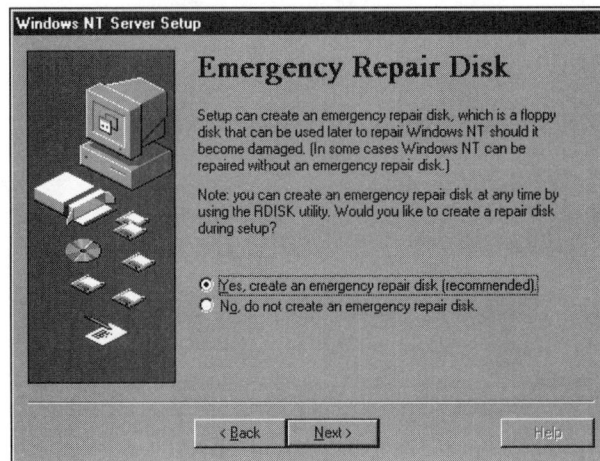

Optional Components

Your last step in Setup is to make your choices from the Select Component screen, shown in Figure 6.13. The install process automatically selects typical Windows NT Server 4 components, but you can add more options. The Multimedia support for sound cards or games may not be necessary on a server, for example. The System Policy Editor, used for managing networked client PC settings, can be installed from here.

These component options are not displayed if you selected a Typical or Compact configuration at the beginning of the install process.

Figure 6.13

Optional components can
be selected during NT 4
Server Setup.

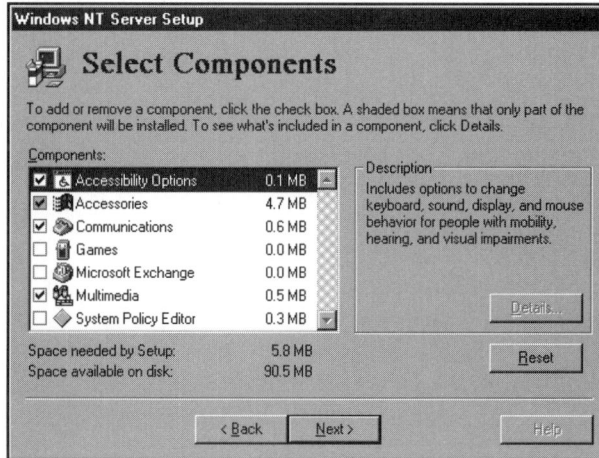

Windows NT Server Setup

Select Components

To add or remove a component, click the check box. A shaded box means that only part of the
component will be installed. To see what's included in a component, click Details.

Components:

☑ 🔧 Accessibility Options	0.1 MB	
☑ 📇 Accessories	4.7 MB	
☑ 🌐 Communications	0.6 MB	
☐ 🎮 Games	0.0 MB	
☐ 📧 Microsoft Exchange	0.0 MB	
☑ 🎵 Multimedia	0.5 MB	
☐ 💠 System Policy Editor	0.3 MB	

Description
Includes options to change
keyboard, sound, display, and mouse
behavior for people with mobility,
hearing, and visual impairments.

Details...

Space needed by Setup: 5.8 MB
Space available on disk: 90.5 MB

Reset

< Back   Next >   Help

- *Network Setup Wizard*

CHAPTER

7

How to Configure Network Options

Y OU CAN SKIP THE NETWORK SETUP WIZARD PORTION OF WINDOWS
NT Server 4 installation for later configuration if you desire. If
there are still unknowns regarding which network protocols or IP
addresses to use, it may be better to wait to run the Wizard till the
rest of Windows NT Server 4 is running properly. It may be necessary to wait if the correct drivers allowing Windows NT to recognize the network adapter aren't available. If either of these are the
case, just press Back on the Windows NT Setup Wizard until the
initial Setup screen with the option "Do not connect this computer
to a network" appears.

Helpful Tip

> *To install the Windows NT Server 4 subsystem after Setup, click on the Network icon in the NT Server 4 Control Panel. If the network setup was skipped the first time around, the Network Setup Wizard will appear. It looks and works identically to the one you used during basic installation. Once Setup Wizard has been run, there's no way to access it again to make changes without first removing all installed services, protocols, and network interface card definitions from the Control Panel. All subsequent network configurations are done through the Network Configuration tool on the Control Panel.*

An added benefit of skipping the network portion of installation is that it's easier to troubleshoot problems with components of the server that don't function properly. On this same principal we recommend that you install only the default networking services and protocols at first. Add other options later through the Control Panel.

If no network device is attached to the machine, you'll have to skip the network service installation, because Windows NT requires at least one network device for network setup.

Helpful Tip

> *If the machine was specified as a domain controller earlier in Setup, networking MUST be installed during basic installation. There's no way for a server to join or create a domain without the networking subsystem in operation. Only stand-alone servers can operate without networking.*

■ Network Setup Wizard

The graphical Setup Wizard, with simplified options and defaults for networking, automatically starts during the Windows NT Server 4 installation.

Wired or Remote LAN Interfaces

The first screen of the Wizard, shown in Figure 7.1, gives the option of either skipping the network setup until later or configuring a wired interface (internal network card). You can also use an option to set up remote access devices, like modems or ISDN cards, as an alternate means of LAN connectivity. As far as Windows NT is concerned, modems are just another network device, capable of running a full range of network protocols and offering services—albeit at a low speed compared to wired solutions.

Figure 7.1

The method of
connecting the NT Server
4 to the network can be
chosen during Setup.

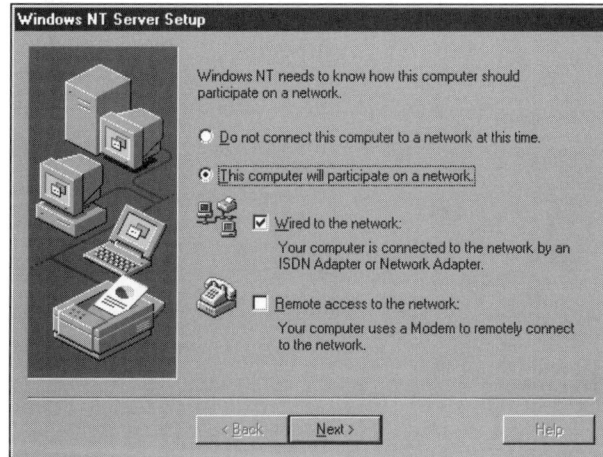

If you're going to use both a modem and network card, we suggest configuring only one device at installation to simplify problem solving. The other can be installed from the Control Panel later.

Installing the Internet Information Server

If you selected them during Setup, the new Internet Information Server (IIS) components will be installed on the server, as shown in Figure 7.2. However, it's still possible to install IIS from the Network icon in the Control Panel after initial setup. In fact, this is the only way it can be installed if you didn't select it during server installation. When you invoke the Network Setup Wizard from the Control Panel after server setup, the IIS installation screen shown in Figure 7.2 does not appear.

Primarily, IIS allows a Windows NT Server 4 to be accessed by any Web browser, such as NetScape's Navigator Gold or Microsoft's Internet Explorer. This feature allows the server to be used as a Web site on the Internet, or on a corporate LAN.

After you select IIS for installation, the Wizard will ask you no further IIS configuration questions until the end of the setup process, when a dialog box asks which IIS components to install. It's a good idea to accept the defaults, installing all components, except, perhaps, the database link, if there are no data systems the Web server will tie into.

Figure 7.2

Internet Information
Server components can
be installed during Setup.

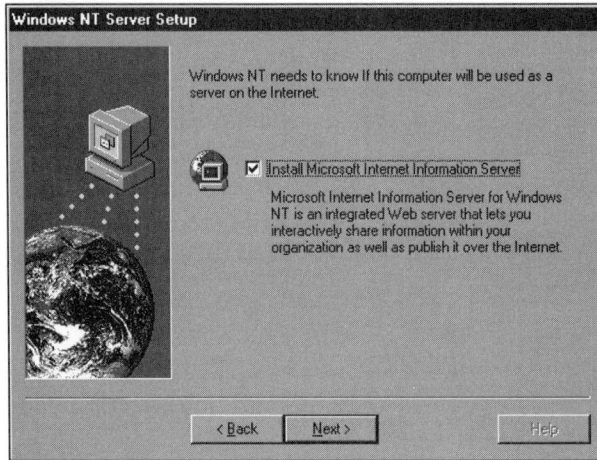

Selecting a Network Card

The Windows NT Server CD-Rom includes support for over 100 network adapter cards. In many cases the Setup Wizard is able to automatically
detect the card. By default, the Wizard only tries to find the first network
adapter card. When you click Find Next on the screen shown in Figure 7.3,
Setup will attempt to find additional cards.

Figure 7.3

Additional network
adapters can be detected
during NT Server
installation.

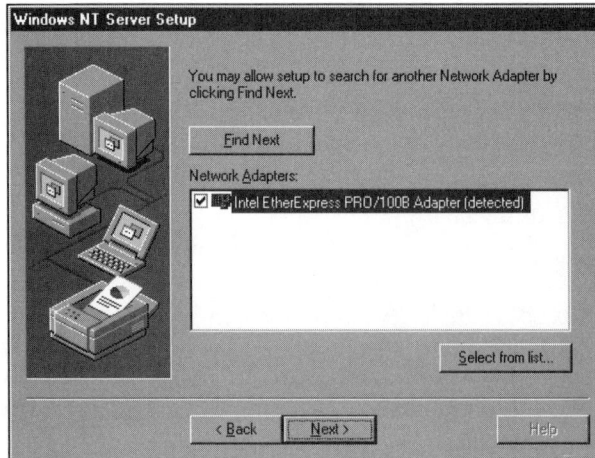

Some network adapters will not be found automatically, and you must choose them manually by pressing Select from list. If your adapter card does not show up in the list that appears, you may need to obtain the appropriate driver from the network adapter card manufacturer. Luckily, adding an unlisted driver is a rather straightforward process. You merely select the Have a disk option in the driver list and then specify the appropriate drive and directory containing the driver.

Helpful Tip

Even if you don't find a network adapter during installation, there's a possibility it might be included in the "/drvlib/netcard" directory on the Windows NT Server 4 CD-ROM. To find out, check the Windows NT Server 4 Hardware Compatibility List. Clicking on the listing for a given adapter will bring up a small pop-up window that specifies the location of the driver. The Hardware Compatibility List is hcl.hlp and is found in /Support. This file can be viewed from any other Windows PC as a standard help document.

At this stage of Setup, you can't select remote access devices, like modems, attached to a serial port. This includes internal cards that use a COM port. However, you can detect internal remote access cards, complete with network adapter card drivers, that are designed to work as LAN cards. (For our purposes, PC cards are also internal.)

NOTE. *A growing number of ISDN cards and other remote access technologies, such as Frame Relay, do not use serial COM ports and do use the same NDIS drivers as standard LAN cards. This allows remote communications to occur at higher speeds than is possible with a serial port. The UART serial port chip, common in most PCs, restricts serial ports to a mere 115.2Kbps. Analog modems and other communications devices that use a serial port (both internal and external) rely on the Windows NT 4 Telephony API and require .INF files.*

When you proceed to the next portion of Network Setup, Windows NT 4 will check the network adapters for their configurations and ask for verification if necessary. Peripheral component interconnect (PCI) extended industry standard archiecture (EISA) and network adapter cards require no manual parameter selection, since the these relatively advanced system buses resolve interrupts and memory addresses between cards automatically. With older industry standard architecture (ISA) adapters, however, Windows NT 4 will display some configurable interrupt request line (IRQ) and memory settings in a dialog box. Be careful to select only those settings that

The Microsoft Network Driver Model: NDIS

The network card drivers for Windows NT follow the network driver interface specification (NDIS). NDIS was initially developed by Microsoft and IBM and is still used by OS/2. However, IBM and Microsoft have modified the standard to their own needs over the years, and drivers for one will not work with the other.

The NDIS model in Windows NT Server is version 4 and should support drivers from Windows NT 3.51 Server. Earlier NDIS drivers for Windows for Workgroups (version 3) or LAN Manager will not work.

the network adapter card is configured for. If an ISA network card is set for IRQ 3, for example, and you select IRQ 10 during Setup, the network services will not initialize properly.

When using ISA cards, conflicts between system devices must be resolved before network installation. It may be necessary to consult the adapter's documentation for appropriate jumper settings. In other cases, such as Intel EtherExpress or 3COM EtherLink III adapters, you can select configuration information through software that requires running text-based DOS configuration programs provided by the manufacturer.

Unfortunately, these network adapter card configuration utilities can't be run from inside Windows NT Server. Keeping a bootable DOS floppy around may prove invaluable.

Selecting Network Protocols

Windows NT Server supports several network protocols that enable it to co-exist in mixed computing environments. For example, if the existing network is configured to handle Internet Packet Exchange (IPX) for NetWare servers with IPX routers between segments, the protocol of choice would likely be IPX. Windows NT Server can also work well with either TCP/IP or NetBEUI, and basic Windows NT networking can be accomplished with any of the three. However, in WANs with hubs or routers between multiple local area network segments, IPX and TCP/IP are the only options; NetBEUI cannot be routed. If, however, there is no need to access a Windows NT Server from other subnets, the NetBEUI protocol is also an option.

By default, the Windows NT Server 4 Setup Wizard will automatically select the TCP/IP protocol for installation. NWLink Internet packet exchange/sequenced packet exchange (IPX/SPX) and NetBEUI are the other selections, as shown in Figure 7.4. Pressing Select from list will give you the options of the Data Link Control (DLC) Protocol that's used for both host connectivity to IBM mainframes and printing to networked HP printers, plus a couple of others. These additional protocols have only limited functionality in Windows NT, so be sure to select at least one of the three primary choices, as well.

Figure 7.4

Setup makes it possible to choose from a variety of protocols.

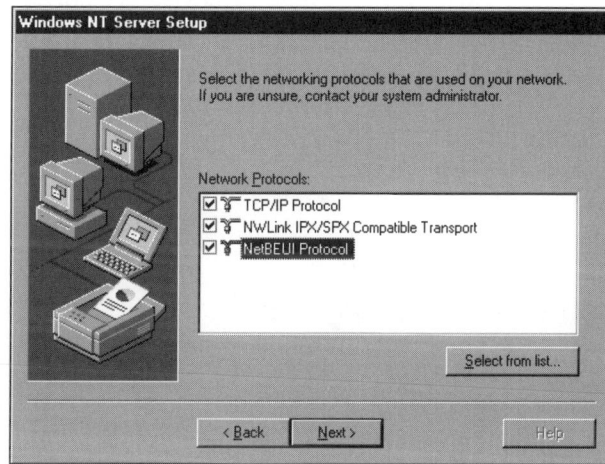

If necessary, you can run more than one network protocol under Windows NT. It's quite common to have at least two protocols selected, and possibly three or four. The amount of system overhead required to execute these extra protocols is minimal.

Helpful Tip

Your client PCs must be configured to run at least one of the same protocols as the server. Windows 95 and Windows for Workgroups can both use NetBEUI, TCP/IP, and IPX.

When selecting protocols, keep in mind that although basic Windows NT networking can work with any of the primary choices, there are specific network services that will work only with specific protocols.

For example, TCP/IP is necessary for running either Hypertext Transfer Protocol (HTTP) or File Transfer Protocol (FTP) services. Novell NetWare integration services, such as Gateway Services for NetWare (GSNW) won't work without IPX.

It isn't critical, however, to select all the correct protocols during installation. When adding additional services, such as the Web service, later on Windows NT Server 4 will automatically add the necessary protocols if they're not already in operation.

NOTE. *Additional network protocols can also be run under Windows NT Server 4, but their functionality is somewhat limited. Appletalk can be run, but it's used only to allow Macintosh computers access to server resources. Actual communications between NT Servers and other PCs can only be accomplished using NetBEUI, IPX, or TCP/IP. However, if multiple network adapter cards are installed in the Windows NT Server 4 across different subnets, Appletalk can also be routed. The DLC protocol is included with Windows NT Server 4 to allow communications with networked printers and IBM host systems like the AS/400. Even more protocols can be used with Windows NT 4, but they must be supplied by a third party. For example, Banyan provides NT drivers for access to their Vines IP network.*

Helpful Tip

The Network Setup Wizard will automatically bring up the TCP/IP protocol configuration box at the end of the network installation process (provided it was selected, of course). Further configuration of protocols is possible from the Control Panel once the network setup is completed.

Selecting Network Services

Like all Windows NT services, such as hard disk drivers, installed network services run in the background at all times. Whether a backup program is being run from the server console, or other administrative functions are being performed in the graphical user interface, network services keep functioning, handling end-user requests, or taking care of network maintenance. Each of these services takes a toll on system performance to varying degrees, and if a great many of the server's network functions need to run, it may be wise to spread them amongst several servers.

For example, one could run the remote access service (RAS), handling connections from remote users over modems, and another could be running Dynamic Host Configuration Protocol (DHCP) and Windows Internet Name Service (WINS). The decision on how to split up work loads between servers is also a function of the size of network. In very small LANs with only ten users, there may be no problem setting up a single Pentium class PC as a primary domain controller and DHCP host running RAS as well, to allow dial-up access to a single modem.

However, even if there's no serious system degradation on a given server running multiple services, it may still make sense to establish a second or third server, just to be redundant if nothing else.

The Windows NT 4 Setup Wizard automatically installs four services that can't be deselected, as shown in Figure 7.5. (They can be removed later from the Control Panel, but their removal can cause erratic behavior in the system.)

Figure 7.5

Various network services can be selected during installation.

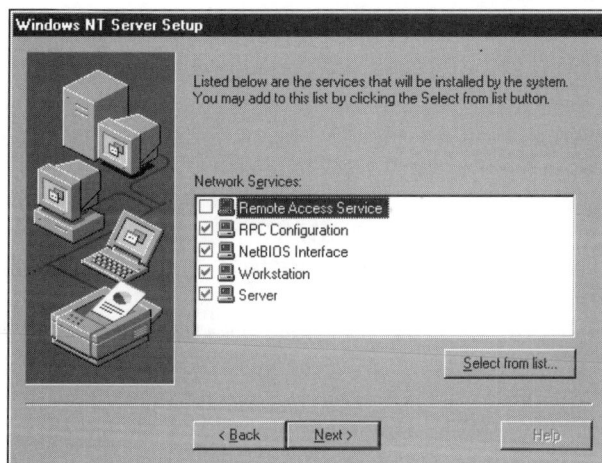

Required Network Services

RPC Configuration   Remote procedure calls (RPC) make it possible for programs to access other machines on the network. Specifically, the RPC configuration service makes it possible to remotely administer a given NT server from any other NT server or NT workstation on the network, provided they have security rights. Several Windows NT administration tools, such as User Manager for Domains, provide the option of choosing a remote system to administer and do so by taking advantage of RPCs.

NetBIOS Interface   All communications over the network between Windows machines (Windows for Workgroups, Windows 95, or Windows NT) rely on network basic input/output system (NetBIOS). NetBEUI is a close relative of NetBIOS, but they've diverged to the extent that NetBIOS can run on top of most Windows protocols. Any time a network connection to a remote shared volume or document is printed, it's done using NetBIOS. The only exceptions to this are when the user is accessing network services not specific to Windows. NetBIOS is not used for connections to NetWare servers. The TCP/IP services in Windows NT don't use NetBIOS either.

Workstation and Server   These are core networking components of Windows NT Server that make it possible to share and access resources between networked PCs.

Optional networking services can also be selected in the Network Setup Wizard by clicking Select from list. However, we recommend that extra services be added later through the Network icon in the Control Panel. This makes it easier to debug installation problems.

Optional Network Services

DHCP Relay Agent   This is a new feature in Windows NT Server 4 that allows DHCP broadcasts for automatic allocation of network TCP/IP addresses to be routed across network segments. This is only useful if there are DHCP hosts on the network, and the Windows NT Server 4 has multiple network adapter cards routing traffic between network segments.

The Routing Information Protocol (RIP) for IP routing service must also be installed for the DHCP relay agent to function. The older BOOTP configuration protocol broadcasts can also be routed across segments with this service.

Gateway (and Client) Services for NetWare   This service allows Windows NT Server 4 to access NetWare file servers to share data and printers. An additional feature to traditional NetWare client support, however, is that GSNW makes it possible to re-share NetWare resources to Windows PCs that are not running NetWare client software.

In Windows NT 4, GSNW supports connections to NetWare Directory Services (DNS), as well as the traditional binderies.

Microsoft DHCP Server   Rather than having to keep track of TCP/IP addresses for each computer on a network manually, DHCP makes it possible to set up a bank of addresses that are automatically assigned to computers that request them. Without DHCP, end users must wait for an administrator to give them a number before they are able to use their computers on the network.

Other network protocols such as NetBEUI and IPX create addresses on the fly by reading the burned-in media access control address of the network adapter card. (Every network adapter has a unique number burned into the circuitry when it's manufactured.) This makes simple networks easy to set up, but it has limitations on host computers that need fixed addresses.

Microsoft Domain Name Service (DNS)   Originating on UNIX systems, DNS was devised to act as a database for the resolution of text-based host names with their numbered TCP/IP addresses. With DNS it's possible to specify the name of a TCP/IP host you wish to access, such as a Web site, without having to remember a lengthy number. This new feature in Windows NT Server 4 allows Windows NT to provide DNS services to a network rather than to traditional UNIX hosts.

Microsoft Internet Information Server 2   Windows NT Server always had built-in FTP service. Version 4 also sports a full fledged HTTP service to help you create a Web site on the Internet or corporate intranet.

Microsoft TCP/IP Printing   The TCP/IP printing service allows Windows NT Server to both access or emulate UNIX line printer remote (LPR) print queues. Existing UNIX hosts on a network will make use of this to send their documents to Windows NT Server print queues, and Windows NT can re-route its own print queues to UNIX LPR. Macintoshes can also benefit by having their print jobs directed to UNIX hosts via a Windows NT Server.

Network Monitor Agent   Once installed, you can configure the Network Monitor Agent to capture packets on the network attached to the network adapter card or cards in Windows NT. With the Network Monitor Agent installed, you can analyze traffic remotely, using the Network Monitor Tool from the Microsoft Systems Management Server platform. The Network Monitor Tool that comes with Windows NT 4 Workstation and Server are not capable of remote monitoring.

You can set security options for the Network Monitor Agent under the Services tab in the Network icon of the Control Panel. Passwords can require any remote users to be authenticated if they wish to monitor the network traffic.

This agent is particularly useful for watching network traffic across subnets. The SMS Network Monitor Tool can track packets to and from any network adapter on a given subnet, but unless it can remotely manage a network monitor agent on a separate subnet, it will be blind to traffic.

Nearly all network packet types can be captured for analyses by the Network Monitor Agent, including NetBEUI, IPX, TCP/IP and Appletalk.

Network Monitor Tools and Agent   Selecting the network monitor tools and agent service will install both the Network Monitor Agent, which provides the intelligence to capture raw packet transmissions over the network, and the Network Monitor Tool for actually configuring and viewing captures.

The Network Monitor Tool provided in Windows NT Server is a subset of the Network Monitor Tool in Systems Management Server. The Windows NT 4 version of the Network Monitor Tool can only sniff packets going to and from the network adapter cards attached to the specific server the tool is running on.

Packet capturing can only occur when the Network Monitor Tool is active, after being loaded from the Administration Tools menu. Filters can be defined to narrow the amount of packet data that is sniffed, making it easier to pinpoint problems. The space available for captures can be set, but is ultimately limited by the available RAM. (Captures are not spooled directly to disk.)

Remote Access Service   Windows NT Server can be configured to use analog modems or other remote communications devices, such as ISDN and Frame Relay adapters, to handle remote connections to the network. By using the Dial-Up Networking feature of Windows for Workgroups, Windows 95, or Windows NT 4 Workstation, any remote system can connect to the network as if they were locally attached to the LAN.

Using RAS, it's not only possible for remote systems to use resources on the Windows NT Server, but also to access UNIX or NetWare hosts. Because RAS uses the standard PPP, even non-Windows computers, such as Macintoshes or UNIX workstations, can use it to gain access to the network. Although RAS can route multiple protocols to a remote computer, it can't route traffic between LANs.

Routing Information Protocol for Internet Protocol   Windows NT Server 4 is the first version able to route traffic between network segments, out of the box. Windows NT Workstation does not support routing.

NOTE. *LAN-to-LAN routing, using RIP over switched WAN connections with devices such as analog modems, ISDN, or Frame Relay adapters is not currently supported in Windows NT Server 4. However, network traffic can be routed to individual remote clients. It's also possible to configure static routing over dial-up RAS connections, but this requires a number of changes to the registry. Consult the Windows NT Server 4 Resource Kit for more detailed instructions.*

Routing makes it possible for computers on one network segment to both view and access resources on a different segment. For routing to work, multiple network adapters must be installed in the Windows NT Server 4, attached to different segments. The RIP service only routes IP traffic (including the entire IP family of protocols). Other services must be installed to route the IPX and Appletalk protocols.

NOTE. *The RIP routing service can still be installed in systems with only one network adapter card, but it's of little use. With a single network adapter card, RIP operates in silent mode, scanning the network for routing information to build a routing table that can be viewed but serves no other function. If a Windows NT Server 4 is running RIP in static mode (i.e., with only one network adapter card), a change in the registry must be made for RIP broadcasts to start, if a second network adapter is installed. Change the SilentRip Registry parameter to 0.*

Even without installing the RIP service, Windows NT 4 will automatically route IP packets between network segments in static mode (provided that multiple network adapter cards are installed). For simple networks, in which Windows NT is attached to all segments, static routing may be all that's necessary. In more complex environments, however, RIP is necessary to maintain a dynamic table of routes that changes automatically in response to network alterations. To disable static routing, deselect Enable IP forwarding under the TCP/IP Configuration Services tab.

A text-based route.exe utility can be used to both view and manage the routing tables, with either static routing or RIP.

RIP for IPX/SPX Compatible Transport   The multi-protocol routing support in Windows NT Server 4 can also handle IPX traffic. As long as two or more network adapter cards are installed in a server, IPX traffic can be automatically forwarded between subnets using RIP. Static IPX routing, with hard-route definitions, isn't possible with Windows NT Server 4. However, the RIP for IPX service will enable dynamic routing of both IPX and Service Advertising Protocol (SAP) between networks, where the router will continually change its route table definitions to correspond to changes on the network.

Using the Route Command

route [-f][-p] [command] [destination] [MASK netmask] [gateway] [METRIC metric]

Available options are:

1. f   Clears routing tables of all entries

2. p   Enables persistent routes

3. command   Choose one of the following:

4. print   Displays route table on screen

5. add   Adds a new route to table

6. delete   Removes a route definition from table

7. change   Modifies an existing route definition

8. destination   Host or network to route

9. netmask   Input the subnet value to use with the route entry. If this value is absent, a default of 255.255.255.255 is used.

10. gateway   The router address that acts as the gateway to the destination for the route.

11. metric   A value to represent the relative cost of the route. A large number will cause most traffic to use a different route. If no number is specified, 1 is the default.

Settings for routing are made in the Network icon of the Control Panel. To enable IPX routing, click on the Protocols tab. Under IPX/SPX Compatible Transport, choose Properties. Next, select the Routing tab and then Enable RIP Routing. For IPX routing to function properly, each network adapter card in the server must be given a unique network number, chosen from Properties for the IPX/SPX Compatible Transport.

Since many NetWare servers broadcast their services using SAP, the SAP Agent should also be installed, to ensure that other network segments can access resources across the whole network.

Unfortunately, Microsoft has not yet implemented filtering features for IPX routing to cut down on needless traffic. In large networks the volume of SAP traffic can be quite large, easily overwhelming low bandwidth remote connections. If IPX spoofing and filtering features are necessary, network managers may still want to consider traditional routers.

Routing over dial-up connections is not yet supported in Windows NT. However, it can support routing on fixed WAN links, such as a T1 line, in which internal adapters with NDIS LAN drivers are used.

RPC Support for Banyan   For integration with Banyan Vines networks, RPC support makes it possible to remotely administer Banyan servers.

Service Advertising Protocol Agent   The SAP is used by NetWare servers to broadcast their presence and available resources over a network. The Windows NT Server 4 SAP Agent makes it possible for the NT multiprotocol routing components to carry SAP packet traffic across network segments. The SAP Agent is of no use without the RIP for IXP/SPX service.

Services for Macintosh   Windows NT Server 4 can integrate well into a Macintosh network using the Services for Macintosh. This service allows NT Server to share its resources in the native Macintosh networking protocol, Appletalk. The Windows NT Server becomes transparent to Macintosh clients, so they can access the server through their control panels, in the same way they use LocalTalk laser printers and Appleshare file servers. Windows NT Server will even convert Macintosh print jobs from PostScript into the language of any other Windows NT printer. The Windows NT Server Macintosh services also make it possible for PC users to share Macintosh printers.

Both PC and Macintosh users can use the same network directories for sharing files. However, for data to be shared, users on both platforms must be using the same software. Microsoft Word and Excel, for example, have both Macintosh and PC versions with the same data file formats.

Windows NT Server can automatically detect the Appletalk protocol configuration on your network if it has already been set up with a router or server. If necessary, however, Windows NT Server can create the Appletalk network by "seeding" the LAN.

Seeding can be explained this way. Unlike TCP/IP networks, which require all the appropriate addressing information to operate, Appletalk computers sniff the network to find appropriate network subnet information. One device on a subnet must be configured with the appropriate network addresses and assigned by the administrator so all the Appletalk devices can function.

With the inclusion of multi-protocol routing support, Windows NT Server 4 can route Appletalk traffic across subnets if it has more than one network adapter card. Just as with IPX routing, the Windows NT Server network configuration requires adjustment to route Appletalk properly. Different Appletalk network addresses must be specified for each network adapter card under the Network icon in the Control Panel.

Simple TCP/IP Services   Support for even relatively obscure TCP/IP network features has been provided with Windows NT Server 4. Some of the supported features are Quote of the Day, Discard, Echo, Daytime, and Character Generator. These simple TCP/IP services are of use only to respond to requests from other hosts.

Simple Network Management Protocol (SNMP) Service   With the SNMP Service installed, Windows NT Server 4 can be remotely monitored from any industry standard management platform on the network, like Hewlett Packard's Open View or Sun Net Manager. If the SNMP agent on a Windows NT Server 4 has been configured to allow access, an administrator on a UNIX workstation running a network management package can monitor the status of the Windows NT server and check such things as usage levels.

Windows NT cannot yet be managed remotely via SNMP. Only passive monitoring is possible, although remote management is possible using the Microsoft NT management tools. Security can be set on the SNMP agent to specify which remote hosts, by IP address, and which SNMP communities are allowed to monitor the system. Configuration is accomplished under the Services tab of the Network icon that appears on the Control Panel.

Windows Internet Name Service   Microsoft developed WINS as a means of resolving the NetBIOS Windows network host names with their TCP/IP addresses. Without designated NT servers acting as WINS hosts, the only way to access resources in a Windows network using TCP/IP was by entering the specific IP addresses of the hosts in the host file on the local PC.

On a TCP/IP Windows network, you can't browse lists of all the networked PCs, as you can when the NetBEUI protocol is used. When the IP stacks of client Windows PCs have the IP address of a WINS host specified, they'll be automatically registered in the WINS table, and users can browse and make network access requests via the central table. If the client PCs obtain their addresses automatically via DHCP, it's possible to configure a WINS host variable to be propagated throughout the network.

WINS can be easily linked to the new DNS in Windows NT Server 4, allowing all Windows clients to be automatically registered in the DNS. Along with the DHCP and DNS service, WINS can help automate the management of host names and addresses across Windows networks.

Configuring Network Protocols

If you selected the TCP/IP protocol, the Network Setup Wizard will bring up a configuration window towards the end of the installation process, requiring some basic information about the network addresses. Other protocols like IPX/SPX and NetBEUI don't require additional information, since they are able to automatically determine the appropriate address information by scanning the network.

After installation, all network protocol parameters and settings can be further modified through the Network icon in the Control Panel.

NWLink IPX/SPX Compatible Transport

Over the history of the development of NetWare, its creator, Novell, Incorporated, has developed improved network protocols using different frame types. These protocols aren't compatible with one another, and client PCs will only be able to detect network services using the specific IPX frame type they were configured for.

By default, the NWLink IPX/SPX protocol driver is set to auto-detect the IPX frame types on the network. In some cases, however, if the NT 4 Server cannot see NetWare servers on the LAN, you may need to configure the frame-types manually from NWLink IPX/SPX Properties window under the Network icon of the Control Panel, shown in Figure 7.6. You may need to find out from a network administrator which frame types should be selected.

Manual frame-type selection is a requirement for setting up IPX routing between LANs, using the RIP for IPX/SPX network service. The IPX frame type and network number must be specified for each network adapter card.

Another important option in the IPX/SPX Properties screen is the Internal Network Number parameter. When Windows NT Server 4 is used merely as a NetWare client with Gateway Services for NetWare, the IPX Internal Network Number can be set to anything. However, when the NT Server is used as a host for NetWare services or as an IPX router, the Internal Network Number must be unique so that no conflicts arise between other NetWare servers on the LAN.

NetBEUI Protocol

There are no user-definable parameters for the NetBEUI protocol. NetBEUI is a very simple protocol without multiple frame-types, as IPX has,

Figure 7.6

The IPX frame type can
be selected under
NWLink IPX/SPX
Properties.

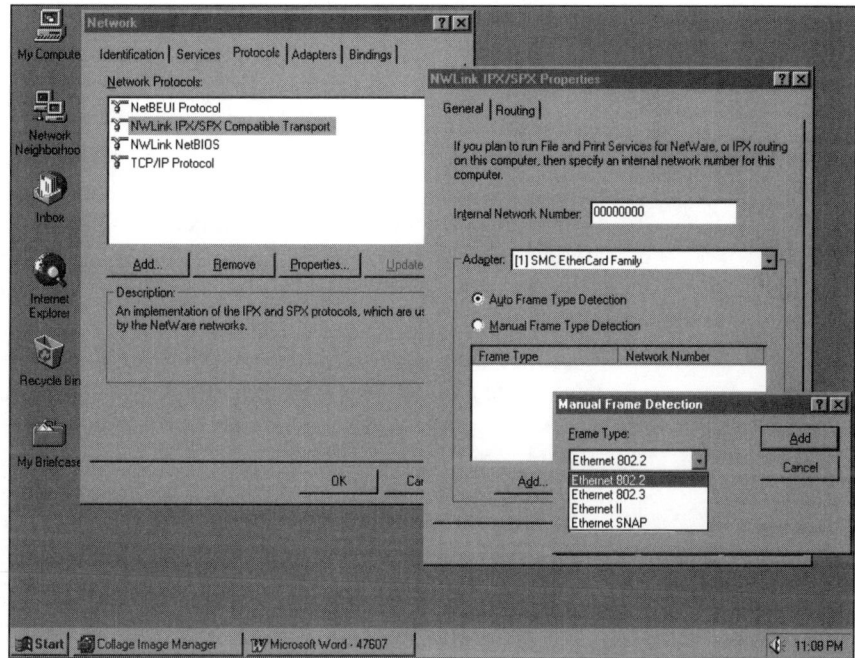

and no need for specified addresses, as TCP/IP has. This protocol, however, is
not routable, and only works on a single segment.

TCP/IP Protocol

If a DHCP host on the network (usually another Windows NT Server), is already assigning IP addresses, the TCP/IP configuration windows can be by-
passed during installation. The Setup Wizard offers a dialog box asking if the
IP address should be obtained dynamically via DHCP. Answering no to this
question will bring up the IP configuration screens. If Setup refuses to proceed further after you click on Yes, it indicates the NT Server was unable to
discover a DHCP host on the network, and the information needs to be entered manually.

Whether the IP address is entered manually or obtained automatically
over the network, the NT system requires it for the TCP/IP stack to function.
If no DHCP host is available, an IP address must be obtained from a network administrator to proceed with the installation.

It's possible to enter a false address into the IP stack by picking numbers
out of the air, just to finish the system installation, but this can be dangerous,
since picking an address already in use by another host can cause serious

problems on the network. If the Windows NT Server is the first system on a given subnet to be configured with TCP/IP, you can choose a number that will be changed later.

Even if a DHCP host exists on the network, administrators may prefer to have all servers manually configured with TCP/IP so a fixed address can be assigned to the new NT server.

The new IP address management tools may help simplify network administration and system installations, but their dynamic natures may be problematic when applied to the main servers on a network. It may be fine for the DHCP host to assign new IP addresses to Windows 95 clients frequently, but it can be a nuisance on servers. It's a good idea to keep servers at the same address so users know where to reach them.

The TCP/IP configuration windows are filled with boxes for parameters, but the only value absolutely essential for installation is the IP address itself. IP addresses are split into four groups of numbers, known as octets. The first two sets typically remain the same for a given network; the last two octets may change from machine to machine in the same building.

TCP/IP numbers are precious resources managed by a central Internet governing body known as the InterNic. Typically, InterNic will assign a range of IP addresses to a given company, and the local system administrators then choose which numbers to give to which machines. This whole process is designed to ensure that no two machines on the Internet have the same address.

Often, however, companies build their own IP networks using fictitious numbers. This works as long as the corporate LAN remains separate from the Internet. As soon as a link to the global Internet is planned, however, these companies are faced with having to reconfigure all the addresses on their entire network. If DHCP and automated IP management systems are used, it may be relatively simple to change all the system addresses in a company, but there are always problems with routers and computers that don't support DHCP.

Another solution to this re-addressing nightmare is to use translation devices that sit between the corporate network and the Internet, translating valid addresses from the Internet to the invalid ones inside the company. These address translation products used to be very expensive, but the price has dropped considerably, and address translation has become a standard feature in most firewalls. Address translation will become increasingly popular, since there are few IP addresses left that aren't already reserved.

NOTE. *A whole new TCP/IP protocol, known as IPv6, has been developed to vastly increase the number of available address space. Unfortunately, IPv6 won't be available for several years.*

A large company might be assigned a class B address like 140.244. This means that every computer running TCP/IP on the corporate LAN will begin with 140.244. By segmenting the LAN further, administrators may decide that all computers in the San Francisco office will have an address of 140.244.68. All the computers in San Francisco can then be given addresses ranging from 1 to 254 (since IP addresses work on the hexidecimal, or HEX, numbering system, numbers can't go beyond 255).

NOTE. *Class B addresses specify the first two octets, leaving the last two for internal administrators to allocate. Class C addresses specify the first three octets.*

The subnet portion of the IP address configuration window must be filled in, as well. The subnet mask plays the critical role of allowing minute segmentation of IP networks. It has become a requirement so the computer recognizes only the IP addresses it should. An IP address can be entered correctly but still not function because the subnet mask was improperly specified. Usually, each octet of the subnet mask has only the numbers 255, filling up as many octets as the class of the IP network. All the computers in a class B network would use 255.255.0.0 as the subnet mask. Class C networks would use 255.255.255.0.

The IP address and subnet mask must be set for each network card in the Windows NT Server 4. The network adapter card being configured is displayed in the Adapter list box. You can install additional cards by clicking on the down arrow here to show the available choices.

Another piece of information to place in the IP stack is the address of the default gateway. Without specifying a gateway address or router that bridges your local subnet with the broader network, it will only be possible to communicate with computers on your local subnet. In a small company with only one subnet this is not a problem, but as soon as you link to the Internet or other company LANs, you may need to add a gateway address into the IP stack configuration in order to communicate across the entire network.

TCP/IP Protocol 1: Advanced TCP/IP Settings   The built-in TCP/IP stack in Windows NT Server 4 supports sophisticated functionality that has hitherto been maddeningly difficult to configure in the UNIX systems that pioneered TCP/IP. In the Advanced IP Addressing window, you can configure multiple IP addresses to the same network adapter card (this is known as multihoming), set packet filtering, and define additional gateway addresses. A new feature, unique to Windows NT Server 4, is the ability to configure a network adapter card for the Point-to-Point Tunneling Protocol (PPTP) that allows secure encrypted connections to a corporate network from remote users on the Internet.

Multihoming   You can add IP addresses easily by clicking on Add.

Most NT 4 Servers only need one IP address per network adapter card, but there are cases where you may want to consolidate servers with new hardware and give a Windows NT Server multiple addresses to avoid end-user disruption. This feature is particularly useful to Internet service providers that may have multiple, outsourced, corporate Web sites, each needing a separate identity.

Additional Gateways   Another advanced function is the definition of alternate gateway addresses, or routers, that link the Windows NT Server LAN to other subnets. The default gateway, specified at the main TCP/IP configuration window, will always be used first; the alternate addresses are tried if no response is found from the default.

PPTP Filter—Virtual Private Networking   Rather than maintaining banks of modems for remote users to call into for e-mail and network access, Microsoft has taken the first steps towards building virtual private networking technologies into Windows NT Server 4. This allows secure remote access to the corporate LAN over the Internet; users in remote offices can use whichever Internet service provider they choose to access the corporate data, using encryption. Not only can companies save on administrative overhead because they no longer need to maintain modem banks, but they can eliminate the expense of long-distance calls to the head office. Even a salesman on another continent can connect to the head office with a local call.

It's always been possible to hook up servers to the Internet, but because of security concerns, few companies have done it. The Internet is like a massive party-line. Anyone can watch, or eavesdrop on, traffic between computers. The Microsoft PPTP technology uses 40bit encryption to scramble the data in all the packets going to and from the Internet.

For Windows NT to accept PPTP connections, an additional network adapter card must be dedicated to the purpose. One network card is attached to the corporate LAN and the other to the router that's linked to the Internet. In this fashion all Internet traffic must pass through the PPTP configured network adapter card on the NT Server.

Unfortunately, no other types of Internet connectivity can occur on the network segment behind the NT that's acting as the PPTP host. A second Internet connection and a firewall may be necessary to allow internal corporate network access to the Internet for such things as Web browsing and FTP.

PPTP works closely with RAS and the Dial-Up Networking service of Windows NT Server. Remote users accessing the corporate LAN from the Internet must configure their Dial-Up Networking session to use PPTP. The Windows NT Server 4, configured for PPTP, authenticates remote users with the NT domain users, based on the Windows User ID and Password. The need to maintain only one set of user IDs can help reduce the administrative work necessary in traditional remote access systems.

One of the big drawbacks to PPTP is that only Windows NT Workstation 4 currently supports PPTP. Windows 95 and Windows for Workgroups remote PCs are out of luck (as are any other non-Windows computers). Microsoft does have plans to introduce Windows 95 PPTP support sometime in early 1997.

Enable Security—Packet Filtering   IP packet filtering is another new feature in Windows NT Server 4.

By selecting Enable Security in the Advanced IP Addressing window, you can send rudimentary filters to prohibit unwanted types of network access. Packet filtering security works on a lower, more fundamental level than standard Windows NT challenge/response authentication.

With normal Windows NT security, access is controlled by checking User IDs and Passwords. However, this does not prevent unauthorized users from attempting to logon by guessing access codes. With packet filtering, you can specify that only certain types of IP network traffic are even allowed access to the NT Server in the first place.

From the TCP/IP Security window, it's possible to specify which logical IP ports are allowed to be used, and for which IP family protocols (such as UDP and TCP). Unfortunately, Windows NT only offers a very basic packet filtering subset. It isn't possible to restrict host access by IP address, for example (ensuring that only network traffic from a specified computer is allowed access).

TCP/IP Protocol 2: Domain Name Service configuration   The DNS tab of TCP/IP Configuration allows you to specify the DNS hosts on the network. The Host Name field will already show the computer name, because it was specified during system setup. The Domain Name field, however, is for the domain name. It isn't so critical for you to fill in this name, and not assigning it shouldn't prevent normal functionality of Windows NT Server 4. However, when the server is to be used as an Internet host, it can be useful to properly specify the full domain. For example, the host name for an engineering server in the Boston office is bosteng, while the domain name for the registered corporate Internet domain name is fabchoc.com.

The IP addresses of DNS servers on the network can also be specified under the DNS Configuration tab of the TCP/IP Properties window.

DNS hosts resolve the commonly known names of IP hosts with their numbered addresses. Without a DNS server on the LAN, you must enter the full IP address to access any machine. Imagine having to type in a 12 digit number to access a Web site instead of www.website.com.

TCP/IP Protocol 3: WINS Address   Use the WINS Address tab under TCP/IP Properties to enable the use of WINS hosts on the network. In TCP/IP networks, WINS hosts are essential to allow browsing of resources. The IP addresses of established WINS servers can be specified in the Windows NT

Helpful Tip

> *A local host table can be maintained in the \%ntsystem%\system32\\
> drivers\etc directory, where frequently used host names can be entered
> with their IP addresses. This may be useful if no DNS exists on the LAN
> or if systems need to be accessed that are not in the DNS list.*

Server 4 IP stack. There are fields for both a primary and secondary WINS
servers. Another option in the WINS Configuration window allows for the
use of a DNS for Windows name resolution as well.

For additional name resolution, individually maintained host files, listing
IP addresses, and host names can be imported for use in Windows host name
resolutions. You can even maintain a central host file on one server that all
the NT servers point to for name resolution. However, if you want centrally
managed name resolution, it would be far easier, and ultimately superior, to
set up an NT Server running WINS and DNS somewhere on the network.

(TCP/IP Protocol)4: TCP/IP troubleshooting tools   Several text-based
TCP/IP tools are automatically installed with the TCP/IP protocol. They can
be very useful for troubleshooting network connections and IP network status.

Perhaps the most useful of these tools is the PING command. When you
input an IP address or host name as a parameter, PING will attempt to find
the specified machine on the network. PING is an invaluable tool to ensure
that basic network connectivity is working. Examples are PING 206.66.184.204
or PING www.pcweek.com.

If the specified host is found on the network, PING will respond, showing the replies. When the host cannot be found, PING hangs for several seconds and then reports that the specified IP address is bad.

You can use the PING command to check for rudimentary network functionality and the Windows NT Server the network is running on. This is a procedure known as "pinging onself." If there is a response, it shows that the
network protocols have at least been properly bound to the network adapter
card. After you check the internal network adapter card with PING, you can
ping other computers in the local subnet. If this works, try pinging hosts on
other subnets, or ultimately on the Internet.

The PING utility is very useful to help pinpoint where network problems
are. If all machines in the local subnet are pingable but hosts in a separate
subnet can't be reached, there may be a problem with the gateway or router.
Try pinging the router to see if it is functioning. Another possible problem is
that the DNS may not be functioning properly, making it impossible to ping
names like www.pcweek.com. In such a case, using the hard coded IP address
instead of the name should work. Try pinging the designated DNS host to see
if it's still running.

The TRACERT command works in the same fashion as PING, but gives more detailed information about the path used for the network transmission. When pinging a host on the Internet, for example, it's not uncommon for the packets to travel through 15 to 20 routers and network segments along the way. TRACERT gives you the ability to follow these paths.

Quite often, some of the parameters for the DNS host and default gateways haven't been set properly in the Windows NT Server IP stack. The IPCONFIG command will display the IP settings. These settings can also be viewed by using the control panel. Using the /all parameter with IPCONFIG will display all the settings for each network adapter card.

IPCONFIG can also be used to obtain new IP address leases from a DHCP host for dynamic IP configuration. First type IPCONFIG /RELEASE, and then IPCONFIG /RENEW.

Another tool that may be of some use is NSLOOKUP. This program returns the host name of an IP address. If you type NSLOOKUP 206.66.184.204, the system should return the name www.pcweek.com. Of course, NSLOOKUP only works if there's a DNS host on the network.

Several other command line tools have been included with the IP stack, which are of less value. For further information consult the Windows NT Server 4 resource kit.

Configuring Bindings

Although the Network Setup Wizard provides a graphical interface, for changing the network bindings (shown in Figure 7.7) we generally recommend that you accept the defaults and finish the installation. It's possible to tweak performance by changing the order of protocol bindings, ensuring that the most frequently used protocols have a higher priority, but the default settings shouldn't affect network functionality. In rare cases, the order of the bindings needs to be changed for third-party NT services to function properly.

Even when changes are necessary for compatibility reasons, it's still best to finish the installation, check the basic network functionality, and then change the bindings from the Network icon in the Control Panel. A fair degree of networking experience is suggested for any attempts to alter bindings.

Joining a Domain

The final step in setting up Windows NT Server 4 networking is to join a domain or workgroup. In order to join an existing domain, the Setup Wizard will require a Domain User ID and Password with appropriate administrative rights to create a domain account for the new Windows NT system. This is shown in Figure 7.8. If a system administrator has already created an account for the new system from the Server Manager, any domain user ID will suffice for installation.

Figure 7.7

The order of network protocol bindings can be altered during Setup.

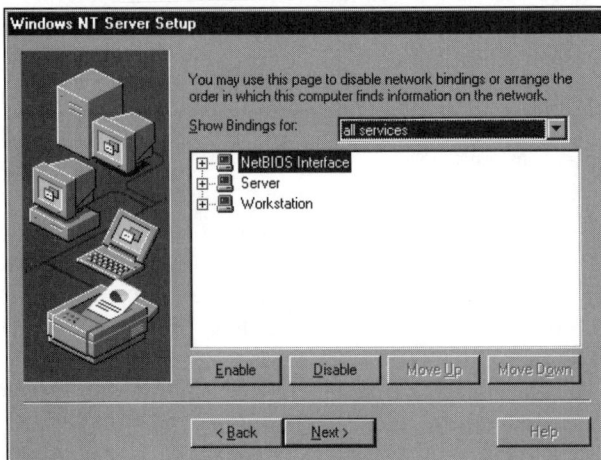

Figure 7.8

A domain name for the NT Server to be part of must be specified during Setup.

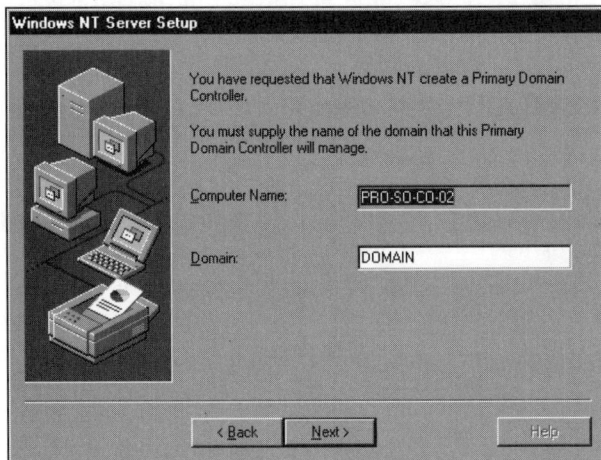

For primary domain controller (PDC) installations, no special user ID is needed, since the PDC will be the first computer of the new domain. A PDC can be installed on networks with existing segments, but the separate domains will act as islands unto themselves unless trust relationships are established. However, the installation will not proceed further unless a unique domain name is specified for the PDC. Unfortunately, it isn't possible for client PCs running Windows 95, Windows for Workgroups, or Windows NT to belong to two domains at the same time.

All Windows NT systems must be given unique names. If a new Windows NT Server 4 is to be configured to use the name of an existing host, you must first remove that machine from the network, or at least change its name. Even Windows NT systems no longer on the network are still registered in the domain; an administrator needs to remove the system ID using the Server Manager before the new Windows NT computer can be given the same name.

Both primary and backup domain controllers (BDC) must be in domains. Backup domain controllers require that a domain already exist, and the installation will not go forward until the system has successfully joined.

Stand-alone NT servers do not actually have to join any domain. In lieu of domains, Microsoft has created a loose network organization system known as workgroups. A stand-alone NT Server can be added to any workgroup on the network or given a new workgroup name. Workgroups do not have any common security privileges or access rights, and anyone can configure systems to join any workgroups they wish. These loose groupings are only relevant from an organizational perspective, putting all the servers in various workgroups together when browsing the network, for example. Each workgroup host is responsible for its own security.

- *RAID Options*

8

How to Choose a Disk File Subsystem

Unlike other microsoft operating systems, such as dos, Windows 3.1 or Windows 95, with Windows NT, you can choose the file system architecture you want to use on your hard disk media. In addition to the traditional File Attribute Table (FAT) used by DOS, a new NT File System (NTFS) was designed for Windows NT.

NTFS makes possible a number of sophisticated features, such as better data recoverability and RAID configurations. NTFS is also far more secure than FAT and is able to store information for each file and directory about access privileges.

Although NTFS is the best choice for use with Windows NT Server, a FAT partition might still be necessary in multiboot systems, where operating systems other than Windows NT will be used on the computer. For example, with a system with OS/2 using High Performance File System and Windows NT using NTFS, at least one FAT boot partition must exist. Windows NT may not be able to recognize additional partitions for UNIX or OS/2, but it won't bother the data, either.

Caution

> *In the case of RISC systems, FAT partitions may be necessary to operate the manufacturer's system configuration software. Be careful not to remove these system partitions.*

For multiboot systems, the other operating systems should be installed before Windows NT. To have a dual boot Windows 95/Windows NT 4 system, for example, Windows 95 should be installed in a FAT partition before Windows NT. The Windows NT Setup will automatically detect the other operating system and add and create an option list at system boot.

However, multiboot systems are useful primarily on desktops; there's little reason to configure servers this way. Remember, there's no way to access data on NTFS partitions without running the Windows NT operating system; Windows 95 or even DOS boot floppy diskettes will not be able to see the NTFS files.

Even in cases where NT is installed on a FAT partition, you should create an additional NTFS partition for data files. Without NTFS you won't be able to set security access privileges on specific data; only general rights can be set on FAT partitions, allowing or disallowing access to the entire volume. NTFS is also required to support long file names.

If no other operating systems than Windows NT are to be used on a system, we recommend that you format all the partitions to NTFS.

When multiple hard drives are available, we suggest you keep the core NT operating system separate from the data drives. This segregation of system files and user data can help in disaster recovery. If a system drive should fail, the data drives could be easily installed on another server, and if the data volumes fail, at least the NT operating system is still functioning, making recovery efforts simpler. Even in cases where large numbers of disks are used in RAID systems, it still makes sense to keep the operating system separate.

For even greater reliability, the NT Server system drive can be set up with a mirror (RAID level 0). The data drives can be configured for RAID, as well (either mirroring or Striping with Parity, which is RAID level 5).

Other than reliability, administrators should strongly consider RAID for optimizing system performance. By using multiple hard drives intelligently, RAID options can improve Windows NT Server responsiveness considerably. Configuration of RAID must be done via the NT Disk Administrator, after initial operating system setup.

■ RAID Options

Built-in support for RAID offers a wide range of options for configuring Windows NT hard drives. Your choice depends on your performance needs, budget, and data integrity concerns. With high capacity disks at relatively low prices these days, even small companies can benefit from the real-time fault tolerance of RAID. Even when good backup data is available, recovering from a failed hard drive and rebuilding the system can take hours, if not days. Hard drives have one of the highest failure rates of all server components, and serious crashes are, by and large, inevitable.

Helpful Tip

As useful as RAID can be, it's no replacement for regular system backups on tape or other media. Hard disk redundancy might prevent catastrophic failures from crashed disks, but it can't recover data lost to user error or other means. If data is accidentally deleted, for example, there's no way of recovering it without a backup.

By definition, multiple disks are required for RAID configurations. Single-disk systems can still benefit from some of the fault-tolerant features of the NTFS file system that offer help to recover from crashes, but the real-time redundancy of RAID is only possible with multiple disks.

Any hard drive can be used with NT Server RAID. However, the standard IDE hard drives and controllers that ship with desktop PCs only support two or three drives, which makes some RAID features impractical. The more advanced SCSI disk specification is more suitable to RAID configurations, supporting up to seven disks, while providing higher throughput of data transfers. Hard drives designed for SCSI do not cost much more than regular IDE models, but the cost for the SCSI controller interface is extra. (You only need one for seven drives.) Many server systems come equipped with SCSI controllers, but in some cases they may be an additional expense.

Windows NT supports RAID levels 0, 1, and 5. Level 0 provides no-fault tolerance but can improve disk performance by spreading data across all disks automatically and spreading the read/write work. RAID level 1 offers mirroring, making one disk the duplicate of another. For more advanced systems with larger numbers of drives, RAID level 5 creates redundancy, by spreading an index across all volumes, and increases performance by dividing workloads among drives.

Hardware vs. Software RAID

Hardware-only RAID options, with built-in circuitry to handle real-time fault tolerance, have become quite popular. As far as Windows NT Server is concerned, the disks in a hardware RAID system will just look as if they are one volume. RAID configuration for such devices are done through the system BIOS over an administrative port or at server boot time.

The big advantage of hardware-based RAID solutions is hot swapability. Defective hard drives can be replaced without even shutting down the server and impacting server up time. When using the inherent RAID intelligence of NT Server, the entire computer must be shut down and powered off to change defective hard drives. This may not be a serious issue for some companies, however, since the maintenance can be scheduled for a convenient time. After all, that's why RAID is used in the first place—so that a disk can fail without affecting overall system operations.

You need to weigh the costs of perfect system availability with the added expense. Hardware RAID systems are considerably more costly than off-the-shelf SCSI controllers and hard drives.

The performance differences between hardware and software based RAID are minor. Of course, the least expensive SCSI controllers and bargain-basement hard drives will likely not perform nearly as well as specifically engineered hardware RAID systems. In some cases server vendors actually recommend software level RAID for maximum performance.

Volume Sets

Technically, Windows NT volume sets don't fit the definition of RAID. A volume set doesn't provide fault tolerance features, but neither do the stripe sets of RAID level 0.

In a nutshell, volume sets make it possible to configure separate partitions across drives, or even on the same disk, so they act as a single logical volume. Rather than three 200MB disks showing up as drives D:, E:, and F:, they all appear as a single 600MB drive D: when combined in a volume set. Existing partitions can even be expanded with volume sets. For example, a new hard drive could be configured to act as an extension of a current partition.

When multiple drives are used in a volume set, performance may improve because the read/write data workload is spread across disks. For optimal performance RAID 0 stripe sets are best, but they require identically sized partitions across all drives.

Volume sets can be very useful because they add a high degree of flexibility in system configuration and maximize disk capacity, but they offer no redundancy or fault-tolerance features.

RAID Level 0 - Stripe Sets

Stripe sets lack redundancy, but no other NT disk configuration option can beat them for performance. By using multiple drives as a single volume, stripe sets write data simultaneously along all drives in the volume. For example, when saving a spreadsheet on a 5-disk stripe set volume, the first bit will be written on drive 1 at the same time bits 2-4 are written on each of the other drives. (See Figure 8.1.)

Figure 8.1

Disks are organized to permit data striping. Data is split into bits/bytes/records/tracks that are recorded in parallel. However, a single disk failure can lead to a large data loss. Therefore, RAID 0 does not provide any fault tolerance/data protection.

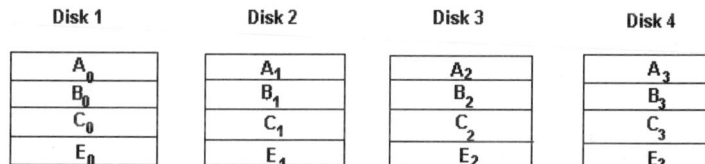

Disk 1	Disk 2	Disk 3	Disk 4
A_0	A_1	A_2	A_3
B_0	B_1	B_2	B_3
C_0	C_1	C_2	C_3
E_0	E_4	E_2	E_3

Similar to volume sets, stripe sets aggregate multiple disks into a single volume; three 1GB hard drives will behave as a single 3GB disk. Unlike volume sets, however, stripe sets are not as flexible at mixing and matching partitions; all partitions must be the same size on different disks. The partition of each drive in a stripe set cannot be larger than the smallest disk.

Helpful Tip

> *Leftover unpartitioned space in a stripe set can be used as a separate partition.*

In theory, the speed of file throughput in a stripe set is directly proportional to the number of drives used; five disks would be five times faster than a single volume. In practice, however, the performance gains aren't quite that good; the more disks you use in the stripe set, the more overhead processing is needed to manage all the reads/writes.

The biggest drawback to stripe sets, of course, is the total lack of redundancy. Technically, RAID level 0 stripe sets offer no form of fault tolerance and exist solely as a means to more efficiently use multiple disks for performance gains.

RAID Level 1: Mirroring

It only takes two disks to achieve fault-tolerant redundancy using disk mirroring, but it's relatively costly because only 50% of available capacity is used (each drive is a duplicate of the other). Since mirroring keeps an exact duplicate across disks there's no loss in performance with a drive failure, unlike Striping with Parity. Of all the RAID options, disk mirroring provides the highest degree of disk reliability. (See Figure 8.2.)

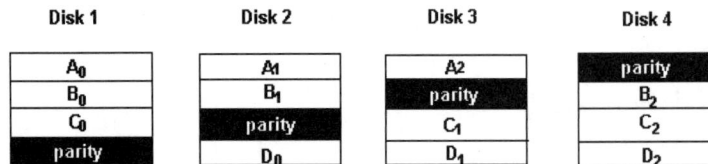

Mirroring makes sense in small NT Server configurations, but in larger environments where three or more disks can be used, RAID level 5 (Striping with Parity) may be a better choice, since it frees up a greater portion of available disk space. Even in larger servers, however, mirroring may be useful for protecting the NT system drive and striping with parity for use on the data volumes.

Each partition of a mirror set must be the same size; available space can be no larger than the size of the smallest drive.

RAID Level 5: Striping with Parity

The more sophisticated features of Striping with Parity offer both the real-time fault tolerance of mirroring, and more efficient use of disk space. Rather than losing 50% of drive capacity, as you do with mirrors, you'll lose the equivalent of only one disk in the set with Striping with Parity. This operation sets aside a portion of each disk in the RAID volume for keeping an index and compressed data to allow the reconstruction of data if any disk should fail. This reserved space is known as parity.

The more disks used in a stripe set with parity, the more efficient the use rate; space equivalent to one of the disks in the striped volume is set aside. In a four-disk system, 25% of the space is taken up for parity; an eight-disk volume loses only 12.5%. (See Figure 8.3.)

Figure 8.3

Disk mirroring is combined with a striped set with distributed parity and two controllers, offering ideal conditions for both fault tolerance and performance.

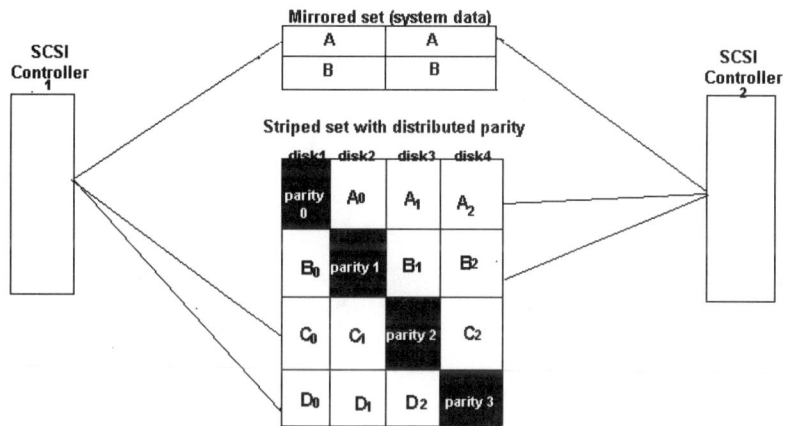

The efficiency of Striping with Parity has a cost in system performance, however. All other NT Server RAID options are slightly faster, and there is a further speed degradation when one of the drives fail; performance returns to normal when a replacement is installed. Windows NT Server also requires a larger amount of system RAM to process the read/write requests in level 5 RAID; servers should have at least 32MB RAM. Striping with Parity is ideal for server applications that rely more heavily on read requests than writing.

- *Upgrading to NT Server 4*
- *Additional Upgrade Notes*

9

Upgrading from Windows NT 3.51

Converting existing windows nt 3.51 servers to nt 4 is relatively simple. Setup automatically reads the configuration of Windows NT 3.51 and keeps all the drivers and registry settings. The system requirements for Windows NT 4 are the same; CPU speed and RAM don't need to be increased, and the disk space requirements are only slightly larger. Of course, if you wish to run several of the new services included with NT 4, you may need to upgrade some hardware to gain adequate performance.

The performance improvements of Windows NT 4 over NT 3.51 are most significant in high-end systems. Small servers with 32MB RAM or less and slow Pentium (or lower) CPUs won't see any gains. The real speed improvements of Windows NT Server 4 are visible in systems with multiple processors and on high speed LANs using fast Ethernet. Overall, however, Windows NT Server 4 isn't dramatically faster than NT 3.51, and in most cases it doesn't make sense to upgrade for speed alone.

Upgrades to Windows NT Server 4 do not have to be done all at once. Individual servers can be migrated to NT 4, and still participate as full partners in existing NT 3.51 domains. Since the domain structure of NT 4 hasn't changed much from NT 3.51, domain controllers, both primary and secondary, are compatible.

Even though most NT 3.51 systems can be upgraded without any modifications or special considerations, it's prudent to spend a few minutes to check with hardware vendors to ensure there aren't compatibility issues with NT 4. Some motherboards require BIOS upgrades, and there are a few cases where drivers for SCSI cards and network adapters must be upgraded to work properly in Windows NT 4. Spending an hour to check the support section on a vendor's Web site can prevent delays when an upgrade is nearly done and the system won't come up.

Helpful Tip

> *The Microsft Web site has a database of known problems called "Knowledge Base" that can provide answers to most questions. A current version of the Windows NT 4 hardware compatibility is also kept on the Microsoft Web site.*

■ Upgrading to NT Server 4

Before upgrading to Windows NT Server 4, make sure there's plenty of extra space on the hard drive. Depending on the options you select, not only does Windows NT Server 4 take up to 50MB more space than Windows NT 3.51 Server, but the installation process also makes a duplicate of the CD-ROM system files. This duplication requires more than 100MB. (The duplicate is erased at the end of the upgrade.) We recommend having about 200MB free space on the system drive before proceeding with the upgrade.

The recommended way to perform Windows NT 3.51 Server upgrades to NT Server 4 is from a running system. From a command prompt window, or the Run option from the File menu in the NT 3.51 Program Manager, run the Winnt32.exe program on the NT Server 4 CD-ROM. Use the /b parameter to skip the floppy disk boot process.

Helpful Tip

If a recent system backup is unavailable, it would be wise to make one before upgrading. The upgrade process should have no effect on existing data, but it never hurts to take precautions on sensitive data. A more likely use for the backup, however, is not to prevent outright data loss, but to get data to users on an alternate server if the upgrade takes longer than planned.

Example: d:\i386\winnt32 /b

After creating temporary system files on the hard disk (a process which can take ten minutes), Winnt32 Setup prompts you for the Windows NT 4 installation directory. If you choose the same directory as an existing NT 3.51 Server, an upgrade will automatically occur. However, if Windows NT Server 4 is installed in a separate directory from the existing NT 3.51 system, it will not touch the existing configuration or set up a dual boot option at system startup. Setting up this latter way gives you the option of testing and debugging NT 4 on your hardware while keeping the old version for a quick fallback.

However, installing NT 4 in a separate directory will use more disk space (since the old version of NT Server will also be on the disk) and can take more time to properly configure, since you must select all options for drivers and components during the installation. You must also give a separately installed NT Server 4 a different system name than the existing NT 3.51 Server, even if only one runs at a time. (This has to do with NT domain security.) The network administrator must remove the previous server name from the domain before a new system can assume it.

In the upgrade, Windows NT 4 will keep existing NT 3.51 drivers for video cards, network adapter cards, and SCSI adapters. After the installation, it's a good idea to upgrade to newer versions, if they're available.

■ Additional Upgrade Notes

- Upgrading the DNS from the NT 3.51 resource kit requires registry changes. Check Windows NT 4 TCP/IP Help.

- NT 3.51 Server WINS, DHCP, and Remote Initial Program Load databases are automatically upgraded to a new format under NT 4.

- Some computers might need BIOS upgrades to handle Windows NT Server. In the case of some servers, such as Compaq's Proliant 5000, you may need to specifically choose NT 4 as the operating system in the BIOS.

- Previously used High Performance File System volumes are no longer supported under NT 4. You must run the Windows NT 3.51 Convert.exe utility to migrate to NTFS before upgrade.

- Some hardware, such as the Intel EISA fast Ethernet card, is no longer supported.

- Not all the Windows NT 4 drivers show up in the main list anymore. Those that don't are in \Drvlib on the CD-ROM.

- NT 3.51 servers running on 80386 CPUs cannot be upgraded, since Windows NT Server 4 no longer supports these processors.

10

How to Migrate Applications

Software migration issues with NT 3.51 upgrades are not all that relevant for existing NT server installations that are only using the built-in Windows NT services. However, when additional client/server software is installed, you should check with the software vendors for compatibility problems before loading Windows NT 4. Even if the applications come from Microsoft, there could be newer versions recommended for use in Windows NT 4.

End-user programs that happen to be stored on an NT Server for shared network access will work the same under Windows NT 4. E-mail programs like Microsoft Mail or Lotus' CC:Mail only require a storage repository—all the applications are run on the client PCs—and are unaffected by upgrades to NT Server. Office automation tools, such as spreadsheets and word processors, are also client applications that require no changes with NT Server upgrades.

Client/server applications that are actually executed on NT Server—Lotus' Notes, Microsoft Exchange, Oracle SQL Server, NetScape's Commerce Server and the like—may have compatibility issues with Windows NT Server. In most cases there shouldn't be any problems, but it never hurts to check with vendors for known problems. The Microsoft Web site may also have some tips.

Most Windows NT 4 migration problems occur with add-on network services. Network fax or serial port sharing programs could require new versions under Windows NT. Programs that must be upgraded are Microsoft's own NetWare integration software, File and Print Services for NetWare, and Domain Services Manager for NetWare.

The good news is that Windows NT 4 Server is more compatible with Windows 95 than is Windows NT 3.51 Server.

3

Configuring the Windows NT
Server 4

- *Creating Partitions*
- *Formatting Partitions*
- *Volume Sets*
- *Configuring RAID*
- *Repairing Disks*

How to Use Disk Administrator

Unlike DOS, Windows NT does not have an FDISK tool for partitioning disks; instead, NT relies on a graphical Disk Administrator program that has a far greater degree of sophistication. Windows NT can use a more advanced file system, called NTFS, than the limited DOS FAT.

Disk Administrator can manage FAT partitions, but it can also take advantage of the special features of NTFS to create logical volumes out of multiple hard disks. RAID is configured through the Disk Administrator.

Many of the management functions in the Disk Administrator can be accomplished through other utilities of the Windows NT environment. You can do formatting, error checking, and resource sharing through the Explorer, and command line utilities still exist for most functions.

The Disk Administrator is located under Administrative Tools in the Programs menu. When first started, the Disk Administrator will automatically go through a brief initialization process to store information on the current drive configuration.

■ Creating Partitions

You can configure physical disks as either primary or extended partitions. To a great extent, both types of partitions are similar, but we recommend using extended partitions for most volumes, since they're the most flexible. Primary partitions are needed for operating system installations; and there's always at least one that's automatically created during the NT Server Setup. Multiple primary partitions are only necessary in multiboot configurations, with several operating systems or NT versions running on the same computer system. There can only be one extended partition per disk, but a single extended partition can be subdivided into numerous smaller subpartitions and logical drives if necessary.

You can create partitions by first selecting the disk to be configured in the graphical display of the Disk Administrator, and then choosing either Create or Create Extended under the Partition menu. (Right-clicking on the disk also shows these options.) Use Create for setting up primary partitions and Create Extended for extended partitions. The Disk Administrator will ask the amount of space on the disk to be set aside for the partition.

Before partitions can be formatted or used for RAID, the newly set partition information must be stored. The Disk Administrator will automatically prompt you for permission to commit the changes when it is quit, but Commit Changes under the Partitions menu will store the settings as well.

Helpful Tip

The primary partition where Windows NT Server 4 was installed can't be modified from the Disk Administrator.

Creating Logical Drives

Subpartitions called logical drives can be created with extended partitions. To create a logical drive, select available free space in an extended partition and use Create under the Partition menu, as shown in Figure 11.1.

Figure 11.1

An extended partition can be subdivided into multiple logical drives.

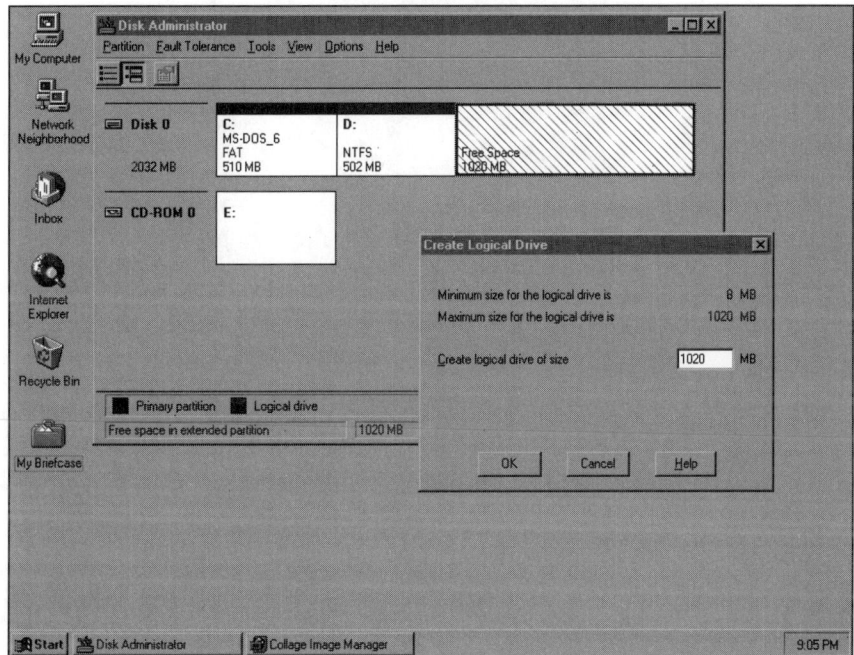

Marking Partitions as Active

You can select Mark Active under the Partition menu to set a primary partition for booting. Only one partition can be marked active, and only partitions with an operating system installed should be selected. This is useful primarily in multiboot systems with several versions of NT on different partitions.

■ Formatting Partitions

Once you've created the partitions—and committed the changes—you must format them before use. (See Figure 11.2.) You can format by selecting the Format option after right-clicking on a selected drive, or choosing Format under the Tools menu of the Disk Administrator (right-clicking on a drive under the Windows NT Explorer will also bring up the Format options).

Figure 11.2

Low-level disk
configuration options can
be set when formatting.

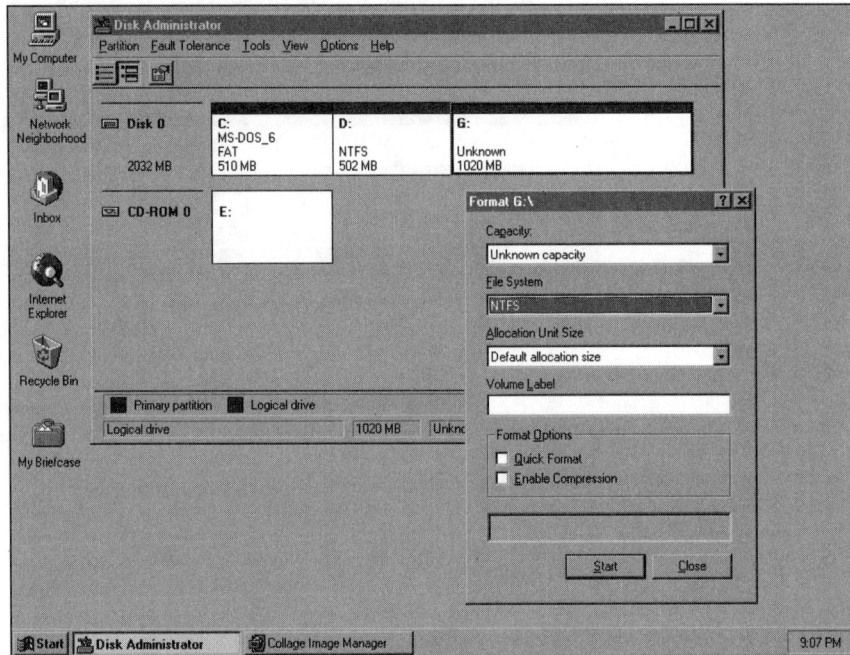

Helpful Tip

*Don't format a partition you're planning on using for a volume set or
RAID until after you've created the aggregate RAID or volume set.*

From the Format window, you can select either the FAT or NTFS file system. In most cases we recommend using FAT for added data safety and security in networked environments. NTFS is required for partitions used in
RAID volumes.

A new feature in Windows NT 4 makes it possible to specify the block allocation size of a drive. This is useful for optimizing performance on high-
end systems. In most cases the default allocation unit size works fine.

Other formatting options are for Quick Formatting (which skips a detailed search for bad blocks) and compression enabling.

Helpful Tip

> *Disk data is stored in logical chunks called blocks. The bigger the blocks, the less searching a drive needs to perform to find all the blocks containing data for a single user file. However, larger blocks use space inefficiently. You have a wider variety of block size formatting options to choose from when using the command line FORMAT utility.*

Helpful Tip

> *Windows NT 4 only supports compression on NTFS partitions. This feature may be useful to help store more information on a volume, but there's a performance penalty since the server must always run the algorithms to compress and decompress data as needed.*

■ Volume Sets

By linking free space in different partitions—even on different drives—into a single virtual drive called a volume set, Windows NT Server 4 gives you a great deal of flexibility in managing disk space. Volume sets make it possible to use bits of leftover space on separate partitions as if they were the same disk.

Volume sets are created by simultaneously highlighting more than one section of free space in extended or primary partitions (hold down the control key while clicking to allow multiple selections) and selecting Create volume set under the Partition menu. You can then format the volume set for use.

Unlike other types of Windows NT partition aggregation types (such as RAID stripe sets), you can modify volume sets after creation to add more space to the logical drive. Do this by choosing Extend Volume Set, after selecting the additional free space to be used and the existing volume set. Although volume sets can be expanded, they can't be diminished or subtracted from.

Volume sets should only be used to maximize utilization of incontiguous drive space. Because of its improved performance, the Windows NT 4 RAID stripe set feature provides a better way to combine multiple physical drives into a single virtual volume (keep in mind that all the partitions in a stripe set must be the same size).

■ Configuring RAID

Windows NT partitions can be combined for use in RAID volumes. RAID level 0, or stripe sets, provides no special fault tolerance abilities but can combine multiple drives into a single volume (which also improves disk performance). Level 1 RAID is mirroring; it makes two identical disks to prevent a system outage or data loss in the event of a failed hard drive. The third level of RAID, striping with parity, allows multiple drives to be used as a single volume, while keeping a portion of each disk set aside for recovery information. This information allows the data for any disk to be reconstructed in case of drive failure.

Helpful Tip

> *The fault tolerance possible with RAID is no substitute for good backups of data. RAID is an excellent means of preventing system crashes and down time, but it doesn't protect data from becoming corrupted through user error or software malfunction. If a user accidentally deletes their data, for example, the only way to recover it is from a backup.*

Stripe Set

Select available free space in separate partitions on multiple disks in the Disk Administrator (hold down the control key for multiple selections), then choose Create Stripe Set on the Partition menu.

The Disk Administrator will prompt for the amount of space in each partition, to be used in the stripe set; this value can't be larger than the size of the smallest set of free space available. For example, if the smallest selected partition is only 1GB, then the stripe set partition size can't be larger than 1GB, even if one of the selected areas of free space is 4GB.

Stripe sets don't offer any fault tolerant features, but are the best means of maximizing throughput over multiple disks.

Mirroring

Disk mirroring offers excellent fault tolerance by making identical clones of two or more disks. If any disk in a mirror set should fail, the other disks keep working and users should notice no difference. A failed disk creates error messages in the Event Viewer.

Mirroring is a relatively wasteful means of redundancy, since 50% of disk space is lost. You might want to consider striping with parity as an alternative, since a smaller portion of disk space is reserved for recovery purposes. However, striping with parity is only useful in systems with three or more drives.

By selecting free space in separate partitions (hold down the control key for multiple selections) on different disks, a mirror can be set up by choosing Establish Mirror under the Fault Tolerance menu. The chosen sizes of the mirrored partitions, which are requested by the Disk Administrator, can be no larger than the smallest block of free space in the mirror set. Different sized disks can be used for mirroring, but in unmatched mirrors, larger disks will have space left over for other uses.

Striping with Parity

The most efficient means of fault-tolerance in Windows NT Server 4 is striping with parity. It reserves a smaller portion of disk space for recoverability logs, or parity, than mirroring. Unfortunately, striping with parity is a bigger drag on performance than mirroring, and can require more system memory to work well. Striping with parity also requires three or more hard disks in the stripe set.

You can configure striping with parity by selecting Create Stripe Set with Parity under the Disk Administrator Fault Tolerance menu. (Select the free space across multiple drives first.)

In the case of a drive failure, overall system performance will degrade until you replace the failed hard disk and regenerate the stripe set with parity.

■ Repairing Disks

Access the Tools tab of the Properties window by right-clicking a selected drive or selecting the Tools menu on Disk Administrator. The window shown in Figure 11.3 will be displayed. Here you can check disks for errors and have detected errors fixed automatically.

If you choose the system drive for a check, the scan will be scheduled to occur the next time the NT Server is restarted; system drives cannot be analyzed while the NT operating system is running.

You can also use the CHKDSK command line utility to check disks for errors. Use the /f parameter to automatically repair problems.

Figure 11.3

Drive diagnostics can be run from the Disk Administrator.

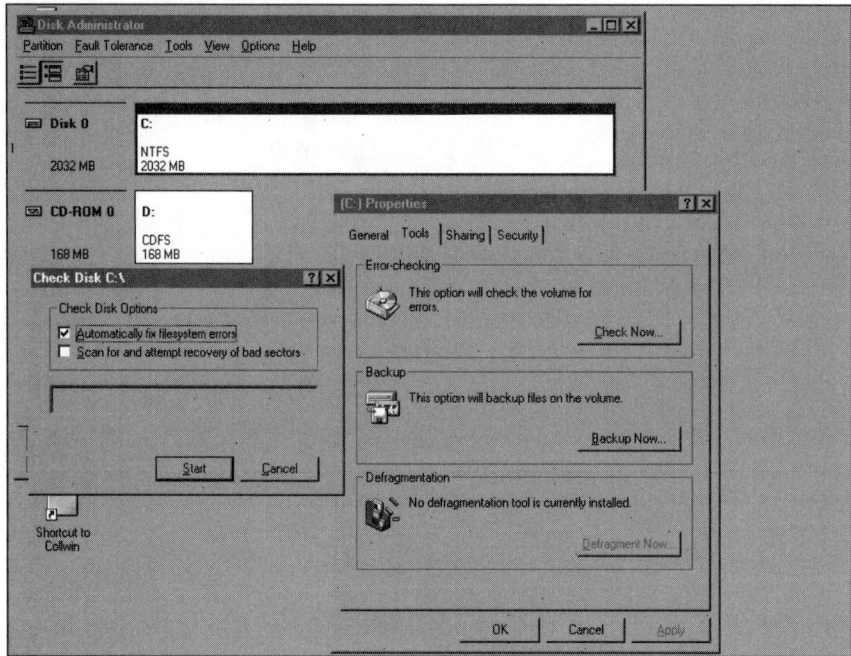

- *Installing a Printer Using the Wizard*
- *Configuring a Printer*

12

How to Set Up Printers

LIKE OTHER NETWORK OPERATING SYSTEMS, WINDOWS NT SERVER can allow networked users to share the same print devices. However, NT Server excels in its ability to act as a glue for disparate client computers to access the same printers. Both Macintosh and UNIX clients can easily access NT print queues; NT Server can even re-share print queues on other operating systems, such as NetWare.

Because Windows NT 4 supports multiple printing protocols, users on an NT 4 network can transparently access printers on other networks.

A wizard has been built into Windows NT Server to simplify printer configuration.

■ Installing a Printer Using the Wizard

There are two ways to access print queues. As shown in Figure 12.1, from the Start menu, choose Settings and then the Printers tool. Or, choose the Printers icon from the Control Panel. Either way brings up the Printers window; clicking on the Add Printer icon automatically invokes an easy-to-use Add Printer Wizard.

Figure 12.1

Printers can be installed via the Add Printer Wizard.

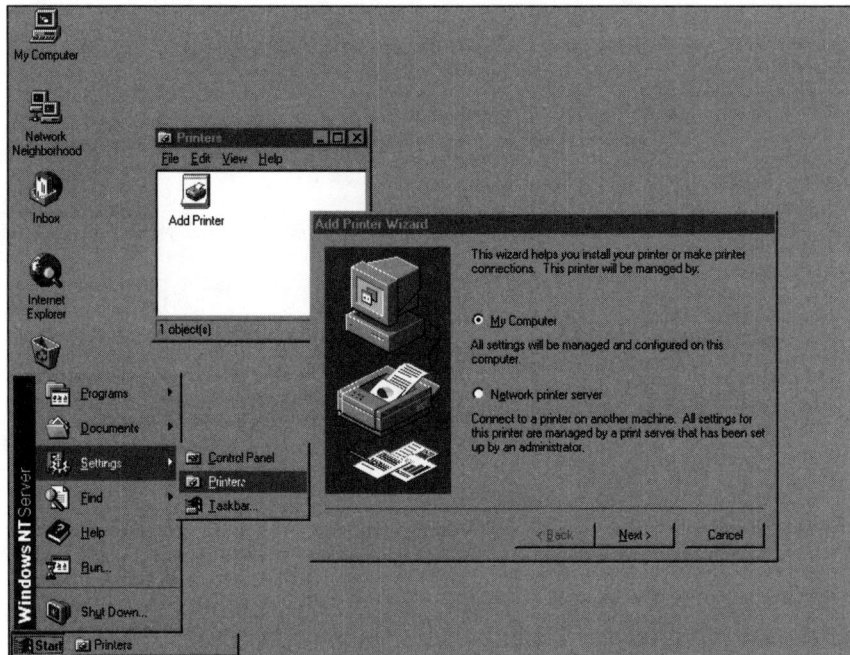

Activate the radio button for My Computer and click Next. (The network printer server is for using print queues on other NT Servers.) This brings you to the screen shown in Figure 12.2. If the new printer will be directly attached to the server, select its connection port.

If the printer has built-in networking and is attached directly to the LAN, click on Add Port... to see a list of supported network printers. This list

Figure 12.2

Add Port... allows
connections to networked
printers.

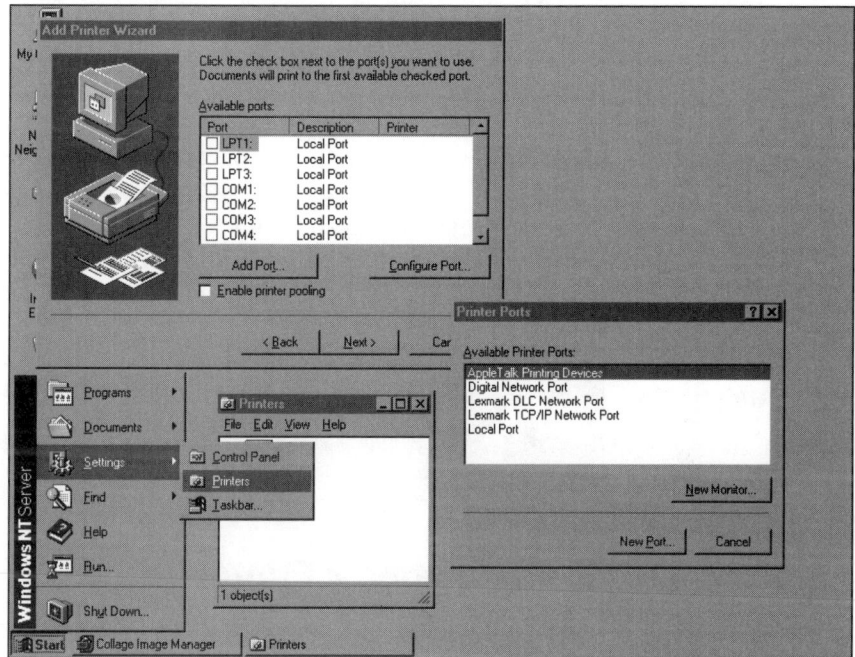

will vary depending on the network protocols and services installed under
the Network section of the Control Panel. To use a Macintosh printer, for example, Services for Macintosh must be installed as an option under the NT
Server network configuration screens.

For LPR printer support in UNIX environments, you must first install
TCP/IP and TCP/IP Print Services from the Network icon in the Control
Panel. Additionally, for networked Hewlett Packard printers, you must in-
stall the data link control (DLC) protocol.

When you click Next, you'll have the opportunity to choose a driver appropriate for your printer. Even though the driver list is large, some newer
devices may not be listed. You may need to contact your vendor for proper
Windows NT support software.

Helpful Tip

*Always check the vendor's Web site for the latest printer driver, as the
driver on the NT Server CD-ROM may be outdated or not included.*

To make the printer available to other users on the network, you'll need to select Shared and give the printer a name. Next, a screen gives choices to install drivers for all of the operating systems that will access this printer.

Newer Microsoft operating systems, such as Windows 95 and Windows NT, no longer must have network drivers installed on each client PC in order to use networked printer resources on NT Servers. Driver support for each client type must be installed on the NT Server, however. For example, if both Windows NT 3.51 Workstation and Windows 95 client PCs will be sharing the same printer, drivers for both NT 3.51 and Windows 95 must be installed on the server. This does not apply to WFW, Win3.X, UNIX, or Macintosh users, who can still print but must load the driver on their individual machines.

Helpful Tip   *When adding a new printer driver to your NT Server, you do not have to reboot for the print driver to become effective.*

■ Configuring a Printer

Once you've installed a printer, you can configure its properties by accessing the Printers window through the Control Panel, then right-clicking on the Add Printer icon.

Properties

Under the General tab, you can choose to enable or disable the separator pages that can be printed out before every print job. Choosing a print processor is also an option, although we recommend leaving this at its default configuration. Other options are for helping in compatibility issues, such as support for LAN Manager print queues.

Under Ports you can enable or disable printer pooling to allow for more than one printer on the same printer queue. Technically, networked users never print to a printer but, instead, to a print queue.

Scheduling lets you configure the printer's availability. Additionally, you can configure to print directly to the printer so that no pooling is allowed and, as a result, all the print jobs wait there.

Under Sharing you can choose whether a printer is shared or not and select the drivers that are available.

Like File Sharing, Print Sharing security features let you adjust permissions, ownership, and auditing. Assuming you have administrator rights, you can configure who can use the printer and specify what print activities are logged on the Event Viewer.

Device settings are very specific to the printer itself and allow configuration of options such as the types of paper available to users and downloading extra font types.

- *Creating a Windows Accessible Volume*
- *Creating a Macintosh Accessible Volume*
- *Disabling File Sharing*

13

How to Create Shared File Volumes

WITH NT SERVER YOU CAN EASILY ACCOMPLISH THE BASIC NET-
working feature of sharing files over the network. They can be
made available over the network for PC users as well as Macintosh users.

Windows NT can also be used to share files with other computer systems via TCP/IP. A built-in FTP service is included, and
third-party vendors sell Network File System add-ons to make NT
volumes available to UNIX workstation.

■ Creating a Windows Accessible Volume

For file sharing, previous versions of Windows NT used options found in the File Manager. Although you can still set up file sharing this way, we recommend using the NT Explorer.

In the Explorer, right-click on the directory you want to share. Then choose the Sharing tab, as shown in Figure 13.1; the directory will show up as a separate volume, To Client Computers, even though it's on the same drive. Make sure to activate the options you want, then type a Share Name and add your description in Comment.

Figure 13.1

Permissions can be set by which users or groups can view the shared folder.

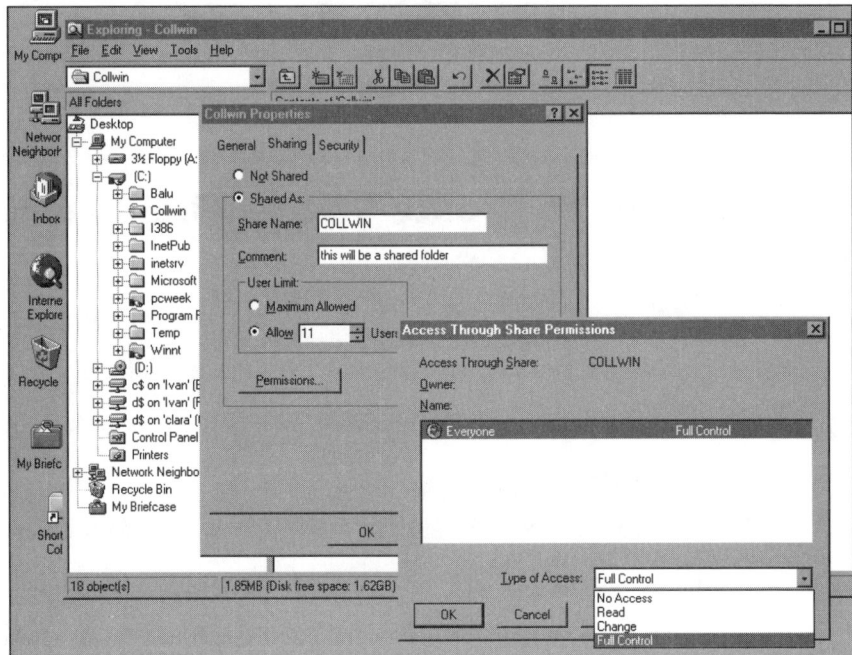

Helpful Tip

When creating share names, you can add security by including a $ after the share name (example: \\Chicondman\$). Adding a $ makes the drive volume become invisible to browsing from client PCs. In other words, a user would have to both know the full path name, and type it in to get access.

If you need to limit access to the shared folder, click Permissions... and choose which users or groups can view the contents of the shared folder.

Helpful Tip

Windows 95 clients can access NT Server shared directories. However, they don't have access to administrative functions such as changing permissions. There's a utility that can be downloaded from the Microsoft Web site that will remedy this.

Other available file sharing configuration options include those under the General and Security tabs. In General, you'll find basic information about shared files and about setting attributes. The Security tab options allow you to set permissions.

Helpful Tip

We recommend that shared volumes be created only on NTFS partitions. FAT partitions have limited security and cannot store permission information for individual files or directories.

Other features under Security include Ownership and Auditing. Ownership allows granting of permissions for files and directories. Only administrators, however, can take ownership. Use Auditing to tag events so they'll show up on the Event Viewer.

■ Creating a Macintosh Accessible Volume

Shared files and directories created for the PC on a network aren't accessible to Macintosh clients; you must create separate shared volumes for them. Instead of using Explorer, use the File Manager (run winfile.exe). To do this, however, you must first install Services for Macintosh as a network service, using the Network icon in the Control Panel.

Helpful Tip

As far as Macintosh users are concerned, the NT Server shows up as a standard Appleshare shared volume. Macintosh users must go to Chooser to select the NT Server they wish to access.

To set up file sharing for the Macintosh, select the directory or file you want to share in the File Manager and then select Create Volume under the MacFile menu. Next, input a directory name, a volume name, and a path. By typing in a password, Macintosh users will be prompted for a user ID and password before gaining access to the shared directory. Additionally, you can configure Permissions to give access to selective groups and users (see Figure 13.2).

Figure 13.2

Macintosh shared volumes are configured from the File Manager.

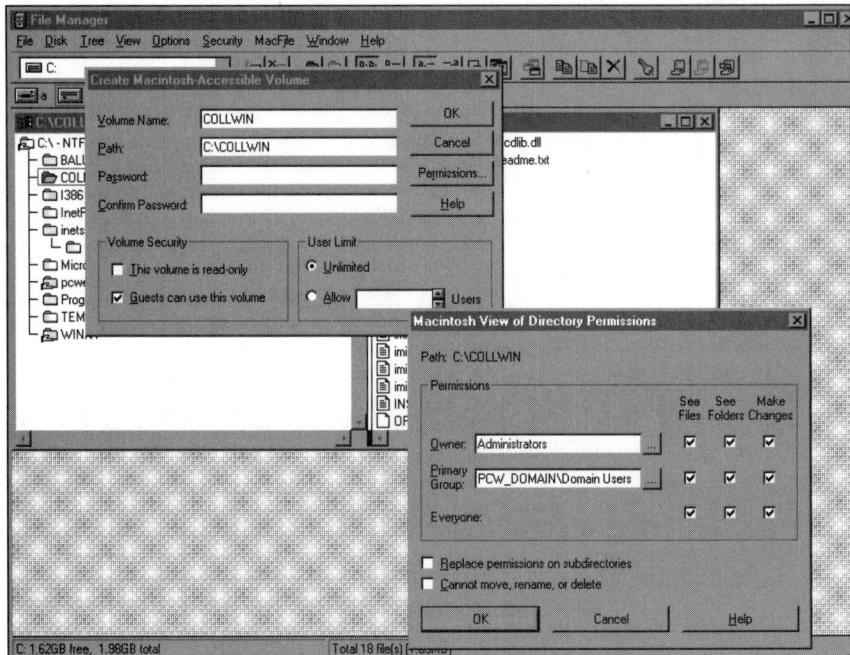

Helpful Tip

Although the shared volume name can be different for both the Macintosh and PC networks, we recommend using the same volume name for both to avoid confusion.

■ Disabling File Sharing

To disable a PC user's shared directory, go to Explorer and select a shared volume (all shared volumes are marked by a hand). Right-click on the directory to see Sharing. Simply click Not Shared to disable file sharing.

For Macintosh shared volumes, disable the files using the File Manager. Click on the directory or file and choose Macfile. Then choose Remove Volumes, and all of the available volumes will be displayed. Highlight the file and click Cancel to disable file sharing.

- *System*
- *Security*
- *Application*
- *Message Types*
- *Using the Event Viewer*

14

How to Use the Event Viewer

THE EVENT VIEWER CAN BE AN INDISPENSABLE TOOL FOR TROUBLE-shooting and diagnosing problems with NT 4. Windows NT Server keeps track of many types of events, such as failed hardware or user file access. These events can be viewed through the Event Viewer.

The Event Viewer logs any significant occurrences in the system or in a program that requires you to be notified. There are three different log files that can be viewed here: System, Security, and Application. They're all located under the File menu.

■ System

The System page of the Event Viewer shown in Figure 14.1 notifies you about the status of services on your server; it shows you which services are running. For example, when your computer starts up, the Event Viewer logs the process. It also tells you about hardware problems.

Figure 14.1

Hardware problems can be diagnosed in the Event Viewer.

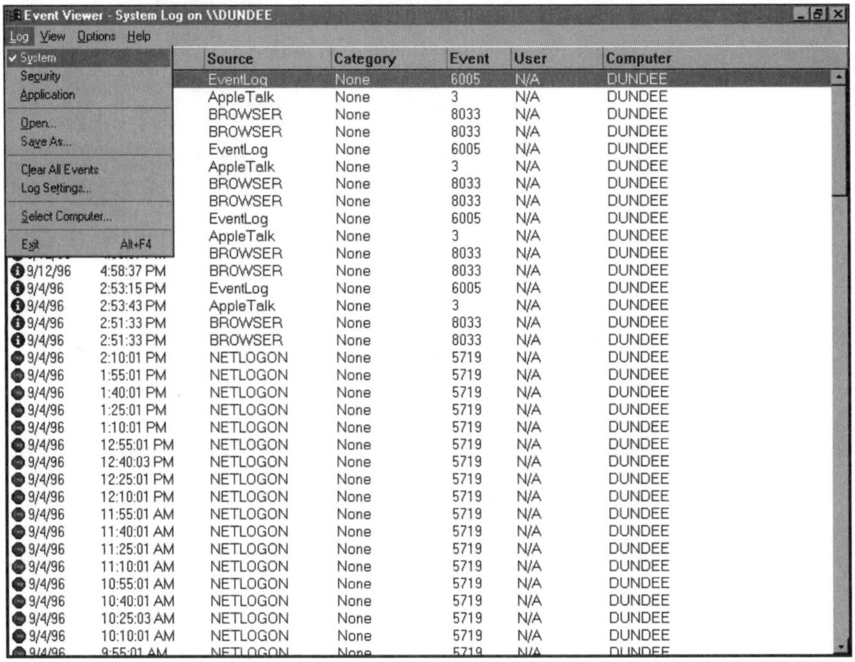

■ Security

Administrators can view user activity, such as accessing files or directories, using the Security log. The monitored activities can be set through Auditing options in the Explorer, or through several other NT administration tools. In the Explorer right-click on a file or directory and choose Properties. Under the Security tab, select Auditing.

With auditing you can add and configure events to be recorded in the Security log. This is how you determine what Security events will be recorded. Unless you've configured auditing, not much is going to show up under Security.

Breaches of security will, however, show up. For example, if someone tries to log into an account unsuccessfully, it will be automatically logged. Additionally, remote access dial-ins are automatically recorded.

■ Application

The Application page alerts you about critical and non-critical events that are application-specific. Your programs must have this feature built in. Applications like Oracle, Sybase and Lotus Notes may be able to generate events that can be seen under the Application page in the Event Viewer.

■ Message Types

The Event Viewer uses icons to notify you of the severity of an event. For example, the informational blue icon tells about services that have started or completed successfully, like a print job. The yellow exclamation point icon tells you something, such as a network adapter card, needs to be configured. The red stop sign shows you there's an error, such as Windows NT Server being unable to bind the network drivers to a network adapter card because of an interrupt conflict.

Double-clicking on the messages will give a more detailed description of the problem. There are thousands of possible event messages. Use the Windows NT Resource Kit as a reference book for their definitions.

Helpful Tip

For critical events, such as lack of disk space, you may see a screen message in addition to an icon in the Event Viewer.

■ Using the Event Viewer

Recent events are not automatically updated in an open Event Viewer window. Press F5 to refresh the screen for events.

The Event Viewer has a buffer that can be configured to the amount of space desired. Old events will be deleted and replaced by newer ones once the buffer is filled up. To change the maximum buffer space size, go to Log Settings under the Log menu. The Event Viewer can also be configured to automatically remove events that are over a certain date.

You can look at the logs of different NT computers on your network from any one machine, using Event Viewer, provided you have administrator privileges. To do this, use Select Computer under the Log menu, and type in the computer name of the other NT computer.

Helpful Tip   *When accessing event logs remotely over slow connections, select Low Speed Connections under the Options menu. By doing this you will disable browsing of the network, which is slow on WANs or on 28.8 modems.*

Log files can be saved for future reference with Save As... in the Log menu. To view a saved log file, click on Open in the Log menu.

Helpful Tip   *Saved log files can also be imported into spreadsheets, as a means of graphing messages. For example, by selecting only remote access messages from the Security log, you can put peak usage of RAS in a graphical view.*

- *Performance*
- *Processes*
- *Applications*

15

How to Use the Task Manager

Y OU CAN EXECUTE THE WINDOWS NT TASK MANAGER BY PRESSING Control+Alt+Delete and clicking on Task Manager. New to Windows NT 4, the Task Manager can be used when your computer is hung and there is no other way to end an application or process. It also gives a quick, graphical overview of system performance.

Caution

> *Because data will not be saved when you end a process or application from the Task Manager, we recommend using it to stop a process only under emergency circumstances, such as when a program hangs. Whenever possible close an application via the standard exit procedure. For example, if you want to quit Microsoft Word 7.0, choose Exit from the File menu. Word automatically asks for confirmation and saves data if it hasn't been saved.*

There are three parts to the Task Manager: Performance, Processes and Applications.

■ Performance

The Performance tab shown in Figure 15.1 gives a view of the overall, aggregate system performance. CPU Usage and Memory Usage are available at a glance in graph form. If you have multiple processors, the GUI screen will change to accommodate more CPUs.

Figure 15.1

The Task Manager's Performance Tool shows CPU and memory use graphically at a glance.

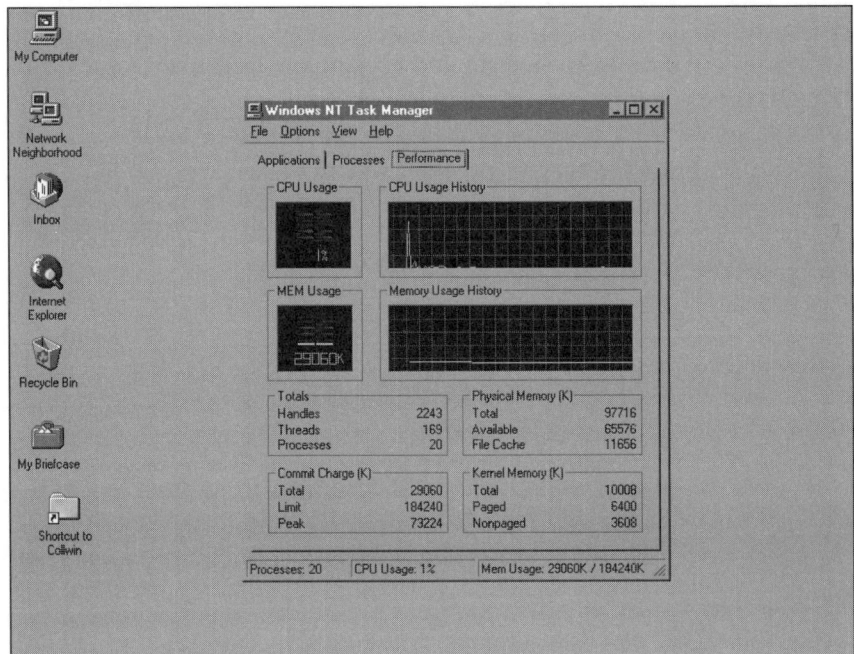

Like the Performance Monitor Tool, the Task Manager shows you over-all CPU and memory performance. However, with the Task Manager you can also stop processes and applications that have hung.

Helpful Tip

Double click anywhere on the Performance screen within the Windows NT Task Manager to enlarge the CPU graph to full size.

■ Processes

The Processes tab shown in Figure 15.2 allows you to dynamically check run-ning background and foreground processes, see their status, and terminate them if necessary. This option shows you, in list form, how much memory and CPU cycles each process is using.

Figure 15.2

Task Manager's Processes tab shows the status of all processes running and allows you to terminate them.

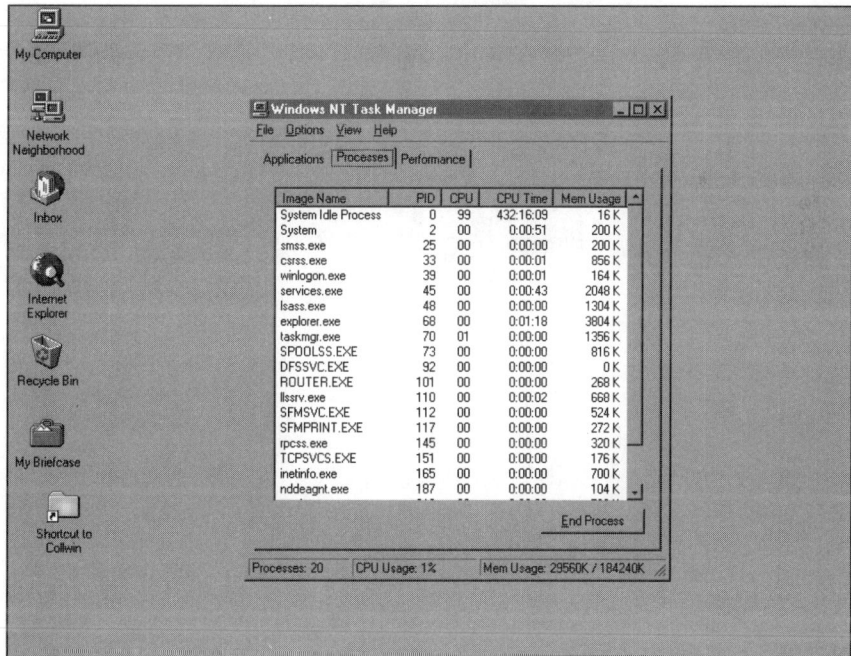

Windows NT Task Manager

File   Options   View   Help

Applications | Processes | Performance

Image Name	PID	CPU	CPU Time	Mem Usage
System Idle Process	0	99	432:16:09	16 K
System	2	00	0:00:51	200 K
smss.exe	25	00	0:00:00	200 K
csrss.exe	33	00	0:00:01	856 K
winlogon.exe	39	00	0:00:01	164 K
services.exe	45	00	0:00:43	2048 K
lsass.exe	48	00	0:00:00	1304 K
explorer.exe	68	00	0:01:18	3804 K
taskmgr.exe	70	01	0:00:00	1356 K
SPOOLSS.EXE	73	00	0:00:00	816 K
DFSSVC.EXE	92	00	0:00:00	0 K
ROUTER.EXE	101	00	0:00:00	268 K
llssrv.exe	110	00	0:00:02	668 K
SFMSVC.EXE	112	00	0:00:00	524 K
SFMPRINT.EXE	117	00	0:00:00	272 K
rpcss.exe	145	00	0:00:00	320 K
TCPSVCS.EXE	151	00	0:00:00	176 K
inetinfo.exe	165	00	0:00:00	700 K
nddeagnt.exe	187	00	0:00:00	104 K

End Process

Processes: 20   CPU Usage: 1%   Mem Usage: 29560K / 184240K

■ Applications

The Applications tab (see Figure 15.3) shows the visible programs that are running and their status. If a program hangs, you may want to exit the program via the Task Manager's Application tab.

Figure 15.3

The Application tab of Task Manager shows the status of all applications.

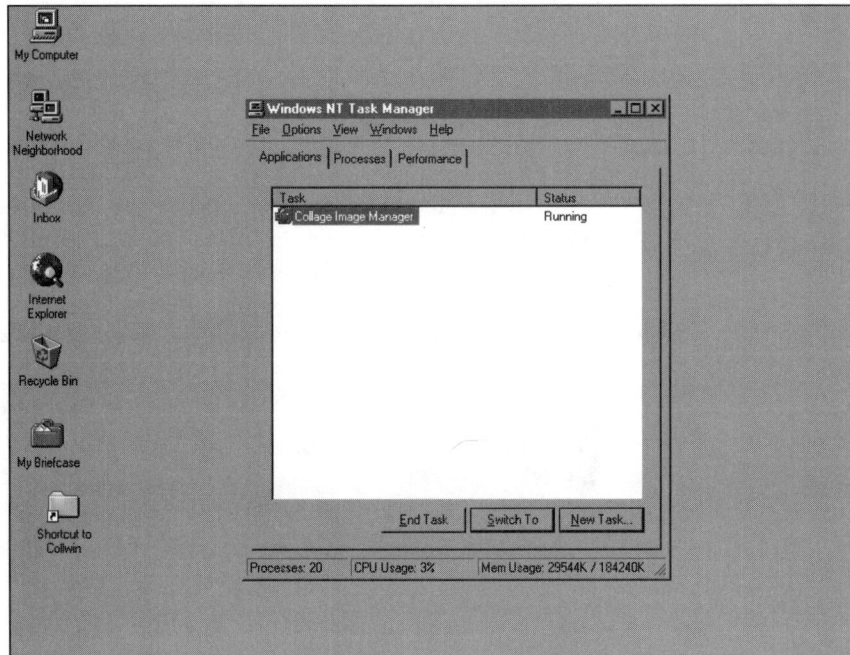

- *Using the Registry*
- *The Registry Editor*
- *More Registry Editor Uses*

16

How to Use the Windows NT Registry

U NLIKE EARLIER 16-BIT VERSIONS OF WINDOWS, WHICH USED TEXT-
based .INI files for storing and configuring information, Windows
NT and Windows 95 use a new architecture called Registries to
store system information. Registries are like databases that contain system-specific information regarding installed hardware, selected parameters, and security.

Most changes to the registry occur automatically when software is installed or options are selected in configuration windows
in various NT applications. For example, installing a new network
protocol will make changes to the registry.

■ Using the Registry

We suggest that administrators don't make changes to the registry themselves. However, there are cases when you must make vendor-recommended changes. It's not uncommon to add a parameter in a dialog box for a third-party program that wasn't included as an option—for example, increasing buffers for improved performance. On the other hand, it can be dangerous to remove or change parameters you're not sure about. Most of the entries in the Registry are cryptic and require intimate knowledge of the system before changes are made.

Helpful Tip

> *Windows NT Registries are not compatible with Windows 95 Registries. Although the same editing tool can be used to work with both, they're not directly analogous.*

■ The Registry Editor

Windows NT comes with a Registry Editor, shown in Figure 16.1. It's not located on any menu, but rather resides in the main NT directory under System32. It's called Regedt32.exe. You can run the Registry Editor by using the Run option under the Start menu; then type: Regedt32.

The database is structured in several subfile sections, such as hardware information and user profile data, which determines colors and wallpaper each user can have. Table 16.1 lists and defines each of the registry's subfiles.

Helpful Tip

> *The Windows NT 4 Resource Kit has a more detailed explanation of specific values for the registry.*

■ More Registry Editor Uses

It's possible to save portions of your registry to the disk for future use by selecting Save under the Registry menu.

You can remotely access and modify the registries on other NT Server machines. Go to the Registry menu, choose Select Computer, and type in the name of the machine.

Figure 16.1

The Registry Editor can
be used to change
system options.

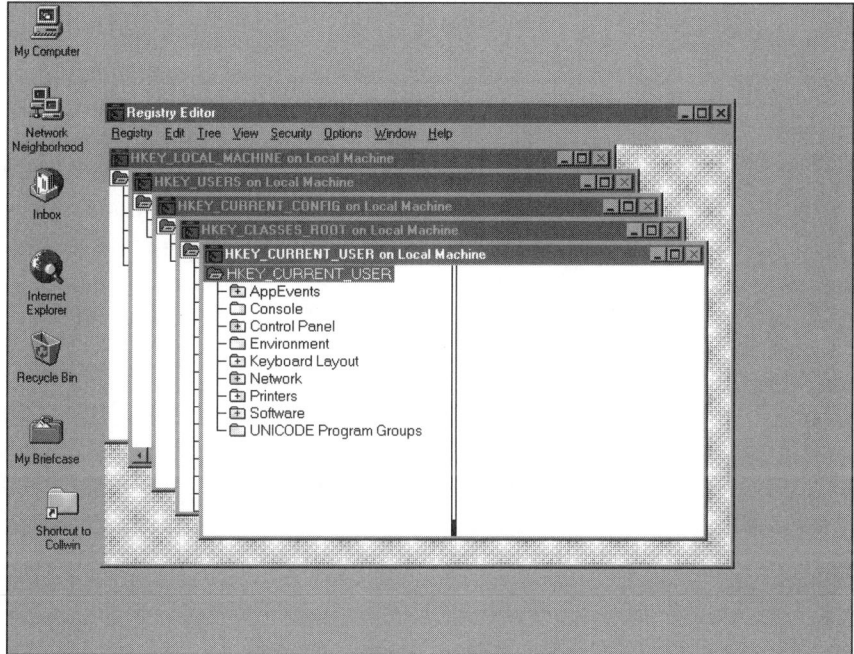

Table 16.1

Registry subfiles

ROOT KEY NAME	DESCRIPTION
HKEY_LOCAL_MACHINE	Hardware and operating system data information about your local machine resides here.
HKEY_CLASSES_ROOT	OLE and file class association data is stored here.
HKEY_CURRENT_USER	Contains user profile information for the user currently logged on. This includes desktop settings, network connections, and application settings.
HKEY_USERS	All actively loaded user profiles reside here. Users who access the server remotely do not have profiles on the server under this key.
HKEY_CURRENT_CONFIG	Here you'll find hardware profile information used by the local computer at startup. You can use this information to configure settings such as device drivers or display resolution.

Under the Security menu, you can set permissions for registry access and specify users or groups who you want to access the registry.

You can also specify auditing and configure it so that any time changes are made, the Event Viewer logs the events.

Helpful Tip

You must reboot after changes are made in the editor for them to take effect.

- *Disaster Prevention*
- *Backup*
- *Other Disk Recovery Options*

17

Backup and Disaster Recovery

Microsoft has built many features into NT 4 to assist you recover from a system crash. Some of them work automatically, but some require planning to use them.

Although no one ever expects their system to crash, it inevitably happens, and it's best to be prepared. When it comes to preventing a disaster, a little preparation can help a great deal.

■ Disaster Prevention

The NTFS has built-in redundancy and recoverability features that will automatically repair minor data losses and corruption. Sometimes the only thing necessary to repair damaged data is to reboot the server and the NTFS will run repair routines as it detects problems. This is not a fail-safe solution, however, and does require an NTFS formatted hard disk. Automatic recovery is not supported by the FAT file system.

NT Server also supports RAID, which allows multiple hard drives to be pooled together, sharing the data loads and making it possible for the system to keep functioning with no data loss when one drive fails. (See the section on NT file systems in Chapter 8.)

Another way to minimize the damage of system failures is to spread network services throughout the entire network. For example, it may be better to have several small NT servers on your network than one large server. If one small server crashes, some functionality will remain. However, if your only large server crashes, nothing works.

Following this idea, we strongly recommend that at least one NT Server be designated as BDC on the network. If your PDC, used for authenticating users on the network, crashes, users have an alternate way to log on.

Uninterruptible Power Supply

You can use uninterruptible power supplies (UPS) to improve system availability and to ensure that servers don't go down when there's a power surge or outage. It can also protect hardware from power spikes or surges. Along with building systems to avoid disasters, it's also good practice to prepare to recover from disasters when they happen.

■ Backup

There's no substitute for frequent and reliable backups of system data. Even if you use the NT features of RAID, backups are still essential. RAID only provides fault tolerance so a server doesn't crash if a driver fails. But RAID can't recover data that's been inadvertently deleted by a user or corrupted by software problems.

Microsoft includes a software utility with Windows NT Server that can work on a number of output devices, such as digital audio tapes (DAT) or various streaming devices. Unfortunately, the Windows NT Backup Tool is limited in functionality and is really only useful for manual backups. We strongly recommend that administrators purchase backup software from third-party companies, such as Seagate or Cheyenne, which can handle scheduled backups that automatically run at specified intervals. These third-party backup tools also sport myriad extra features that can be very useful.

Helpful Tip

> *It's a good idea to do backups before carrying out any changes to an NT Server, such as adding a new disk or network adapter.*

Installing Backup Devices

NT can support a wide variety of archival devices ranging from DAT to the tape streaming standard and it's well worth the investment to get a backup device that has the capability to hold the information on your server without changing the tape. Support for the tape device drivers is installed through the tape device's option in the Control Panel.

NT Backup Tool

From the Backup program under Administrative Tools, shown in Figure 17.1, you can specify which tape device you want to work with. This is done through Hardware Setup in the Operations menu.

After you choose a backup device, select the data you want to back up. Double-click on the drive you want and tag the directories and files to back up.

You can back up a whole volume by clicking the volume in the drives window under Backup. Additionally, backing up directories and volumes across the network on other machines is possible—even if they're on other types of servers such as Novell NetWare. As long as it shows up as a drive, you can back it up. To back up other servers, you need to go to the Explorer and map to that drive.

Helpful Tip

> *Be advised, however, that NT Backup will only store security information for other NT Servers running NTFS. If you're backing up data from a UNIX or NetWare host, none of the security permissions will be saved. In order to back up security information on NT Servers, the backup user ID must be a member of the backup user's group.*

After selecting the drives you want to back up, click the Backup icon. You can then choose what type of a backup you want to do. The choices are normal, copy, incremental, differential and daily backups. See Table 17.1 for a description of what these various types do.

Figure 17.1

Different archival devices
can be selected for
backups.

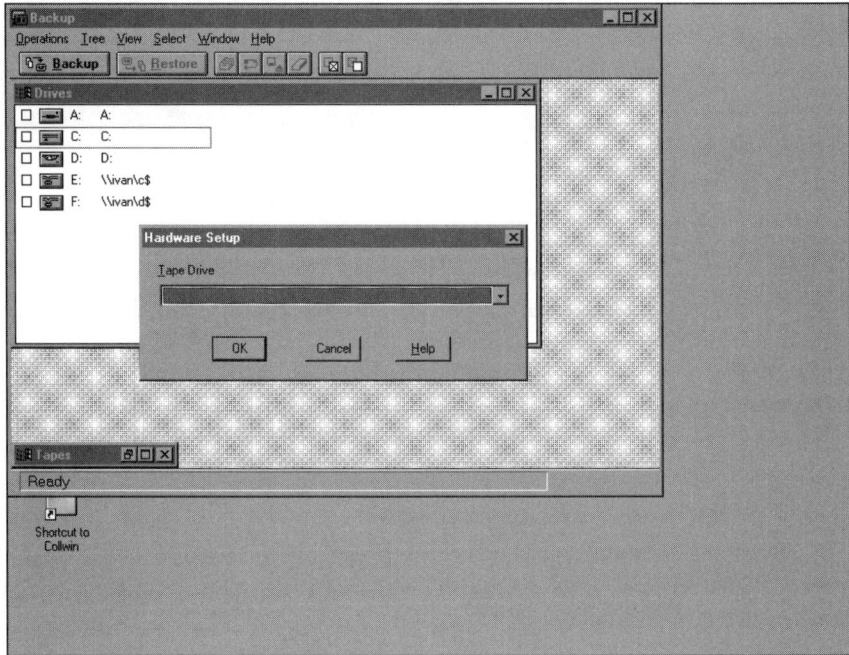

Table 17.1

Types of backups
available

TYPE OF BACKUP	DESCRIPTION
Normal backup	All selected files are backed up, letting you restore files quickly because files on the last tape are the most current.
Copy backup	Copies all selected files but does not mark each file as having been backed up.
Incremental backup	Backs up only the files created or changed since the last normal or incremental backup. It does not mark files as having been backed up.
Differential backup	Files created or changed since the last normal or incremental backup will be copied. Files are not marked as having been backed up.
Daily backup	Copies all selected files that have been modified the day the daily backup is performed. Files are not marked as having been backed up.

Restoring

You can easily recover data from backups. Simply put a previously made backup tape in the drive, and it'll automatically show up in the tape drive in the Backup Tool. Double click on the tape, and an index of all the data on the tape will be generated. You can select the files or directories you want to restore.

Helpful Tip

> *Backing up and restoring files can be a useful way of transferring data from one NT Server to another, while still maintaining security information. If you simply drag directories and files from one network volume to another via the Explorer, the directories and data will be copied, but all of the security information specifying access privileges will be lost. Data restored from backups, however, maintains all of this information.*

Tape Maintenance

You can do basic tape maintenance from the NT Backup Tool. Options under the UPS menu in the Backup Tool allow you to erase and format tapes.

■ Other Disk Recovery Options

It's sometimes possible to recover from crashed disks and corrupted data by using special NT tools and some home-grown remedies.

Windows NT has an RDISK.EXE utility that can generate recovery diskettes, as shown in Figure 17.2. Recovery disks hold critical information about the drive configuration in your system. In the event of a disk failure, the original NT install boot floppies can be used to boot the system and enter a recovery mode. The recovery disk is asked for and a repair process is attempted.

Figure 17.2

The RDISK tool can create recovery diskettes.

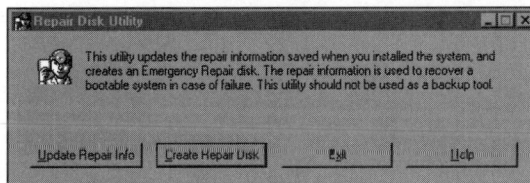

Recovery disks are also generated automatically during system installation, from the Disk Administrator. Every time a change is made to the NT disk configuration, such as adding or deleting a disk, a new repair disk should be made or the existing repair disk should be updated.

For serious problems—for example, an NT Server can still boot up, but there are problems with the data—you can run the CHKDSK command line tool from a command prompt window. Use the /F parameter to automatically correct errors.

Helpful Tip

If CHKDSK /F is run on the system drive when the NT operating system fails, you'll need to reboot the machine for the disk analysis to proceed.

If an NT won't boot and simply gives an NTLDR error, it may be possible to correct the problem by booting the system with a bootable DOS disk and running the DOS FDISK program with the /MBR parameter. This will correct problems with the master boot record and has no detrimental effect on the disk.

It may be necessary in some cases to call Microsoft Technical Support, but the Windows NT Resource Kit, as well as the Microsoft Web site, can provide other tips and specific information.

P A R T

4

Setting Up Users

- *Domain Controllers*
- *Domains in Small Networks*
- *Large Domains*

18

Introduction to Domain Security

An integral part of maintaining any network is the necessity of keeping track of user IDs, their passwords, and which resources they're allowed to access. Early PC networks, such as the bindery technology pioneered by Novell, required that each server or shared network resource have a list of accounts and access information of its own. This worked well in small networks, but now that it's not uncommon to have 4, 5, or even 20 servers on a company network, maintaining the lists of accounts and privileges on all the servers has become an administrative nightmare. If a new user needs access to data stored on ten different NetWare 3.12 servers, the administrator must add the new name ten different times to each of the ten machines. Even simple tasks such as changing passwords becomes an ordeal (all binderies must be altered).

Microsoft, together with IBM, developed a new type of network security model in the late 1980s called domains. It was first introduced with the LAN Manager file server product based on OS/2 and has most recently been the underpinning of the Windows NT security model. Domains make it possible to set up groups of servers that share a common database for user data and security information; each of these groupings is called a domain.

In a nutshell, each time a user requests access to a Windows NT network service, such as a print queue or file volume, a Windows NT Server sends a message to a central security database on the network for verification that the user has rights to the domain. In the old Novell bindery system, each server would only check its internal user database.

As much an improvement as domains were over previous network security models, they've become difficult to work with in the large networks of many companies. Rather than having a small group of servers in a single site, many companies now have hundreds of servers spanning multiple buildings, countries, or even continents. Microsoft has improved the domain security system in Windows NT by introducing trust relationships, allowing users in one domain to use resources in another domain, but this, too, becomes unwieldy in extremely large organizations.

Unlike the truly hierarchical NDS in Novell's latest version of NetWare, the Windows NT structure is pretty limited. Whereas it's simple to organize a network according to organization in NetWare, Windows NT domains work best with simple, flat designs. The more structure a company tries to build into its NT network design, the more hassle administration becomes, with trying to maintain trust relationships and security information between numerous domains. In small environments, with only a few sites and less than 500 users, Windows NT domains can work quite well. With planning, domains can even be made to work in large organizations with thousands of employees.

■ Domain Controllers

Domains require that one Windows NT Server be designated as a PDC. The PDC will maintain a database of all network users and authenticate client computers at logon to ensure that valid user IDs and passwords are used.

There can only be one PDC in a domain, but other NT Servers can be configured to act as BDCs. These BDCs share the authentication workload on large networks as well as provide redundancy to ensure that users can still access the network if the PDC happens to be down. If no primary or backup domain controller is available for user authentication in a given domain, users will be prevented from accessing any network resources, even on other NT servers that are still running.

Any Windows NT Server can function as a PDC or a BDC on top of running standard network services. In larger networks with hundreds of users, it may be necessary to set aside an NT server as a domain controller to prevent performance degradation.

We strongly recommend that NT servers acting as either PDCs or BDCs have a minimum of 32MB RAM. The required memory and CPU speed is highly dependent on the other functions performed by the server (for example, is it also a highly used file or application server?). In large networks with 1000 or more users, 64MB of RAM can improve domain user authentication performance considerably.

■ Domains in Small Networks

In companies with small networks of less than 100 computers and only a handful of NT servers, the network should be configured as a single domain, as shown in Figure 18.1. The LAN administrator can manage the domain security database, as well as all the network resources, such as printers and servers. Multiple domains are necessary when the administrative tasks need to be divided, allowing an administrator in one group to have control over certain NT servers without giving him or her full administrative rights to the entire network.

Since the network usage is low in small environments, there should be no problem on configuring multipurpose NT servers acting as both domain controllers and file servers. If more than one NT Server exists on the network, a second machine should be configured to act as a BDC (along with its other tasks) for redundancy in case the PDC should be inaccessible due to maintenance or a hardware failure.

■ Large Domains

The single flat domain model can even work well in large networks with anywhere from 200 to 25,000 users. Unfortunately, the problem with keeping a single domain in large networks is that all the administration of servers, network resources, and user accounts must be highly centralized. It's not possible to give branch office administrators control of a local server without also giving them administrative privileges throughout the entire network.

Multiple NT domains and corresponding trust relationships between them can be useful to decentralize network administration. If all network management is highly centralized, however, or a company does not mind

Figure 18.1

Single domain model in a
small network.

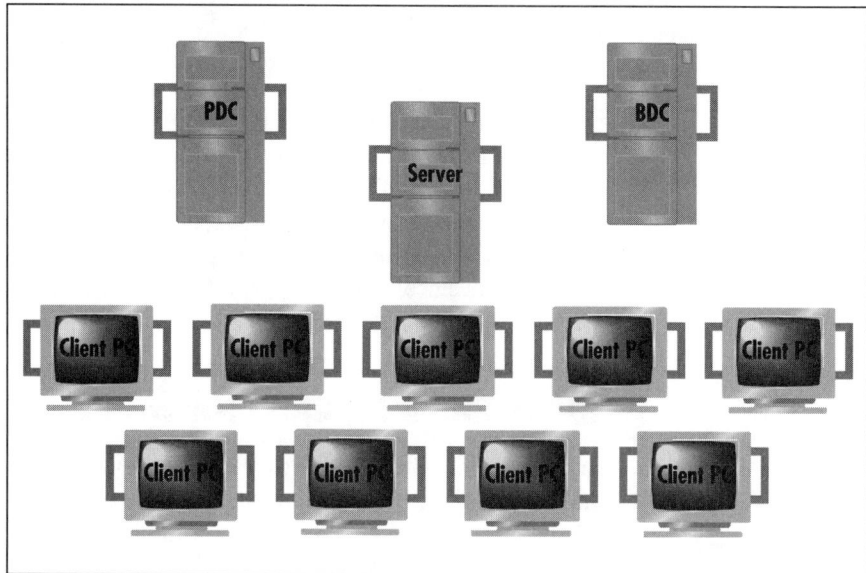

granting regional administrators full network access, the single domain
model is the best solution. Multidomain structures bestow no performance
or scalability advantages and are, in fact, more difficult to maintain.

In either case, the end user sees little difference. When the LAN is properly constructed, a user should be able to connect to it from a laptop at any
office throughout the company and automatically be signed on, with access
to the same standard data as they have at the home office.

Using a Single Domain Model

The critical factor in ensuring an NT network can handle large numbers of
users is the availability and performance of domain controllers. In a single domain as shown in Figure 18.2 there's only one PDC, usually at the head office,
but there can be numerous BDCs throughout the network. By keeping BDCs
at remote sites, client PCs don't have to send messages over slow wide area
links to the PDC, since all authentication is conducted locally at the BDC.

Using Multiple Domains with Trust Relationships

Multiple domains, such as the one shown in Figure 18.3, can be created in
large networks for the primary purpose of decentralizing administration.
One way in which trust relationships can be established between each of the

Figure 18.2

Single domain model in a
large network.

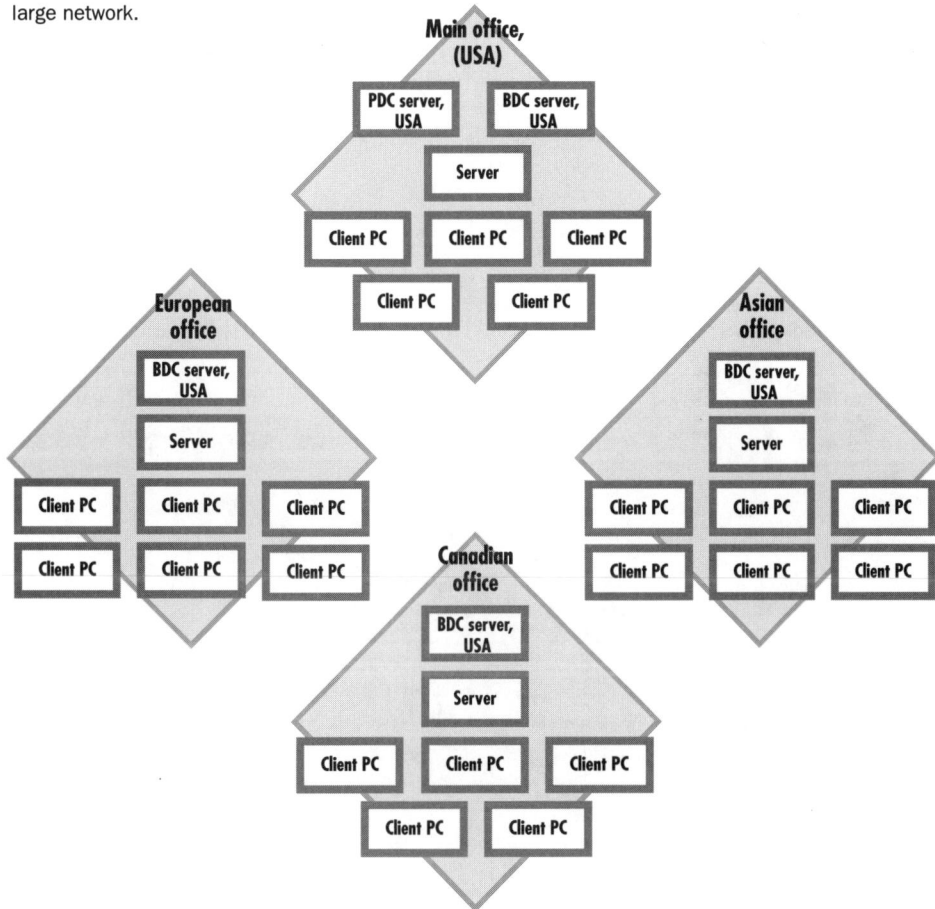

sub, or resource, domains is to allow users to access resources throughout the
company LAN.

Multidomain structures can be constructed according to how much decentralization is wished throughout the LAN. Typically, many companies use
the master domain model, where there's a central domain with centralized
user machine accounts, and one-way trust relationships to subdomains. This
allows user IDs to be centrally maintained, to prevent duplication and allow
global groupings of users, while the management of regional domain resources is delegated to local computer staff.

Figure 18.3

Master domain model in a large network.

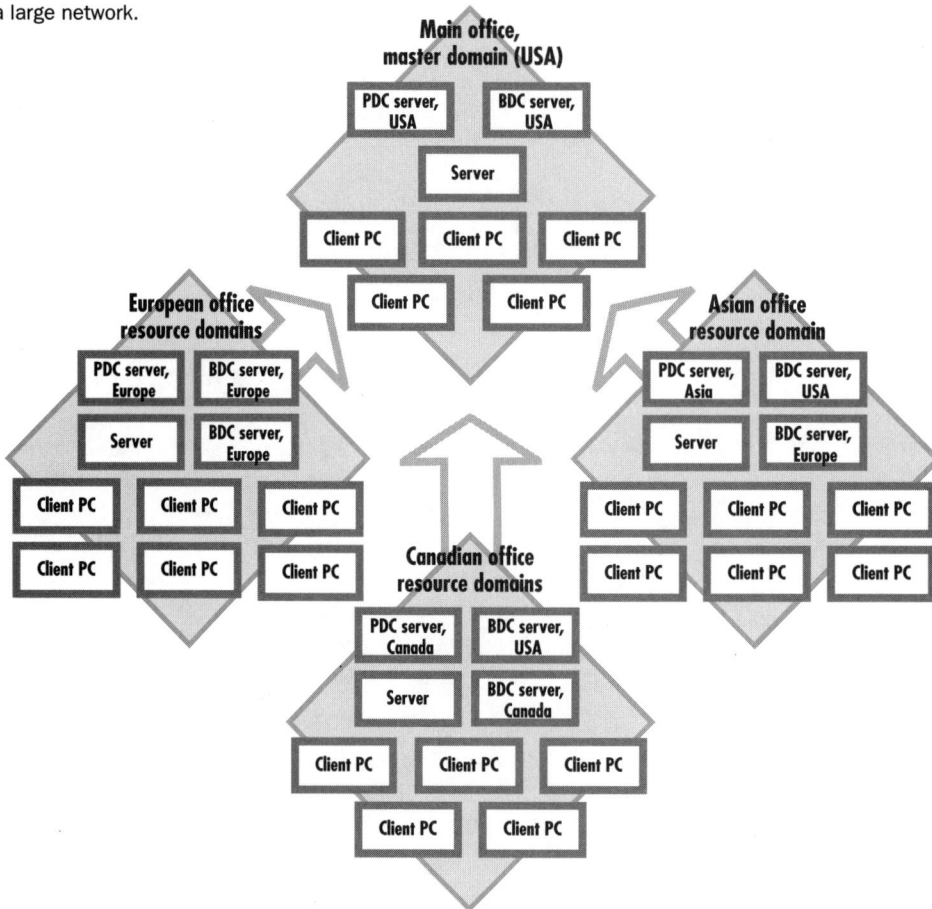

In general, however, even when a multiple domain scheme is chosen, it's advisable to keep the proliferation of new domains to a minimum. The fewer the domains on the network, the less administrative hassles.

In the master domain model, each of the subdomains has not only a PDC and BDC for its local domain, but each one also has a BDC of the master domain. By strategically locating BDCs of the master domains throughout the LAN, you can overcome any performance concerns of requiring authentication that occur over slow wide area network links.

The master domain model can be expanded for further decentralization by creating multiple master domains with their own subdomains. However, each additional master domain increases the complexity of the trust relationships by an order of magnitude, since each subdomain must maintain a one-way trust relationship with each of the master domains.

Helpful Tip

A master domain is simply a logical definition for a domain and does not require any special options to create. Every domain is functionally equal and is only distinguished by the corporate policy of administrating it. There's nothing preventing user accounts from being added to a subdomain, for example; it simply becomes unnecessary if all accounts are maintained in a central domain linked by a trust relationship.

19

How to Use the User Manager

T HE GRAPHICAL MANAGEMENT TOOL, USER MANAGER FOR
Domains, is used in Windows NT for controlling, managing, creating, and administrating all user accounts, groups, and passwords. It's
also used for administrating trust relationships between domains.

The User Manager, shown in Figure 19.1, is a graphical tool that's very easy to use and makes NT security administration easier than in most operating systems. It can be used to manage both the local security database on a given windows NT machine and the network-wide domain accounts. Individual NT computers have their own local security database that can also be managed from User Manager. By simply specifying the name of the local computer, you can manage local accounts.

Figure 19.1

User accounts and groups can be administrated from the User Manager.

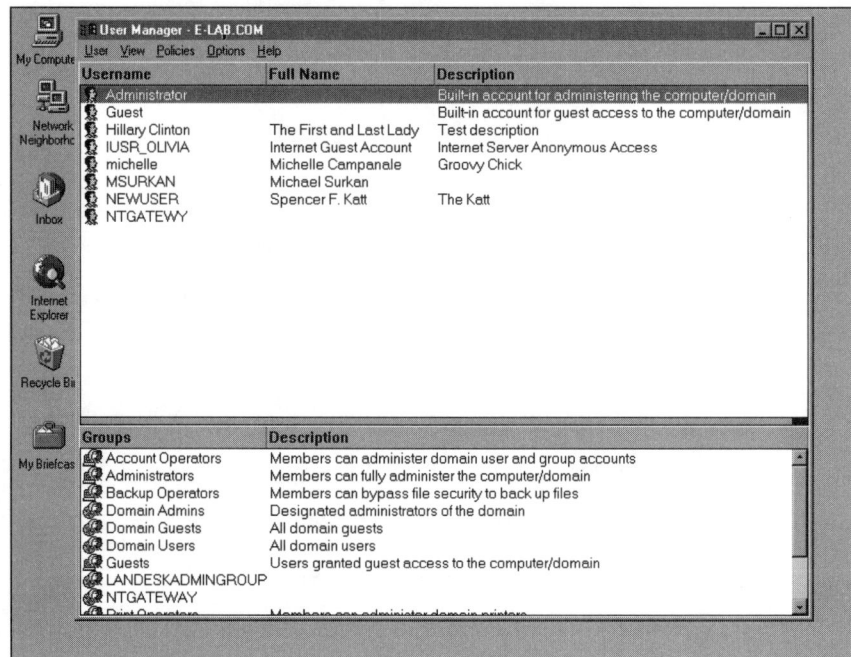

Local user accounts are useful for individual users who want to limit access to users and control their own NT Workstation. A user running NT Workstation on his or her own desktop PC can even lock out domain administrators by using the local security database.

Normally, local accounts aren't used in networks. Instead, the locally administered domain security database is used. Both local or domain security databases can be managed in a similar fashion using the User Manager for Domains.

User Domain Accounts

By default, there's always an administrator and a guest account in NT domains. These can be deleted or altered after installation. Defining a new user account is simple. You can do it by selecting the User menu and choosing New User, which brings up the screen shown in Figure 19.2. Additionally, you can copy the privileges and settings of an existing user account using Copy under the User menu and then selecting New User.

Figure 19.2

New users can be added easily in the User Manager window.

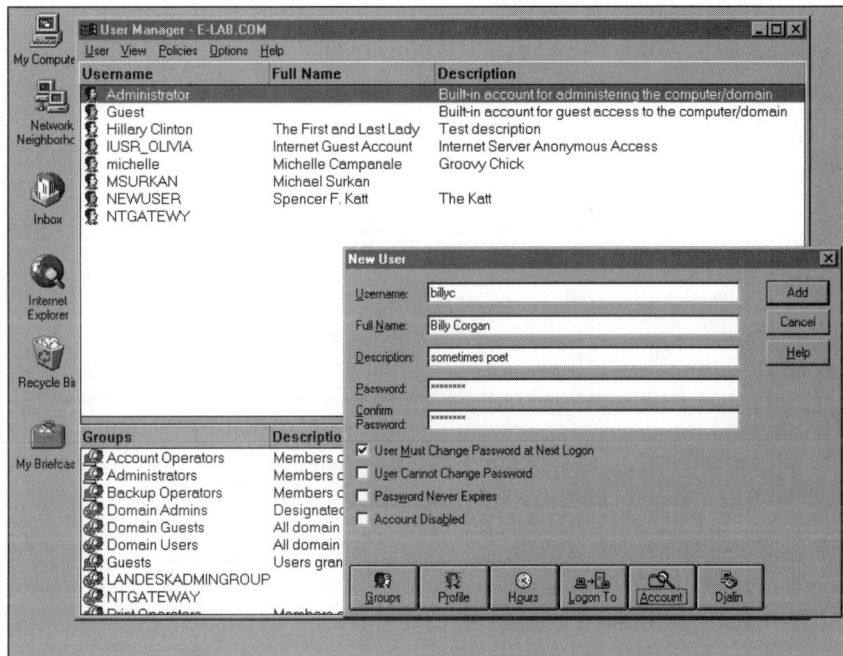

Information must be provided for the new account. The only two bits of information that are absolutely necessary for a User ID are Username and Password. The Username is the word or text string users must enter at logon and by which they'll be referred to in the domain. The username must be a single string of text. Typically, it's a variation of the given user's real name. For example, an account for Mitchel Camp might be mcamp.

Depending on the size of the network and security concerns, you may want to develop a different password scheme. If random text or a numbered code is chosen, it's much more difficult for would-be hackers to break into the system.

Another option is the user's full name. This is useful for administrative purposes so the user IDs don't have to be memorized by the administrator. The Description field can be used for job title. For example, Username is Mitchel Camp and description is HTML Specialist.

In addition to setting usernames, you must set passwords when you create a new user account. After you've created an account with a username, assign a password the user can change later.

We recommend having the user change his or her password at first logon. Properties, under Account Properties, gives you the choice of forcing users to change their passwords. Passwords can also be set to never expire, or prevent user changes. Another option under the New User window allows an account to be disabled altogether.

We recommend that you don't select Password Never Expires. This way, password policies will be governed by settings made under the Account Policies section of the User Manager.

Other password configuration options within New User window include: logon hours, logon workstations, and expiration date. Logon hours, shown in Figure 19.3, specify what times a person is allowed to log on. By choosing Logon To, you can specify which computers a user is allowed to log onto. You can also configure expiration dates—when a user account becomes inactive—as shown in Figure 19.4.

Figure 19.3

Use of the network can be restricted to work hours.

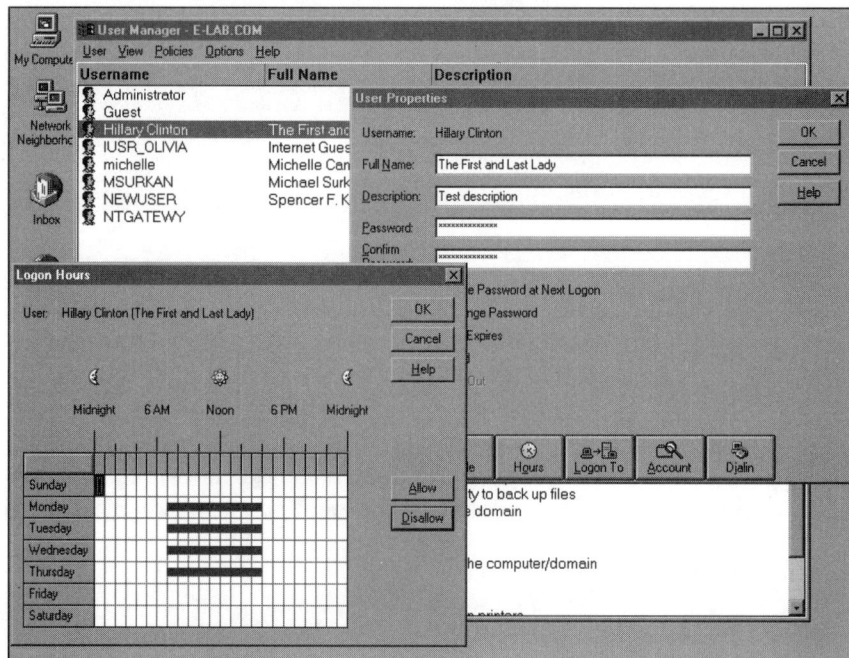

Figure 19.4

Expiration dates can be given to accounts under Account Information, accessed through User Properties.

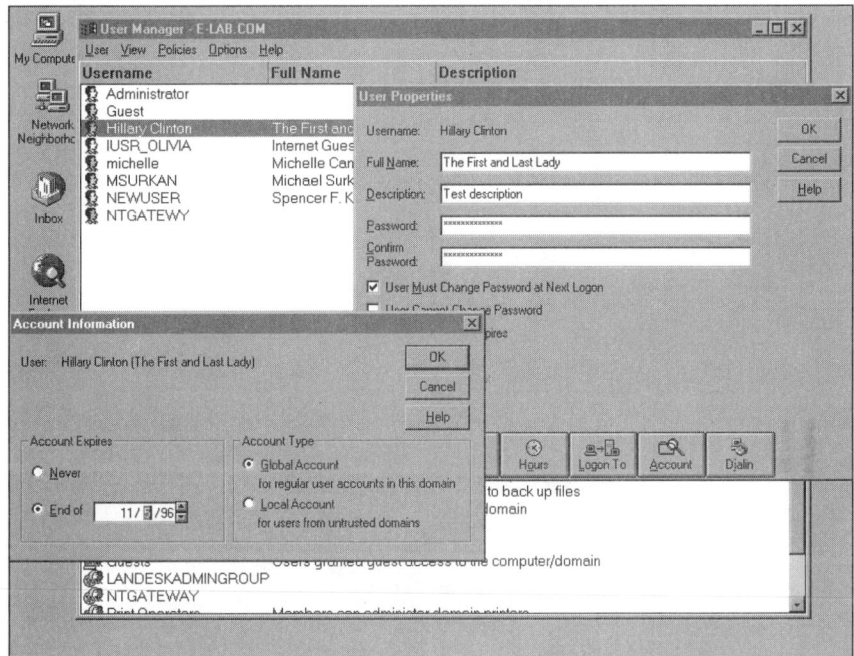

Helpful Tip

The Expiration Date setting within User Properties is particularly useful when creating temporary accounts for contractors. You might forget to disable an account at the end of the contract, particularly if you're an administrator of a large network. With this setting, you can set an account to become inactive on a pre-defined date.

There are additional user account settings that can be activated by clicking on icons located at the bottom of the User Properties window. Two of these, the groups and profile icons, appear by default.

Groups simplify administration. Rather than giving each user access to resources, create a group with multiple users and give them all access via the group, as shown in Figure 19.5. NT domains have default groups, which govern basic access and administrative privileges. They appear automatically. You can create more groups as needed, combining all the finance department users together, for example.

One of the default domain groups is the administrator group, which gives one total access to all resources. In total, there are eight groups to choose

Figure 19.5

Users can be made
members of groups.

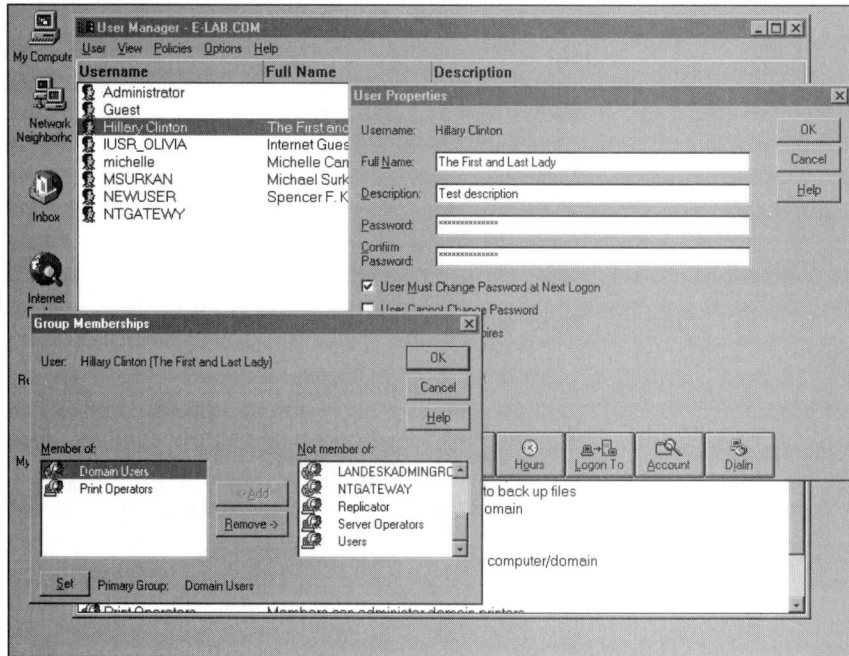

from: administrators, users, guests, account operators, backup operators, print
operators, server operators, and replicators. Table 19.1 explains these groups.

Profile

Windows NT has a user profile feature that's created for each individual user
account. These profiles are best supported by NT Workstation and Windows
95 users. With user profiles it's possible to set up so that your icons, wall paper, color scheme and such remain the same each time you log on, regardless
of what changes a previous user made to the same computer.

Profiles in the User Properties window lets you specify where the profile
is stored. For example, the profiles for Mitchel Camp can be stored on a central server to create a roaming profile, which will give a consistent look and
feel to every user session, regardless of which NT Workstation they log onto
on the network. If you don't specify which server you want a given user ID
profile to be stored in, they'll be stored locally. The user will have to set all
profile settings again the next time they log onto a different machine.

Default directories and logon scripts are also specified under the profile
icon in the User Properties window. Logon scripts are really just batch files.

Table 19.1

Default domain groups

WINDOWS NT SERVER DOMAIN CONTROLLER	DEFINITION
Administrators	This group allows for full control of every NT built-in right and ability. Administrators manage the overall configuration of the domain and the domain's controllers.
Backup operators	Backup Operators can log onto, back up, and restore files on the domain's PDC and BDCs.
Server operators	Server Operators can manage the domain's PDC and BDCs.
Account operators	Account Operators can use User Manager for Domains to create and modify user accounts and groups for the domain.
Print operators	Print operators can create, delete, and manage printers shared on the domain's PDC and BDCs.
Users	Users have rights to perform necessary tasks on their local workstations.
Guests	Occasional or one-time guest users have limited abilities and are automatically and permanently members of the local and global guests groups. They have no rights at domain servers, but they do have rights at their individual workstations.
Replicator	The replicator group supports directory replication functions. However, accounts of actual users should not be added to this group.

Helpful Tip

Profiles are only applicable for Windows NT and Windows 95 client PC users. Older version of Windows and other operating systems do not support profiles.

You can specify the name of the logon script file, a batch file, but don't specify the path for the logon script. The path for all user logon scripts is set under the server icon in the Control Panel.

Other Parameters

Other parameters appear as icons in the User Properties window depending on the network services that are installed. For example, if RAS is installed in the domain, a dial-in icon will appear for setting remote access privileges. Other options will appear if file and print services for NetWare, Microsoft Exchange, or other products are installed.

Local and Global Groups

Groups can be created in NT domains to simplify setting common rights and privileges for users. Rather than specifying each user allowed to access a shared volume containing corporate finance data, you can create a group that has all the members of corporate finance employees contained within. You can create both local and global groups by selecting New local group or New global group under the User menu in the User Manager for domains.

Local groups are inherent to a given domain and can't be accessed across trust relationships in other domains. However, local groups can contain users and global groups from other domains. Global groups can be accessed in other domains linked by trust relationships, but they can only contain users from their originating domain.

Global Groups

Global groups contain accounts from only a single domain. If you had five domains in a trust relationship on a big network, you could make global groups in each domain as shown in Figure 19.6. Each global group would contain the finance users of that region. It's not possible to create an all-encompassing global group of finance users from each domain in the network. If you're in the Boston domain, for example, you couldn't add the users in the San Francisco domain to your global groups.

However, you can use global groups to assign permissions to use resources across domains. For example, you can allow access for all finance users from different domains to a directory within the corporate office's domain. You do this by specifying permissions to each of the global finance groups in the respective domains. In each domain you must create a finance group. In the directory located in the main office domain server, assign permissions to all of those groups—for example, Boston, San Francisco, Chicago—so they can have access.

Local groups can simplify this task of assigning permissions to domain resources in a large network with multiple domains. For example, in a master domain you would make one local finance group and include all other finance groups in other domains, thereby making it part of the local group.

The difference between local and global groups is simple: global groups must specify individual user accounts and can't contain other groups as subsets. Local groups can contain other groups but can't be accessed from other domains.

Figure 19.6

Global groups can contain users from multiple domains.

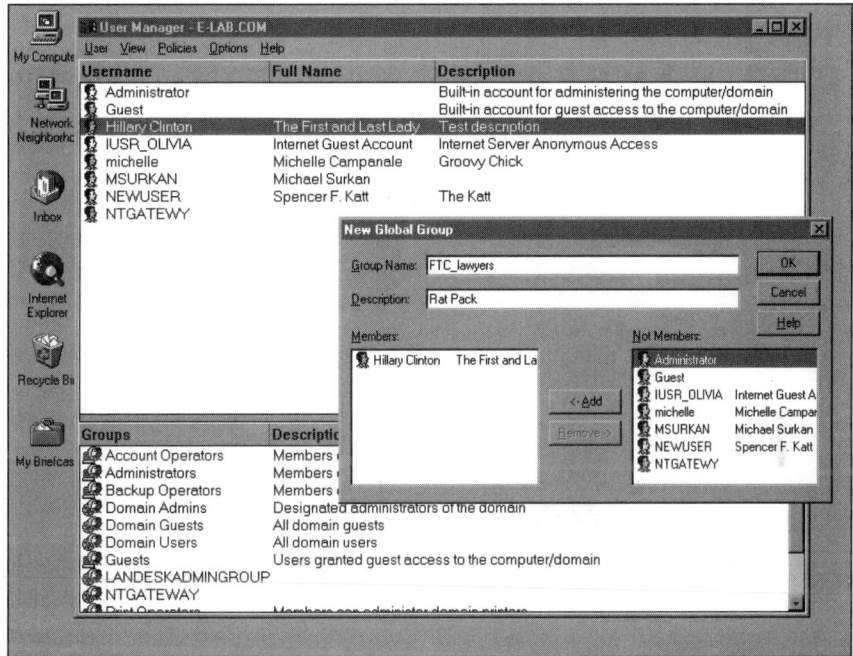

Helpful Tip

Truly global groups, containing users from all domains, are possible in the master domain model. If you have all the user accounts for all users in separate domains, centrally administered, and created in a master domain, it isn't necessary to have global groups in all domains. Rather than a global finance group for each domain, there can be a single global finance group in the master domain.

Local Groups

Local groups simplify the task of granting access to local resources to users in other domains. Local groups can contain user accounts and global groups from other domains, as shown in Figure 19.7. However, local groups cannot be referred to from other domains out on the network. For example, the administrator of the San Francisco domain could not grant file access to a local finance group of the Boston domain. Only if the Boston finance group was global would this be possible.

Figure 19.7

Local groups can contain
both users and global
groups.

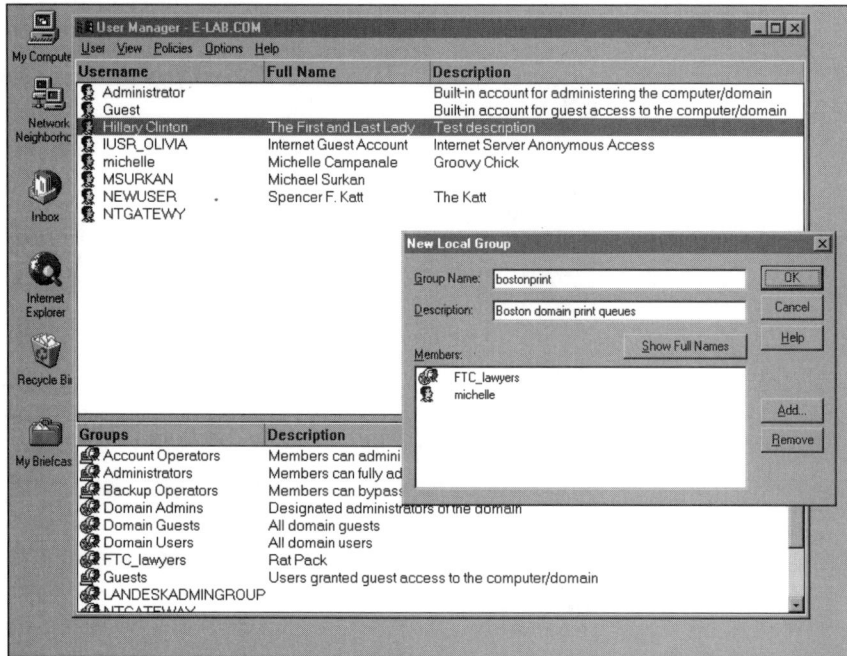

Figure 19.7
Local groups can contain both users and global groups.

In small, single-domain networks, the difference between local and global groups is minimal. However, we recommend that small networks using a single domain create global groups, in case the network is expanded.

Policies

Policies control how passwords must be used by all user accounts for a computer or domain. They can provide different levels of security for user actions on domain controllers and on workstations and member servers.

Account policies can be set in the Account Policy window shown in Figure 19.8, which is located under the Policies menu in the User Manager. In this menu you can choose from three security policies: account policies, user rights and audit policies.

Account policies control how passwords are used by user accounts, including password restrictions, expiration limits, password change requirements, and password length settings. Account lockout, which ensures that intruders can't log on after a certain number of password guesses, is disabled by default and can be set in the policies window.

The user rights section of the Policies menu determines which Windows NT administrative privileges are granted to groups or individual users. You

Figure 19.8

Overall default user account policies can be set in the User Manager.

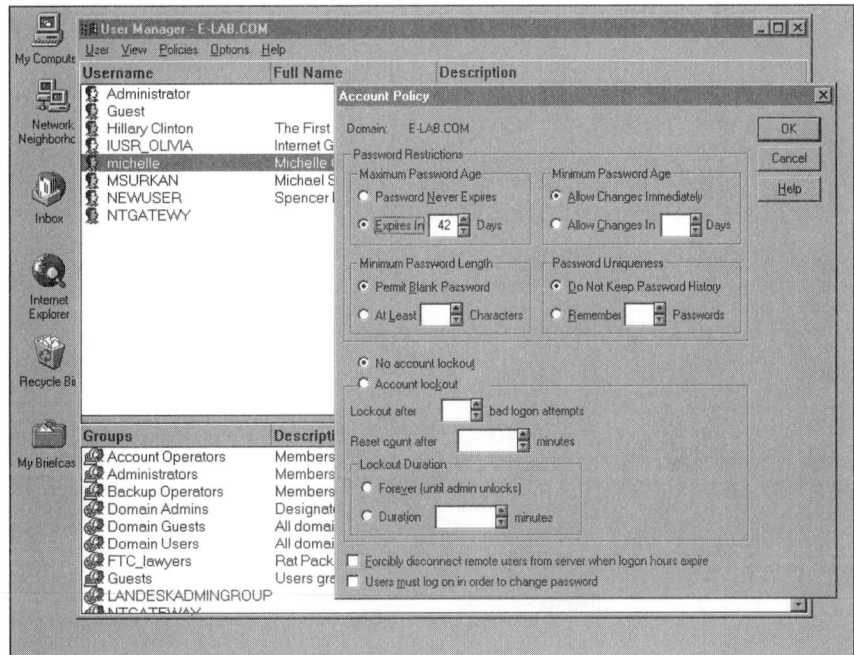

can decentralize network administration, sharing the work by giving specific low-level privileges to users to do backups or create new accounts. By only assigning specific administrative rights, you can minimize the risk of a novice administrator making a mistake or compromising security. It may be helpful to give someone permission to run nightly backups, but give them no further access to the network. Rights differ from permissions, which allow you to use a specific object like a print queue, because they apply to the system as a whole. Audit policies, as shown in Figure 19.9, control what types of events are recorded in the Security log of the Event Viewer.

Trust Relationships

A trust relationship allows a link between different domains so users can share resources across domains. The User Manager for Domains is the tool that manages and creates these trust relationships.

The limit of trusted domains on Windows NT 3.51 Server is 128 trusted domains. Windows NT can support up to 500 trust relationships. The amount of trusts is dependent on the RAM in the server. With 32MB of RAM, a server can have up to 140 trusts, scaling up to 500 trusts with 128MB of RAM.

Figure 19.9

Various types of network access can be configured to show up in the event logs.

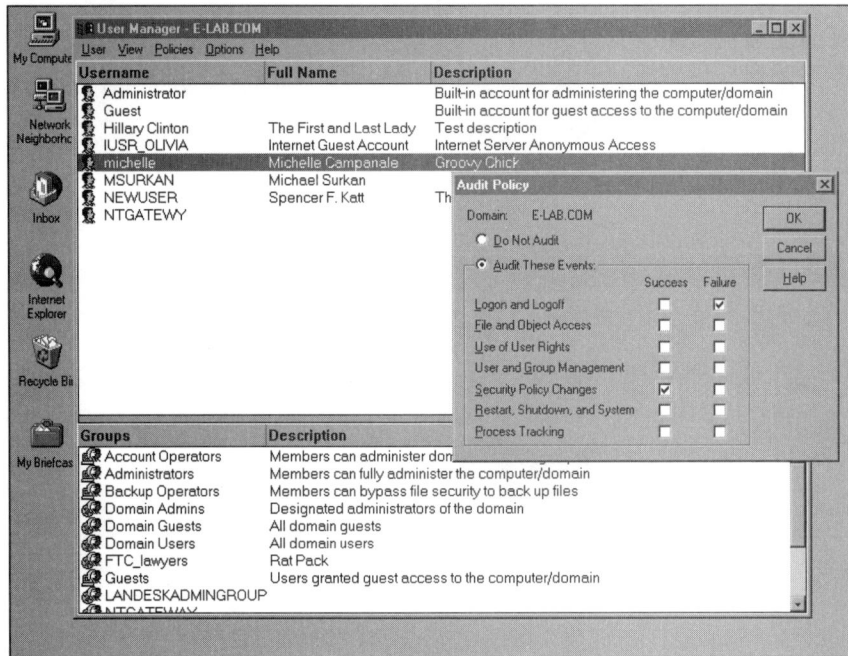

To create trust relationships, choose Trust Relationships under the Policies menu in the User Manager. Trust relationships are always one way, with one domain set up as a trusting domain, which allows trusted domains to access its resources. It's possible to set up a second trust relationship to a given domain in the other direction, creating a two-way relationship that allows all users in both domains full access across domains.

To create a new trust relationship, the trusting domain administrator (that wishes to share its resources with another domain) must add the name of the new trusted domain. To ensure security, a password is specified that must be used by the administrator in the trusted domain, as shown in Figure 19.10.

In multidomain networks with a master domain, the subdomains, or regional domains, will typically have one-way relationships to the master domain. The subdomains are trusted and the master domain is trusting. The master domain will have multiple trust relationships and each of the subdomains will only have a single trust.

Figure 19.10

A password must be given for the trusting domain administrator to enter.

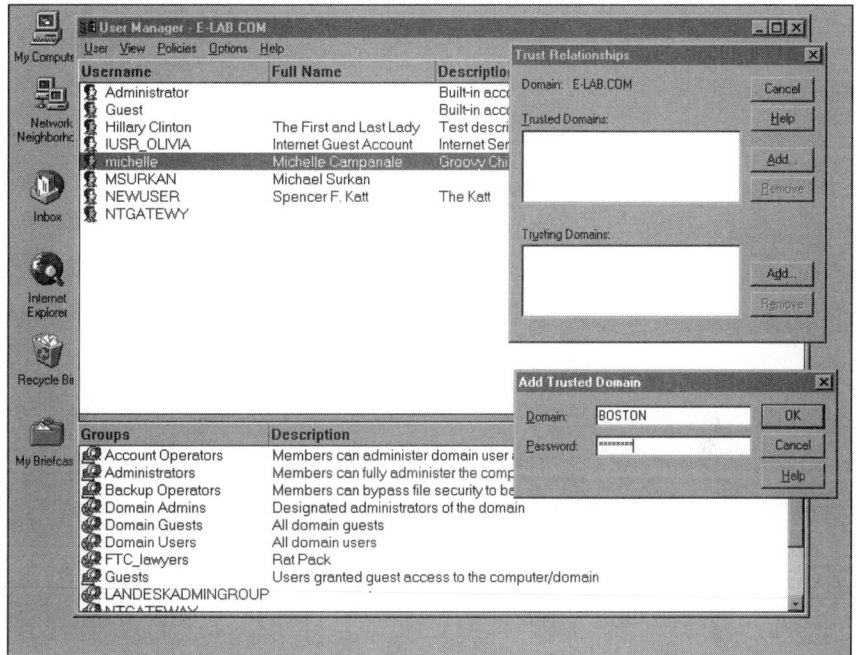

- *Computer Properties*
- *Shared Directories*
- *Services*
- *Send a Message*
- *Domain Controller Synchronization*
- *Removing or Adding NT Computers*

20

How to Use Server Manager

THE SERVER MANAGER IS USED FOR MONITORING AND CONTROL-
ling the activity status of system processes and user activity. It's
possible, from Server Manager, to see which files are currently
open by users and to view shared and opened resources, such as
printers. You can also send alert messages to specified NT servers
and control the replication of directories from Server Manager.

Yet another aspect of the Server Manager is domain administration. NT machine accounts can be removed or added to the domain
as needed. Additionally, domain controllers can be synchronized or
promoted and demoted to and from PDCs and BDCs.

■ Computer Properties

You can look at the properties of any of the NT machines—Server or Work-station—that are registered in the domain. Do this by either double-clicking on the computer name or by accessing the Properties window through the Computer menu of the Server Manager. (See Figure 20.1.)

Figure 20.1

A quick overview of system activity can be seen from the computer properties in the Server Manager.

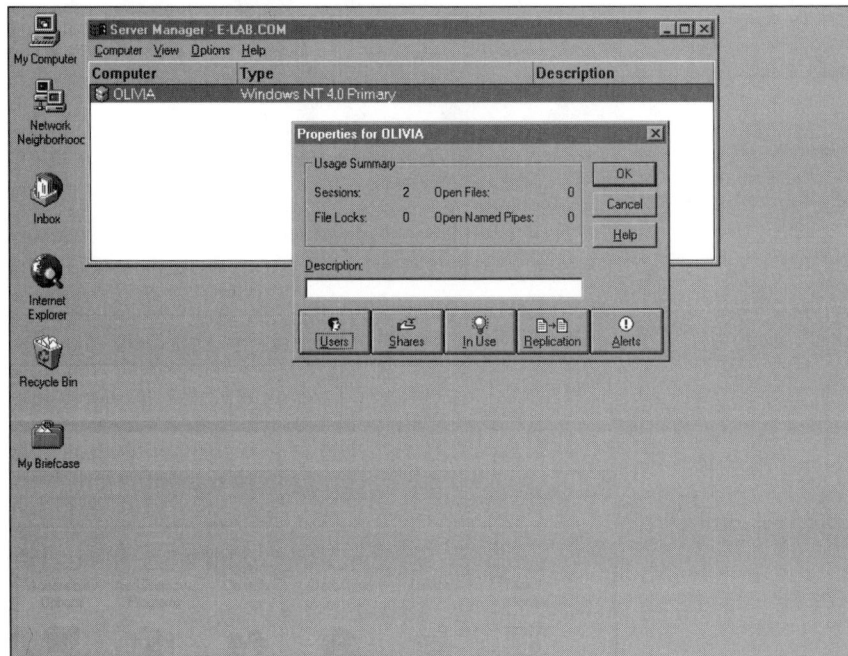

The Properties window shows how many users are logged onto the ma-chine and how many files are open. By clicking on the icons at the bottom of the window, you can select individual user connections or terminate and dis-connect the resource.

Managing Computer Properties

In the Server Manager, under Computer properties, you can view the status of a given computer. You can see who is logged in and what files are open, in addition to sending alert messages and managing replication.

Helpful Tip

> *We recommend that you do not terminate used resources or user sessions through the server manager unless you are certain that there will be no disruption of user work. Termination of open network connections should only be done as a last resort to recover from system hangs. The server manager should primarily be used as a monitoring tool, allowing administrators to find out what is being used on a server.*

The Properties window gives the overall status of the usage summary of a given machine. It shows a system status overview including information about the number of open sessions on the machine. Further information and management of the system usage can be done by clicking icons at the bottom of the Properties window. These options are detailed below.

View or Disconnect User Sessions

Viewing information about a computer can be done by right-clicking the computer and selecting Properties. The Computer properties window will appear, and you can click buttons to view users, shares, current remote connections, replication import and export servers, and to send administrative alerts.

By clicking on Users in the Properties window, you can view all users connected over the network, as well as the resources they're using. As shown in Figure 20.2, you can display user sessions (which can be disconnected) by double-clicking the computer name in the Server Manager window and then double-clicking Users.

Resources in Use

You can assess and manage resource use under the Properties window. There you'll see a summary display of use for the selected computer, as shown in Figure 20.3. Additionally, you can intervene in a user's session using this summary resource.

Sending a Message to Users

Users who are connected to a computer can be sent messages by using Send Message under the Computer menu. The messenger service must be running on both sending and receiving computers. You would use this feature, for example, before you disconnect a user or before you stop the server service on a computer.

Managing Administrative Alerts

Administrative alerts are sent by the system and relate to server and resource use. To manage the list of computers and users that are notified

Figure 20.2

User sessions can be
monitored through the
Server Manager.

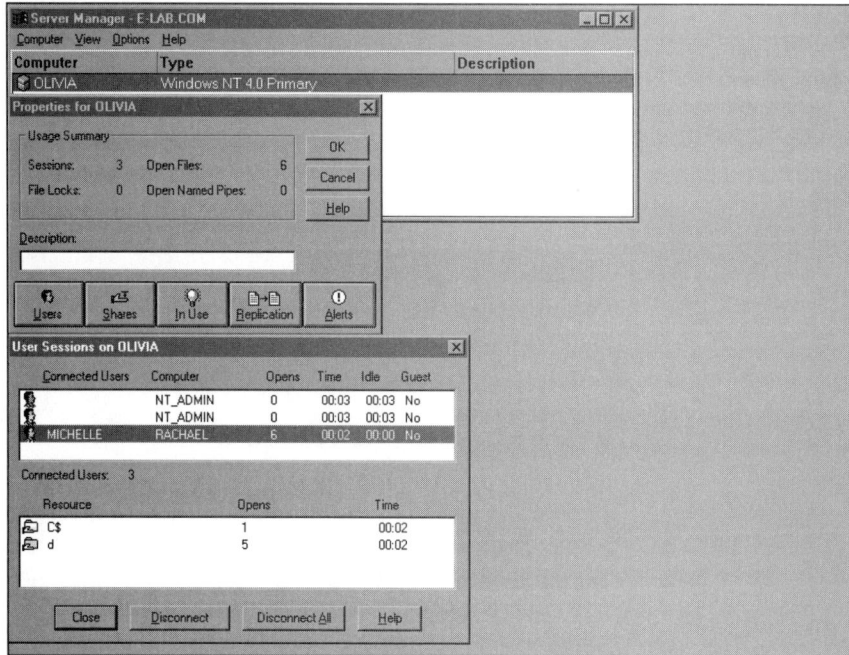

when administrative alerts occur at the selected computer, click on Alerts
at the bottom of the Properties window.

Replication

Domain controller directories can be replicated to other NT servers on the
network. This feature provides a degree of safety by automatically maintaining copies of data, but it's useful primarily for keeping user profiles, policies,
and logon scripts consistent across domain controllers.

■ Shared Directories

Shared directories (Figure 20.4) under the Computer menu shows you all of
the directories that have been set up for sharing. If you want to make a new
shared directory, click on New Share..., then type the share name, the path,
and the permissions. Additionally, this is a good place to stop shares. Click
on any directory and then on Stop Sharing to to disable the shared volume.

Figure 20.3

You can check the
network resources in use
on a given NT Server
from the Server Manager.

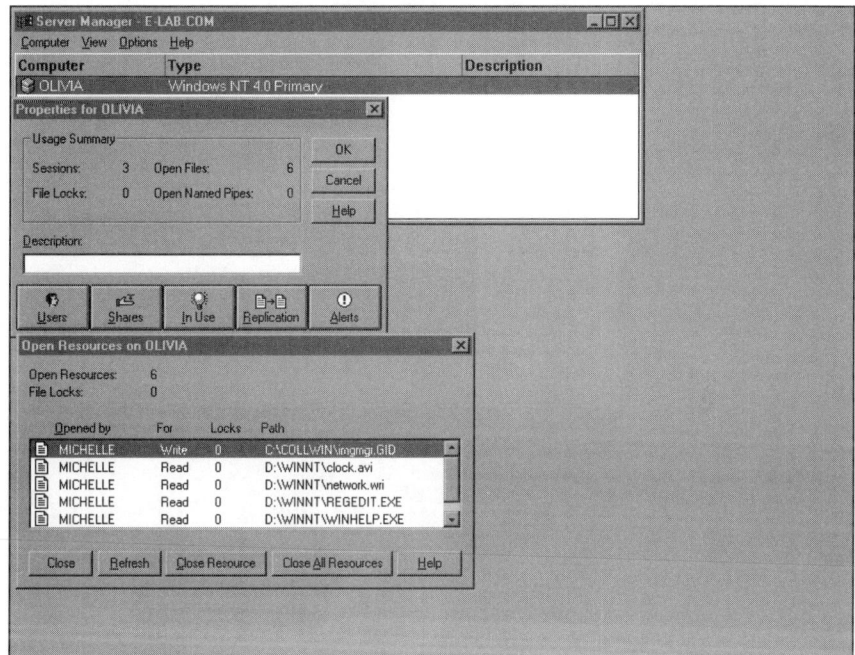

■ Services

The Services menu allows you to remotely access and manage background
services on any NT Server or Workstation on the network. This provides the
same functionality as Services in the Control Panel, but in a remote context.

■ Send a Message

You can send messages to all the users connected to a particular server. This
is useful in cases such as when you're shutting the server down. Unfortunately, messages will not be sent to properly to all computer clients. Currently, only NT or Win95 machines can support this function.

Figure 20.4

Shared volumes can be
created or stopped
through the Server
Manager.

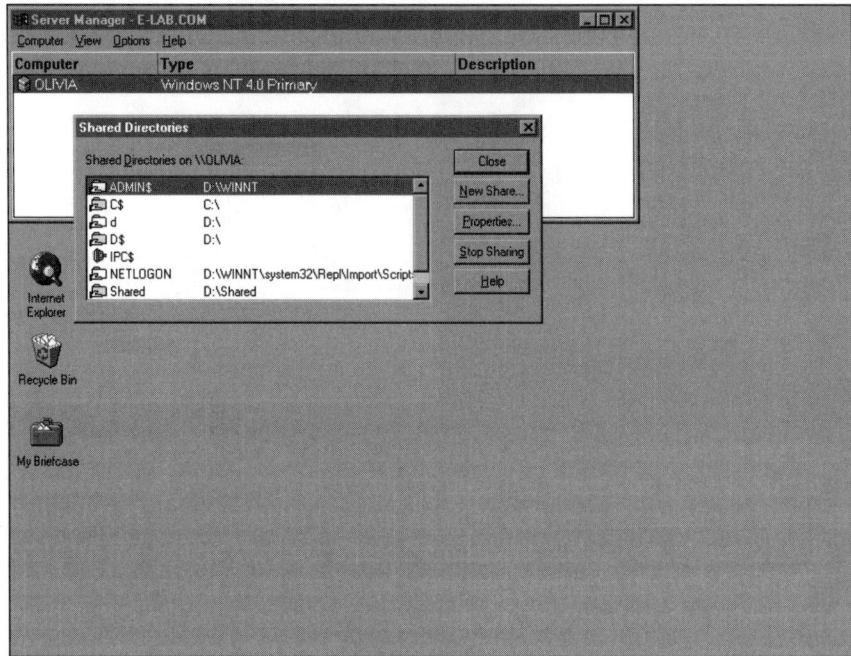

Helpful Tip

*Another menu option called MacFile will appear in the Server Manager
if Mac services are installed. There's a send message option there that can
be used to communicate with Macintosh users.*

■ Domain Controller Synchronization

If you select a BDC and then use this option, the BDC security database will
automatically be synchronized with the PDC. The domain controllers
throughout the network can be fully synchronized by selecting Synchronize
entire domain on the menu.

Synchronization is an automatic process that runs ceaselessly between
controllers without administrator interference. However, these manual synchronization tools exist to help resolve problems when the normal background synchronization fails.

■ Removing or Adding NT Computers

All NT computers, both Workstation and Server, must be registered in the domain to have access. Administrators can use the Server Manager to add the name of new NT computers so they can be installed successfully on the domain. This isn't necessary, however, if the user installing an NT machine has an account with the appropriate administrative rights to add a computer to the domain.

NT computer accounts can also be removed from a domain. Simply highlight the computer you wish to remove and under the Computer menu, select Remove from domain.... This is typically done if a computer name that no longer exists on the network is still registered and a new machine is being installed to take its place.

- *Registry Parameters*

21

Synchronizing Domain Controllers

THE SERVER MESSAGE BLOCK (SMB) SECURITY DATABASE, STORED on primary and backup domain controllers, is automatically kept synchronized as identical copies. Any time a change occurs to the domain account database, the PDC sends a message, or pulse, to the BDCs informing them that an update is necessary. The BDCs then respond to the PDC with synchronization requests.

To reduce network traffic loads, only the changes to the SMB are transferred to the BDCs for a partial synchronization. Full synchronizations are only performed when a BDC is first installed and the SMB account database must be copied from the PDC. All of this synchronization traffic between domain controllers is encrypted, to prevent account information from becoming vulnerable to packet sniffing.

A number of registry parameters, such as the frequency of updates and update packet sizes, govern NT synchronization. To control the synchronization process, you can make settings in the registry for packet sizes and other options. In most cases the default settings should work well, but in large environments with many BDCs, it may be necessary to alter some of them to improve performance or overcome synchronization problems. The most common reason to change these parameters is to improve performance over low speed WAN links. You can use the Server Manager tool to initiate full synchronizations of a single BDC or the entire network.

■ Registry Parameters

The synchronization variables are located in the HKEY_LOCAL_MACHINE\ SYSTEM\CurrentControlSet\Services\Netlogon\Parameters section of the registry. Use the registry editor to change them. Many of the synchronization parameters are not listed in the registry and must be added. All of the following parameters are of the REG_DWORD type.

For these synchronization parameters to take effect, either the PDC must be rebooted or the NetLogon service can be stopped and restarted. Here's a list of these settings, which Microsoft has published.

- Replication Governor: sets the size of buffered data to be used for updates to BDCs. It must be configured separately for each BDC. By reducing the buffer size, synchronizations can be prevented from tying up the entire bandwidth of a slow network connection for long periods of time. The value used in this parameter also determines the frequency of updates. Setting a low value may free up bandwidth, but it also means the remote BDC will be out of date for longer periods of time. The parameter value ranges from 1 to 100, as a percentage of the maximum allowed buffer size of 128KB. A setting of 50 would indicate a 64KB buffer size.

- Change Log Size: determines how many changes can be stored in a temporary change log file on the PDC before being synchronized with the BDCs. This value is set in bytes and can range from 65,536–4,194,304. The default is 65,536. A single change takes up approximately 32 bytes.

- Pulse: sets the frequency of pulses, or messages, from the PDC informing BDCs of changes. The value represents seconds, and ranges from 60–3600; the default is 300.

- Pulse Currency: determines the number of BDCs that can be pulsed at any one time. It can range from 1–500, with the default being 20.

- Pulse Maximum: sets the maximum interval for pulses to be sent to BDCs. The value is entered in seconds and ranges from 60–86400; the default is 7200.

- Pulse Timeout 1: sets the amount of time a PDC will await a response from a BDC before designating it unresponsive and stop updating the BDC altogether. The setting is made in seconds ranging from 1–120; the default is 5.

- Pulse Timeout 2: tells the PDC how long to wait for a synchronization attempt to be completed before aborting. The number is set in seconds and ranges from 60–3600; the default is 300.

- *Configuring Replication*

22

Configuring Directory Replication

Y OU CAN CONTROL REPLICATION OF DIRECTORIES SO THAT ANY directory specified is automatically duplicated to any other NT server you want. For example, you might want to have the logon scripts on your PDC duplicated to all of your BDCs.

Windows NT has the ability to replicate directories and their data across servers. It's possible, for example, to have user data directories continuously updated on more than one server at the same time. Users might access all of their directories on a single server but updated duplicates of the data would be maintained on other servers on the network.

This can be a powerful help in data redundancy and can protect you from system crashes and data loss. Typically, NT replication services are implemented for maintaining user profiles and logon scripts across both the primary and backup domain controllers. The user profiles and logon scripts must be stored on the machine that authenticates them for use.

For example, you may have created user logon scripts on a PDC that work fine as long as the user is authenticated by the PDC at logon. However, if the user is authenticated by a BDC that doesn't have a copy of the logon script, the script won't run.

Helpful Tip   *Replication is no substitute for good backups. If your data is bad, replication will copy bad data. The only way to recover data that users accidentally delete or that has been corrupted, is by using a backup archive.*

■ Configuring Replication

Before you can set up directory replication, you must create a domain user account with appropriate rights. (Make up any name you wish.) Make sure the user is a member of the replication group.

Next, modify the Directory Replication service settings under the Services icon in the Control Panel. To do this, select Directory Replicator in the list of services. The directory replicator's Service window, shown in Figure 22.1, will be displayed. Change Startup Type to automatic. Under Log On As, select This Account and fill in the user name and password to be used by the replication service.

You must configure the replication service in this way on both the exporting and importing servers. Then, use the Server Manager to define which directories are to be exported. Click on the replication icon under Computer Properties in the Server Manager. The Directory Replication window shown in Figure 22.2 will be displayed.

The server that has the directories you wish to duplicate must be configured to export. Activate Export Directories and then under Manage..., choose which directories you wish to export. Unfortunately, you're limited to exporting only one directory and its subdirectories.

For example, if you set the path to C:\Data, you'll only be able to add directories for export that are under the data directory. You must specify the servers you wish to export these directories to. Do this by clicking Add....

You can follow the same process in reverse for import servers. Before an NT Server can import directories from another server, it must be configured

Figure 22.1

A replication user
account must be
specified for the Directory
Replication service.

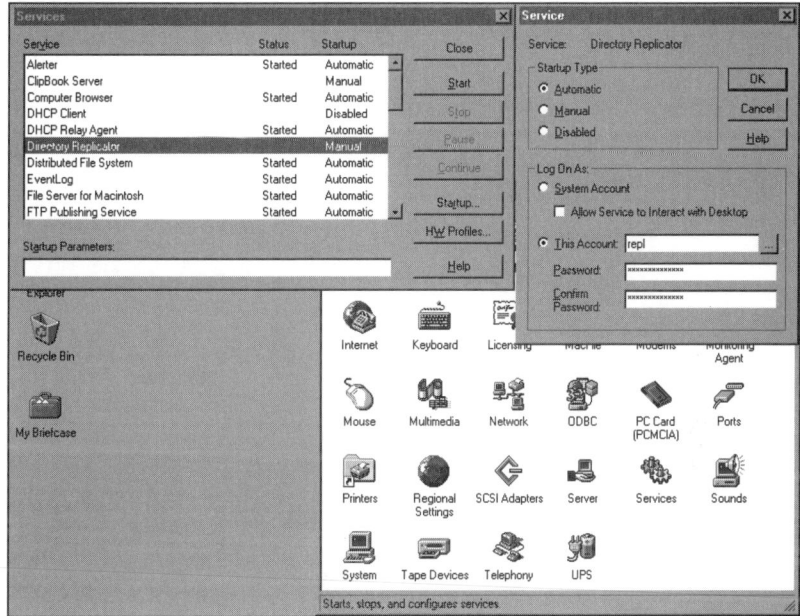

Figure 22.2

From the Server
Manager, directories can
be exported for
replication.

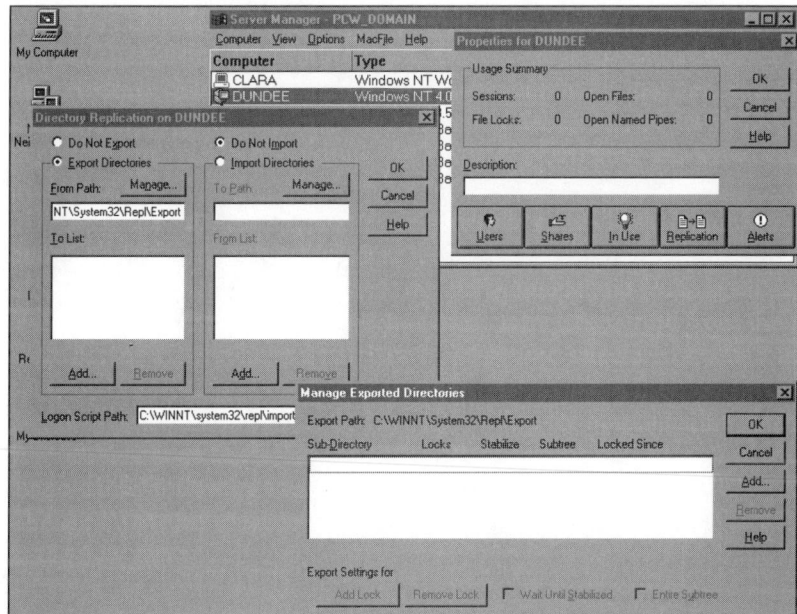

through the Server Manager's Properties window. You must specify the path where the imported directories are to be stored and select the servers the NT server is to receive directories from by using Add....

Once export and import servers are configured and a field exists to specify the logon script path, logon scripts will automatically be replicated.

The built-in replication features of the Windows NT Server 4 are not intended to be used for fault tolerance. Other products exist from third parties that provide real-time duplication of NT Server data across the network.

- *Setting Up NT User Profiles*
- *Configuring User Policies*

23

How to Configure Windows NT Profiles

SINCE ITS EARLIEST VERSIONS, WINDOWS NT SERVER HAS HAD USER profiles that keep track of settings for each user account.

The first time a user logs onto an NT Workstation or Server, a directory containing his or her session setting is created under the profiles directory in the Windows NT system folder. User profiles keep track of connected network sessions to volume shares or network print queues, as well as session settings for the types of wallpaper and screen colors.

Even if several people use the same NT Workstation, each user will see things exactly the way they left it the last time they logged on. It's possible to store these user profiles centrally on a file server so that users have consistent sessions no matter which machine they use to log onto the network. By default, user profiles will be created locally on an individual machine. It's possible for administrators to create standardized profiles that are used by all users on the network or just specific groups.

Windows NT 4 has extended the ability to centrally manage NT user sessions by implementing policies, which were first introduced with Windows 95. Policies enable administrators to restrict user abilities, preventing alteration of such things as Control Panel options, while users can modify user profiles.

Profiles and policies only apply to Windows NT and Windows 95 users. Windows 3.1, DOS, Macintosh, and other client types are not supported by policies and profiles. This chapter explains how to manage and configure profiles and policies for NT users on NT networks. If you'd like to set up profiles or policies for Windows 95 clients, consult the Windows 95 Resource Kit.

■ Setting Up NT User Profiles

User profiles are automatically created each time a user logs onto an NT Workstation or Server. These profiles are stored under the Profiles directory in the Windows NT System directory.

Each user's profile directory will have an Ntuser.dat file that holds these settings. Roaming profiles can be configured by specifying a networked directory for centrally storing user profiles in the User Manager for domains. These directories must be specified for each user account. Before user profiles can be centrally stored, you must create a shared profiles directory on a server.

You can copy an existing user profile to the networked profiles directory that contains all of the settings you want a user to have. You can do this using the System Properties tool in the Control Panel, shown in Figure 23.1. You may wish to change permissions on the Ntuser.dat file to prevent changes from being saved when users exit their sessions.

It's also possible to have more than one user pointing to the same profile, providing a consistent environment for groups. For example, sales staff could share the same profile, which has appropriate icons for sales management applications and drive mappings to sales department NT servers. However, when more than one account shares the same user profile, it's definitely advisable to set file permissions to ensure that no user can overwrite the settings. Otherwise, any changes a user might make to his or her environment will be saved when they exit their NT session.

Figure 23.1

User profiles can be
copied using the System
Properties tool under the
Control Panel.

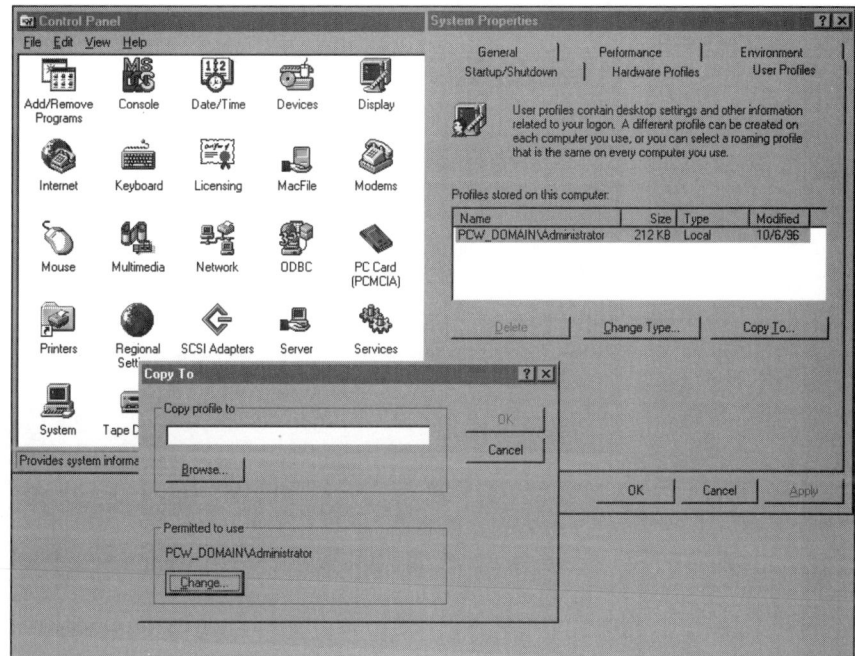

■ Configuring User Policies

System policies are new to Windows NT 4 and are stored in a single file on
domain controllers. System policies supersede whatever is stored in the user
profile and offer administrators much greater flexibility in controlling user
environments and preventing changes in systems. The options available to
you are shown in Figure 23.2.

You can use the same policy editor to create and manage Windows 95
policies, but it must be executed from a Windows 95 machine. Windows 95
policies cannot be administered from an NT console. (This is because the registries of Windows NT and Windows 95 are different.)

Using the system policy editor, you can create a system policy file, Ntcon-
fig.pol. It must be stored in the netlogon directory of the Windows NT system folder of the PDC. If this file is stored in another directory, it won't be
tied directly into the NT domains and set policies won't take effect when
users log on. The policy editor is located under the NT Server's Administrative Tools section in the Programs group.

Figure 23.2

Administrators can set
user policies with the
policy editor.

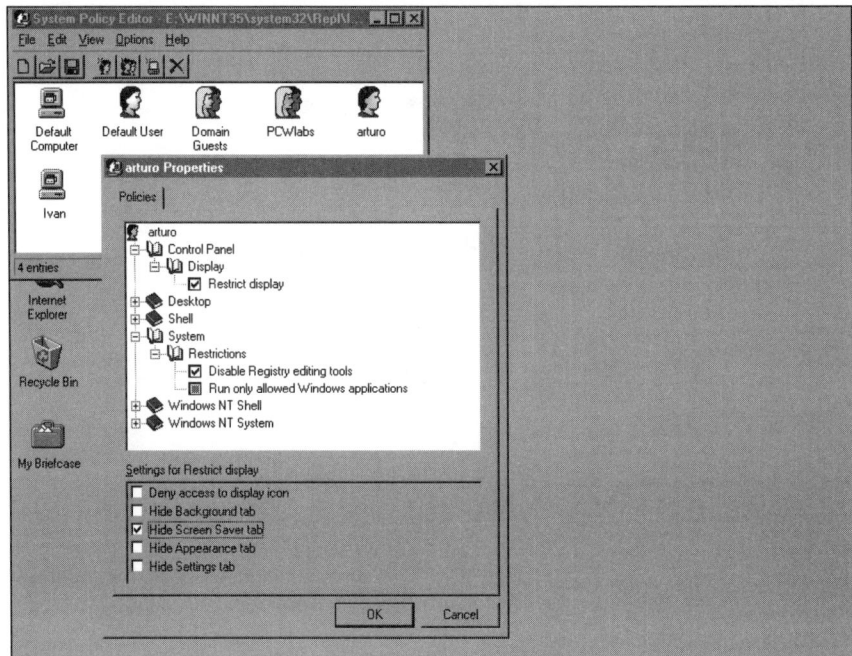

Icons are automatically created in the policy editor for a default computer and user. These will take effect automatically if no specific policies have been set for users or groups. By creating policies for individual computers, you can restrict environment modifications on an individual NT machine.

A copy of the Ntconfig.pol must be stored on each PDC or BDC on the network. If a user is authenticated on a BDC without the policies file, only the user profile will be used for determining their environment settings.

- *Client Support by Emulation*
- *Network Client Administrator*

24

How to Set Up Windows NT Clients

MANY TYPES OF CLIENT COMPUTERS RUNNING NUMEROUS OPER-
ating systems can access Windows NT networks.

Microsoft provides all of the necessary components for their
own operating systems, such as DOS, Windows 3.1, Windows for
Workgroups, Windows 95, and Windows NT 4. Computers with
other operating systems can still access Windows NT OS/2, for example, which has NT-compatible networking built into it. For computers such as UNIX and Mac, Windows NT 4 is able to emulate
the types of networking services that are expected.

There are two ways for client computers to hook up to Windows NT 4. The first is by using the native NT networking protocols and server message block (SMB) technology). All of the Microsoft operating systems come with built-in SMB, excluding DOS, which needs to have special drivers added on that support SMB. OS/2 can connect right out of the box, because its networking components share a common history with NT since the time years ago when it was a joint effort between Microsoft and IBM.

A second way for clients to connect to a server relates to NT's ability to emulate or pretend to be a network service that one of these other clients want to find. For example, both Macintosh file and print sharing features are emulated by Windows NT Server 4. There are also emulations for UNIX services. Out of the box, Windows NT 4 can run TCP/IP services such as LPR printing and FTP.

■ Client Support by Emulation

We've already explained the different systems that Windows NT 4 can emulate. You can also add optional network emulation services to the NT Server so that other clients can access it. Conversely, there's another option available by adding services to the client so it can connect to the server.

Macintosh services is one example of emulation services that can be added in NT 4. Windows NT Server can act as an AppleShare file server, showing up under the Chooser and AppleShare menus. Windows NT Server print queues even appear as AppleTalk printers under the Chooser. A built-in rasterization routine in the NT 4 Server will even convert the standard postscript output from Macintoshes into whatever printer language is necessary.

UNIX emulation can be installed as well. Specifically, the FTP service provides basic file transfer functionality to UNIX machines. The built-in services, such as TCP/IP print services, provide standard UNIX line printer daemon (LPD) print support, allowing UNIX machines to access any NT print queue.

You can accomplish further UNIX–NT integration with third-party software. You can buy Network File System (NFS) server software for NT Server from a number of vendors, such as FTP Inc. or Netmanage. NFS allows an NT server to act like a UNIX file server, where any UNIX host can access NT as if it were a standard NFS host.

More recently, Microsoft has provided additional emulation support—File and Print Services for NetWare (FPNW)—for NetWare servers. If you're running FPNW, the NT Server will emulate Netware 3.x binderies. Any DOS PCs running Novell NetWare's VLM client software can log onto an NT server just as if it were a NetWare server. Unfortunately, Novell's newer Client32 software does not work with FPNW.

■ Network Client Administrator

The Windows NT Server CD includes drivers and client network services for a number of operating systems. In the case of Windows95, the entire code for the operating system is on the CD. Previously, the Windows 3.51 Server CD included the Windows for Workgroups code.

Windows NT 4 has a Network Client Administration tool, which allows you to create network install disks. With these boot disks you can go to any PC on the network, power up, and install the appropriate network client automatically on the local PC hard drive from over the LAN.

However, you must install DOS first. Be aware that this process is only intended for use with DOS and Windows 95 clients. Of course, you can still make your own boot floppies for other operating systems. Just make sure that you have a shared volume on an NT server and that you have Windows for Workgroups or Windows NT Server installation images copied there. Then, make a bootable DOS floppy diskette that runs the Microsoft DOS networking client. If you want to install Windows for Workgroups, NT Server, or NT Workstation over the network, you must make sure that the install CD software is installed in a Clients directory on an NT Server.

Helpful Tip

> *Even though the DOS and Windows 95 clients are installed on the NT Server, you are still legally required to pay the licensing fee for each copy you install. Microsoft does have volume licensing discounts.*

Creating the Installation Diskettes with the Network Client Administrator

You can use the Network Client Administrator to create a bootable network installation startup disk, to create a network installation disk set, or to copy client-based network administration tools to any NT computer. However, the client administrator does not help you if you want to install Windows for Workgroups, OS/2, or Windows NT Workstation over the network. You'll have to look to the vendor for a solution. Additionally, the network client administrator is only of use to Intel-based PCs. The diskettes aren't of any value to other machines, such as RISC machines.

The process of making boot floppies is very dependent on the network interface of your PC. If every client has different network adapter cards and network adapter card settings, you must make a separate disk for each client. So, creating install boot floppies is only of great value if all your machines are identical.

Helpful Tip

The usefulness of the Network Client Administration tool is dubious at best, and often requires manual modifications of the generated boot diskettes to function properly. The number of network cards supported is limited, and there's no way to specify the use of a new driver on a vendor-supplied diskette. You may wish to access the client software directly yourself, under the \clients directory on the NT 4 Server CD.

To start the Network Client Administrator, click Start and then select Network Client Administrator under the Administrative Tools group in the Programs menu. You'll be prompted with four choices that allow you to install or update network client workstations. These options include: Make Network Installation Startup Disk, Make Installation Disk Set, Copy Client-based Network Administration Tools, and View Remoteboot Client Information.

The first time you run the Network Client Administrator, it'll ask you for the path of the files needed, whether they're on CD-ROM, hard drive, or network. Then the administrator copies files and creates the network share volume. A menu appears, shown in Figure 24.1, asking you which installation disks you want to make. Specify what kind of client you want to install, such as DOS or Windows95. After you're prompted for both the client and network adapter cards, you'll be able to create an installation disk for each variation.

DOS Clients

Before you can connect DOS clients to a network, you must install either Microsoft Network Client for MS-DOS or Microsoft LAN Manager Client for MS-DOS. Both are included under the \clients directory of the Windows NT Server 4 CD. The Microsoft Network Client will enable your client PC to interact with the domain controllers and other computers running Windows NT Workstation. The LAN Manager Client has the same functionality as the newer Microsoft Network Client but offers greater compatibility in mixed environments running the older LAN Manager.

The LAN Manager Client takes up more disk space and system RAM than the newer Microsoft Network Client. But it may be more compatible with some networked DOS applications.

Windows 3.1 Clients

There's no built-in NT networking for Windows 3.1 clients. Essentially, Windows 3.1 was a superset of DOS, and Microsoft's DOS networking clients should be used for network connectivity.

Figure 24.1

You can create network
boot floppies for client
installation using the
Network Client
Administrator.

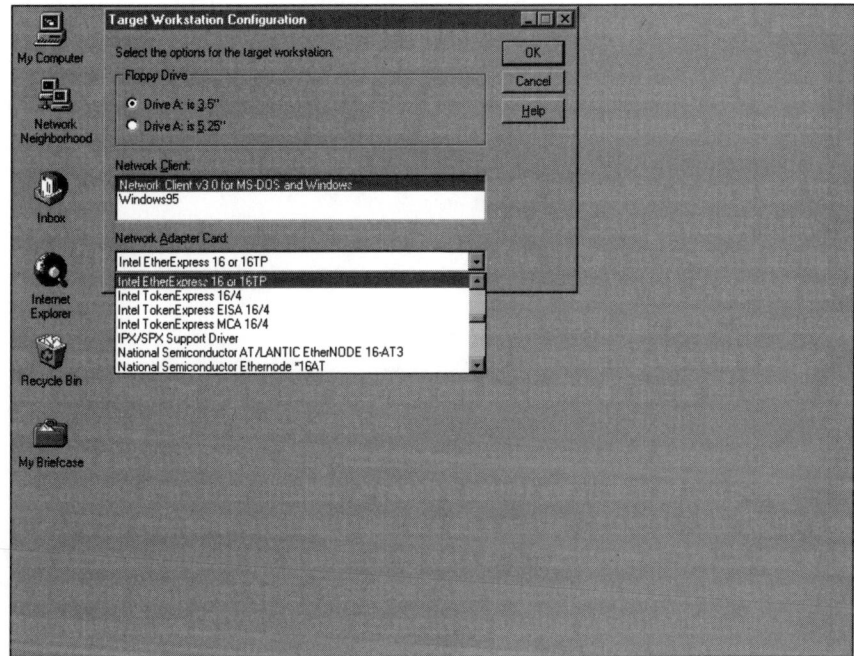

Windows for Workgroups Clients

Windows for Workgroups was Microsoft's first client operating system that
was network-ready out of the box. Windows for Workgroups 3.11 comes
with a built-in 32-bit networking subsystem. You can use the network setup
icon in Windows for Workgroups to install this system, specifying the network adapter and the appropriate settings. The Windows NT Server CD
has a Windows for Workgroups directory of patch updates to various Windows for Workgroups components that can be copied to a Workgroups
client on the network. The path for the updates on the NT Server CD is
\clients\update.wfw.

The NT Server CD also includes a 32-bit TCP/IP stack you can install on
the Windows for Workgroups client. This stack supports the standard Microsoft IP management functions, such as WINS, DNS, and DHCP. Workgroups clients can be fully functional on an IP-only Windows NT Server
network.

Remote Boot Clients

Windows NT Server 4 includes a diskless installation option, Remoteboot. This allows Intel-based PCs equipped with remote program load (RPL) ROMs running DOS and Windows 95 clients to work exclusively over the network, with no local disk drives. You must create profiles for each of the client variations over the network, specifying the network adapter card and IRQ settings for each PC. These profiles are managed using the remote boot profile manager.

You must install the Remoteboot network service through the Network icon in the Windows NT Control Panel.

Windows 95 Clients

Built into Windows 95 is the ability to access Windows NT networks. Its network drivers and configuration options are very similar to those of Windows NT Server. The full Windows 95 code is included in the Windows NT CD under the \clients directory.

You can do remote network installations using the boot disks generated in the Network Client Administrator. Windows 95 machines can also be centrally managed more easily than previous Windows versions by creating policies that govern standardized features to all users on the network. For example, policies can be configured to prevent Windows 95 users from changing Control Panel options.

Although Windows 95 clients are able to share resources such as printers and directories over the network, it's possible for administrators to disable this function using profiles. The peer-to-peer networking services can tie into the domain security database, allowing Windows 95 users to specify who can access their system.

Windows NT

All previous versions of NT are compatible with Windows NT Server 4 networking. As far as the network is concerned, there's very little difference in operation between NT Workstation and Server versions.

Windows NT Server 4 clients can also benefit from user profiles and policies for centralized administration of end-user desktop environments.

25

How to Configure Logon Scripts

LIKE NOVELL NETWARE AND UNIX, WINDOWS NT SERVER SUPPORTS logon scripts. You can create a set of commands that are executed each time a user logs onto the NT domain.

Logon scripts can be of great use to administrators wanting to change drive mappings or access to other network resources such as print queues without having to change settings on the individual client computers. Windows NT logon scripts will only work with PC clients running DOS, Windows 3.1, Windows for Workgroups, Windows 95, or Windows NT.

In essence, Windows NT logon scripts are nothing more than batch files that are stored centrally on a Windows NT server and executed each time a user logs onto the network. Individual batch files can be made for each user, allowing variation in settings, or user accounts can be configured to use the same batch file.

In many cases, logon scripts are unnecessary. Windows NT and Windows 95 clients configured to use policies and user profiles can be centrally administrated by other means. Also, Windows NT network clients will remember their previous configurations with drive mappings and network resource settings, negating the use of logon scripts.

Often, logon scripts are used only rarely to effect basic changes on all clients and are then disabled. For example, in a network where all PCs have a drive mapping to a cc-mail shared volume, you can use a logon script to change that mapping when the cc-mail post office is moved to a different location. Otherwise, you must go to each client on the network to change the drive mappings.

To enable the use of logon scripts you must specify the logon script file name under the user profiles icon when modifying account properties in the User Manager for domains. You must enter the path of the logon script directory under the logon script path variable in the Directory Replication window shown in Figure 25.1. You can access this window through the Server icon in the Control Panel. The default logon script directory is:

C:\WINNT\system32\repl\import\scripts

Figure 25.1

The path name for the logon scripts is specified through the Server settings of the Control Panel.

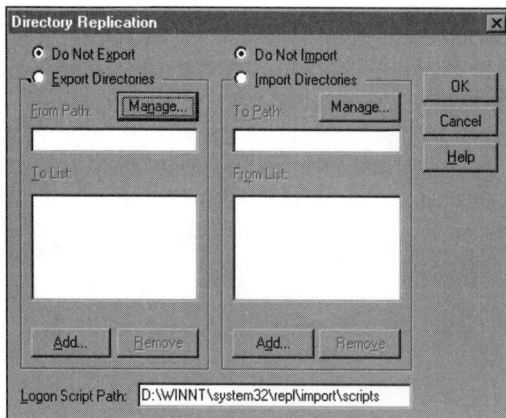

The logon script directory must be replicated to all the domain controllers on the network, both backup and primary. The logon script will not be executed if a user happens to be authenticated on a domain controller that lacks the logon script command files.

Rather than maintaining separate logon script batch files for each user, it's possible to have more than one user account use the same script. For multiple users, simply enter the same location and file name of the logon script under the profile settings in the User Manager.

You can use DOS-like commands for many standard NT networking functions, such as setting mappings to network resources. The NET.EXE program, found on all client PCs running Microsoft's networking client software, is one of the most useful tools. You can view the various NET.EXE functions by checking the built-in help, using the /? Parameter. For example: NET /?

Perhaps the most commonly used function of NET.EXE is to map network drives. An example would be:

NET USE \\ntserver\finance g:

This example would create a network drive g:, which points to user files in a shared volume called finance on the NT Server named ntserver.

You can further customize logon scripts by using parameters to return specific information about network sessions. Table 25.1 lists such parameters:

Table 25.1

Logon script parameters

PARAMETER	DESCRIPTION
%USERDOMAIN%	The domain containing the user's account
%USERNAME%	The user name
%HOMEDRIVE%	The drive letter connected to the home directory from the user's local computer
%HOMEPATH%	The path name of the user's home directory
%HOMESHARE%	The name of a user's home directory share volume
%OS%	A user's operating system type
%PROCESSOR_ARCHITECTURE%	The CPU type of the user's computer

5

Integration with Other Networks

- *Integrating with NetWare Networks*

- *Integrating Windows NT Server into an Existing NT Domain*

26

Cohabitation with Other Networks

IT'S LIKELY THAT AT SOME TIME IN YOUR NETWORK MANAGEMENT career, you'll be asked to configure Windows NT Server to work in a mixed network, an environment where the network infrastructure is pushing packets consisting of more than one or two LAN protocols. Windows NT Server can play well in these environments, and configuration is fairly straightforward at an interoperability level. As yet, Windows NT Server is not a solution to managing a complex mixed environment.

Key to making interoperability work with Windows NT Server is having the appropriate protocol services installed. The NT's TCP/IP and IPX supports are its strengths, and these protocols can be used to communicate with a variety of systems.

Additionally, NT offers a good deal of hardware support. Drivers that aren't included on the installation CD are readily supplied by third-party vendors. This allows Windows NT Server to communicate using a wide array of hardware options, including dial-up lines, Ethernet and wide-area communications adapters.

Sometimes mainframe and minicomputer access can also be provided through host-based gateways that encapsulate other protocols such as Systems Network Architecture (SNA) within TCP/IP or IPX. If your host lacks a TCP/IP or IPX gateway, other products, including the Microsoft SNA Server, can perform gateway functions to upstream hosts using several different types of connection methods. Refer to the third-party solutions page on the Microsoft Web site.

For today's network administrators integrating a new Windows NT 4 Server into an existing office LAN, the integration will likely fit into one of three scenarios:

1. Adding Windows NT Server to a predominantly NetWare environment

2. Adding another NT Server to an existing domain

3. Adding Windows NT Server to an existing TCP/IP network

Helpful Tip

If you're planning a new LAN using Windows NT Server 4, consider your possible future connectivity needs. You may want to set up your system so other LANs are more easily integrated with it. This is especially true in TCP/IP LANs, where the network addressing scheme can be critical.

■ Integrating with NetWare Networks

If you're adding Windows NT Server to an existing LAN, chances are that it's a NetWare LAN. NetWare is still the dominant network operating system, but Windows NT Server can add value to that network through its application serving capabilities.

Windows NT Server 4 has a variety of options that help it play within both NetWare 3.x and NetWare 4.x/NDS environments, though at the time of this writing, there are some limitations. Additionally, a couple of products that are available separately—File and Print Services for NetWare and Directory

Services Manager for NetWare—enable Windows NT Server to more closely embrace NetWare LANs.

Of course, Novell is also participating in NT Server connectivity to NetWare LANs. They've released client utilities for Windows NT Workstation but have yet to support Windows NT Server as an object in NDS.

The following is a list of the Microsoft connectivity components for NetWare LANs, with a short overview of each. A detailed description of the installation and configuration of these components follows in Chapter 27.

NWLink

The NetWare Link IPX/SPX compatible transport is the Microsoft IPX/SPX protocol stack for NetWare networks, and it's included with Windows NT Server 4. Administratively speaking, it's a lot easier to manage a Windows 95 or Windows NT client environment using the Microsoft clients.

Client Service for NetWare

Client Service for NetWare allows Windows NT 4 Workstation clients to connect to and use NetWare File and Print resources. It works with NetWare 2.x and 3.x bindery databases, and the NetWare 4.x Directory Services to enable client logon and printing to NetWare networks. It's the Windows NT Workstation version of Gateway Service for NetWare (GSNW).

Gateway Service for NetWare

At a file server level, GSNW allows a Windows NT server to connect to NetWare servers. It also enables native Microsoft clients to communicate with and access NetWare resources through a Windows NT Server gateway without using Novell client components. This is accomplished by creating Windows NT shares for NetWare volumes.

GSNW is particularly useful for adding NetWare resources to a domain network that's basically Windows NT. When properly installed on the server, a GSNW icon is displayed in the Control Panel. LAN clients see each NetWare disk resource as a Windows NT share. (See Figure 26.1.)

Migration Tool for NetWare

The Migration Tool for NetWare is useful in moving user and group accounts, NetWare volumes, and their contents to a Windows NT server. It's designed to help you physically replace one or more NetWare servers with a single NT server.

Figure 26.1

LAN clients see each
NetWare disk resource as
a Windows NT share
without using NetWare
client components.

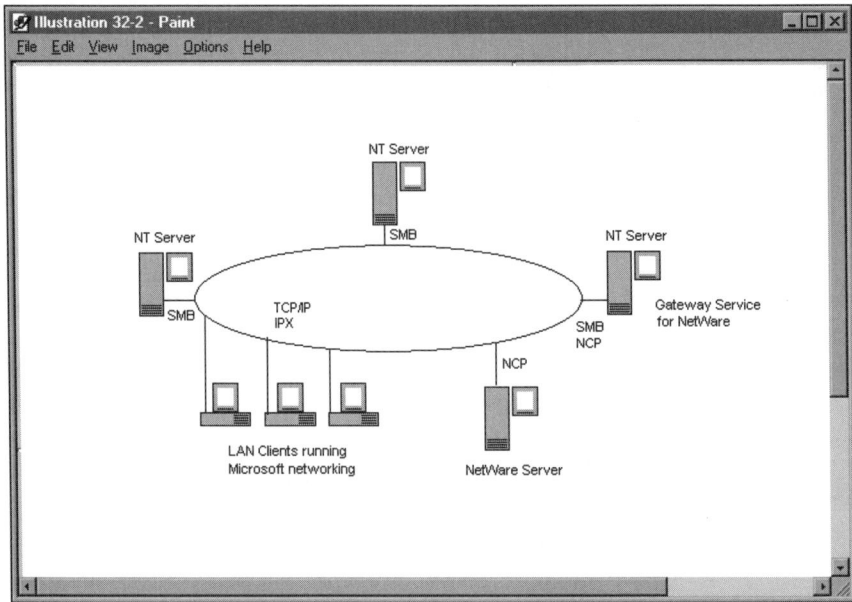

File and Print Services for NetWare

File and Print Services for NetWare (FPNW) makes Windows NT servers
look like NetWare resources to clients running Novell's NETX shell (a DOS-
based shell that coordinates application file requests with network resources)
and virtual loadable module (VLM) networking software. (See Figure 26.2.)
If you want to integrate Windows NT into a predominately NetWare environment, FPNW is critical to your success. With FPNW you can even use the
NetWare utilities such as SYSCON and PCONSOLE to manage users and
output devices running on a Windows NT Server. FPNW is a separately purchased addition to the basic NT Server 4 package.

Directory Service Manager for NetWare

Directory Service Manager for NetWare (DSMN) is a key component to
have if you're planning to add a NetWare 3.x/bindery server to a LAN managed within a Windows NT domain. It allows users to have one logon name
and password for both Windows NT and NetWare networks, which can help
ease general user administration in a mixed NetWare and Windows NT environment. (See Figure 26.3.)

In NetWare 4.x environments, Windows NT Server uses bindery emulation to log on to a NetWare server for collecting statistical data. Both DSMN

Figure 26.2

Running File and Print Services for NetWare (FPNW) on a Windows NT Server enables it to mimic NetWare resources to standard Novell clients.

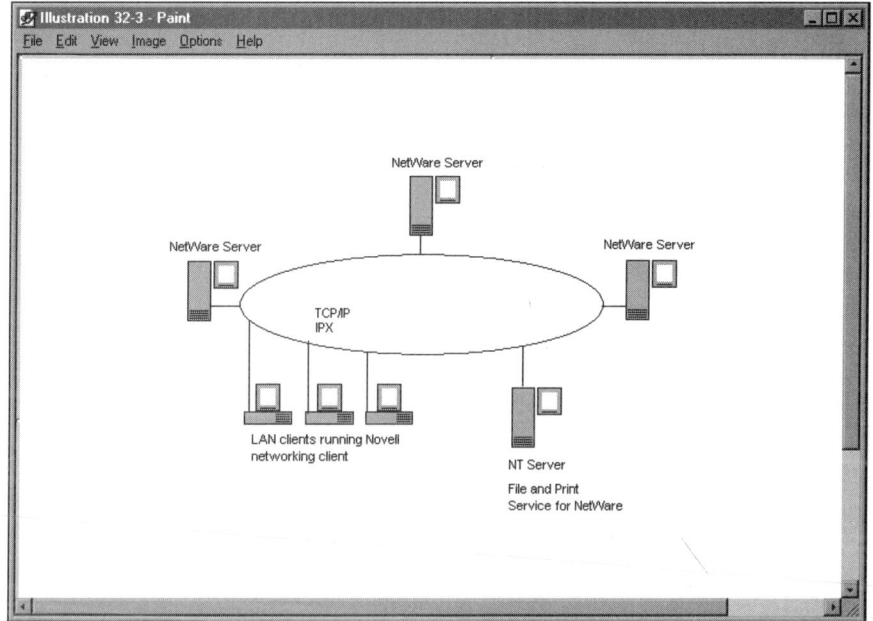

Figure 26.3

Directory Service Manager for NetWare replicates user accounts and access privileges to the NT domain.

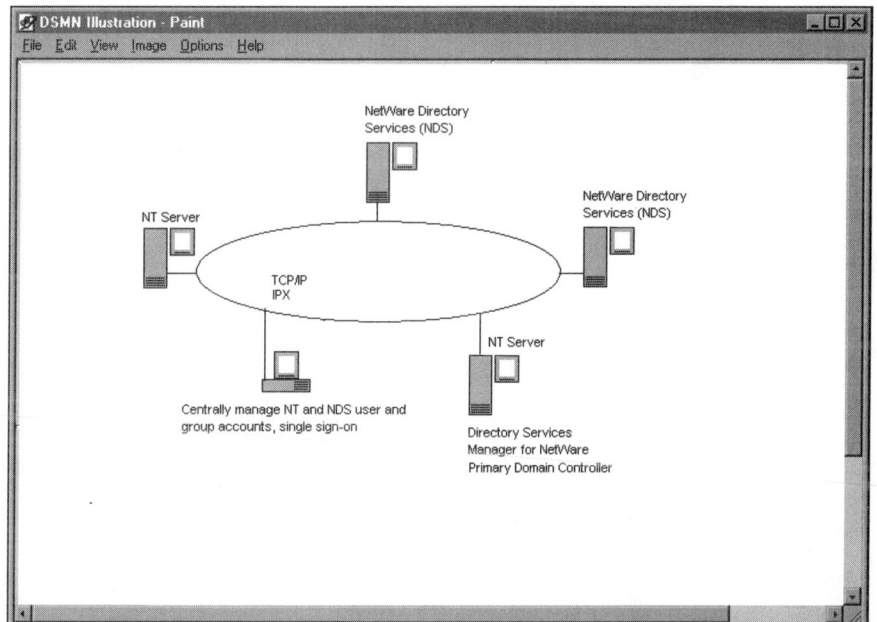

and FPNW are together in a separately purchased package for Windows NT Server 4.

■ Integrating Windows NT Server into an Existing NT Domain

As you would expect, Windows NT Server integrates well into an existing Windows NT domain. The key configuration elements relate to the specific networking issues around the TCP/IP, DHCP, and Name Resolution Services. These configuration elements are covered in Chapter 7: "How to Configure Network Options," and Chapter 36: "Configuring DHCP, DNS and WINS."

For integration into an NT domain as a router, Microsoft includes the Multi-Protocol Router software. This software supports IP, IPX, and Apple-Talk routing using the Windows NT Server operating system components. Routing is a method of connecting separate networks together.

A key element is the Routing Information Protocol (RIP). RIP broadcasts network addresses and forwards IP packets across linked networks. Windows NT supports two RIP implementations, one for IP and another for NWLink IPX/SPX Compatible Transport. These options are installed from the Network Control Panel Services tab.

- *File And Print Services for NetWare*
- *NetWare Directory Services Manager*

27

Configuring Access to NetWare Networks

As we mentioned in the previous chapter, GSNW is best implemented in a Windows NT domain that's accessing Windows NT resources using the Microsoft client set. The management task you least want to perform is to hand-configure each LAN client: adding new protocol support or a special network client. You want access to NetWare-based resources without having to touch the client. That's where GNSW comes in.

Installing GSNW requires the Windows NT Server CD, so have it handy. As with almost all changes to parameters in the Network Control Panel, you'll need to reboot for the addition of GSNW to take effect. To create gateway accounts, you'll also need supervisor or administrative access to each NetWare server.

If this is a NetWare 4.x server, the administrative client must use Novell's network client software, VLM or Client32. Microsoft clients cannot run the Novell Director Service (NDS) management utilities NETADMIN or NWADMIN.

The gateway service must log on to the NetWare environment through either a bindery account or an NDS account.

Often, NetWare LANs can be a mixture of NetWare operating system versions, like 3.12 and 4.1. When integrating Windows NT Server into these types of LANs, it's important to stick with a user and network management decision; don't attempt to straddle the fence as to which scheme you're committed to.

Of course, this will change with future product releases that better integrate NetWare into a Windows NT domain or Windows NT into NDS. Both Microsoft and Novell are making headway in improving the interoperability between these very different LAN operating systems.

Make sure the following conditions exist prior to installing GSNW:

- At least one NetWare file server should be connected to the same LAN segment as the Windows NT server you'll be loading GSNW on.

- The NetWare server should be fully operational, meaning you can log on to it from the administrative client.

- The same protocol must be loaded and running on both Windows NT and NetWare. This can be either IPX or TCP/IP.

- You must be logged on to the Windows NT server with administrative privileges.

Depending on how many NetWare file servers you have and the number of users accessing this service, overall performance of the Windows NT server can be significantly affected by the GSNW load.

Installing GNSW

Open the Control Panel and select the Network icon. When the Network dialog box appears, click on the Services tab, as shown in Figure 27.1. Click Add to add a new service. The Select Network Service dialog box appears, Figure 27.2. Select Gateway (and Client) Services for NetWare from the list of network services. Click OK to install the GSNW service.

Figure 27.1

Gateway Services for
NetWare can be added
from the Network
dialog box.

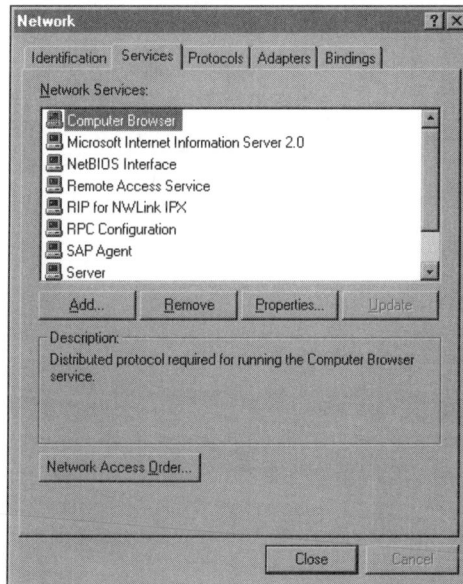

Figure 27.2

This utility adds both
server and client access
into NetWare-based
resources.

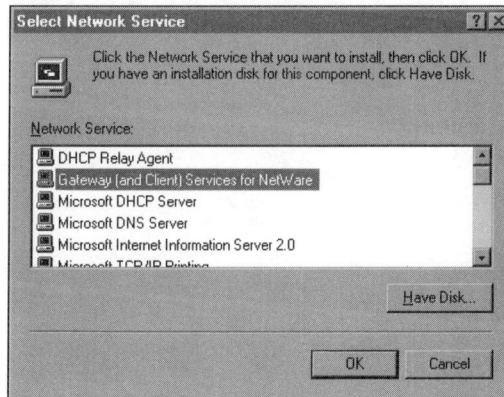

When the installation is complete, the Gateway Service for NetWare will
be displayed among the other services, as shown in Figure 27.3. Click Close
and reboot the Windows NT server.

In the Control Panel (shown in Figure 27.4) you'll notice the addition of
the GSNW icon. Unlike other network components that are managed from
the Control Panel using the Network Properties tab, GNSW has its own icon
for access to the configuration options.

Figure 27.3

Removal of Gateway Services for NetWare is also accomplished using the Network Control Panel.

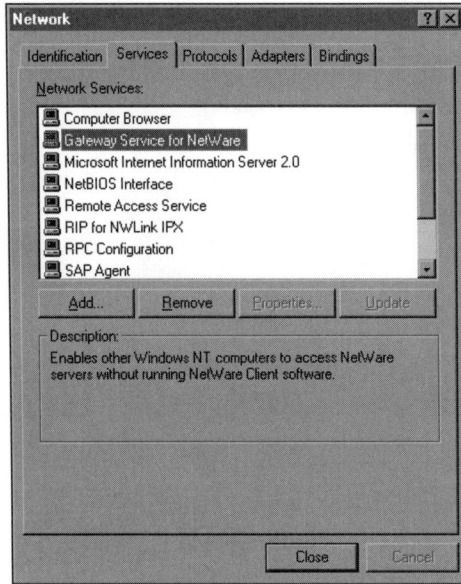

Figure 27.4

After installation, the GSNW icon is used to define and maintain gateway links to NetWare servers.

Select the GNSW icon in the Control Panel to configure the Gateway Service. The Gateway Service for NetWare window shown in Figure 27.5 will be displayed. Depending on the type of NetWare environment you've added connectivity to, after reboot the Gateway Service for NetWare dialog box will appear. You must select either Preferred Server (known as a bindery server) for NetWare environments preceding NetWare 4.x. or Default Tree and Context, if you're connected to a NetWare 4.x/NDS environment. For a mixed NetWare 3.x and 4.x environment, select Tree and Context and use the NDS Tree. It has the capability of allowing gateway connectivity to both types of NetWare servers.

Figure 27.5

Gateway links to NetWare
2.x and 3.x servers as
well as NDS-based
NetWare servers can
be defined.

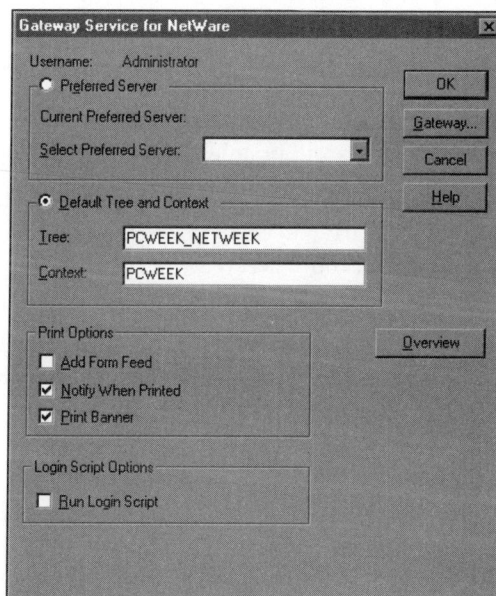

Configuring GNSW

In order to create a gateway to a NetWare server, each server will need a special user account and group membership. Windows NT Server uses this membership to gain access to the NetWare servers it will be communicating with. As the administrator, you define which NetWare resources the Windows NT server will "see." Be careful if you've implemented password expiration policies on your NetWare servers. If a password or user account expires, users will lose access to the shared resources that are NetWare-based.

Before creating the gateway, you must define a dedicated user account and a group account on each NetWare server with the storage resources you want to provide shared access to. This is done using the Novell-supplied administrative utilities, NETADMIN (DOS version) or NWADMIN (Windows version). Strangely enough, you must do this on a DOS or Windows client that's running Novell's networking client software only.

Using one of the two Novell-supplied utilities, do the following to each bindery-based or NDS-based NetWare server you want shared access to:

1. Create the group account called NTGATEWAY.

2. Give the group access rights to the NetWare resources you want available. For example, make sure the group has at least Read and Create rights to volume data.

3. Create a user account. It will be the account the Windows NT server will use to attach to the NetWare file server.

4. Add the user account to the group members list. Access rights to the NetWare resources will be inherited among group users.

5. When finished, you'll be returned to the Windows NT server, in the Gateway Service for NetWare dialog box. You're now ready to create a gateway to one or more NetWare servers.

NOTE. *For NDS-based environments, an NDS volume object must be defined with proper access rights prior to creating a Windows NT share. Create volume objects in NDS for NetWare bindery-based server resources also.*

To add a new gateway to a NetWare resource:

1. Click Gateway... to display the Configure Gateway dialog box of Figure 27.6.

2. Make sure Enable Gateway is checked.

3. In Gateway Account, enter a user name that you defined on the NetWare file server. This can be any user name you want but needs to be identical on all NetWare servers. To confound potential hackers, use a name other than NTGATEWY.

4. Enter the password for the user account. Each character you type will be represented in asterisks (*).

5. Click Add. The New Share window shown in Figure 27.7 will be displayed.

In Share Name, enter a unique share name for the NetWare resource. Our recommended prefix is NW_. In Network Path, specify the server name and volume name of the resource using the \\servername\volume_name:pathname format. In Comment, you can optionally enter descriptive information about the shared resource. In Use Drive, select the drive letter you want

Figure 27.6

Configuring Gateway
Services for NetWare is
an easily accomplished
process.

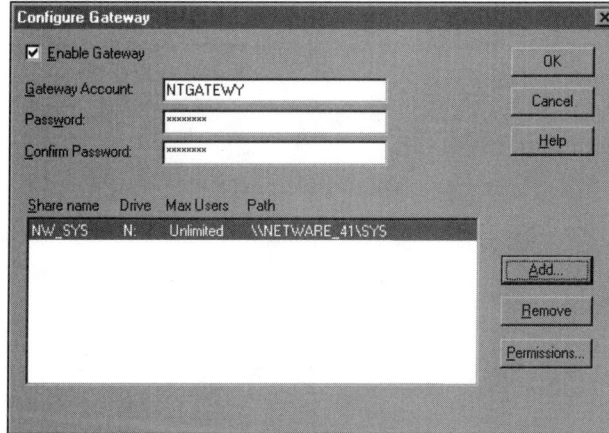

Figure 27.7

Creating an NT share
name for data that
resides on a NetWare
volume is a straight-
forward process.

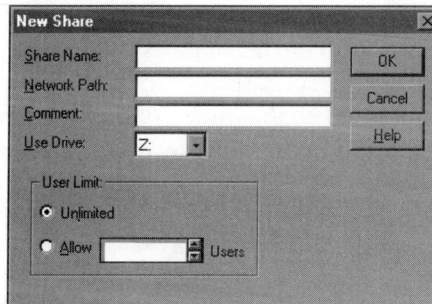

your Windows NT Server to use in accessing the NetWare resource. There
are a limited number of these. If there are user limit considerations, you can
specify it under User Limit. The default is unlimited—which is really the best
choice.

The following conditions must exist to successfully create a gateway
share to a NetWare resource:

- The NTGATEWY user must exist.

- Both the user currently logged on and the gateway must have access to
  each NetWare resource.

- The NTGATEWAY group must exist on the NetWare server you're
  trying to share.

- The current user must have Create rights on the Windows NT server.

When you're finished, the share should look like the one shown in Figure 27.8. Click OK.

Figure 27.8

Preceding the Share Name with NW_ clearly labels the resource as a NetWare device.

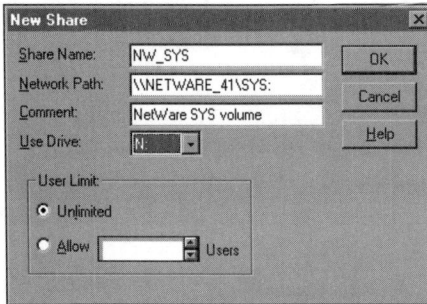

After the gateway and share are created, you'll be returned to the Configure Gateway window. If you want to limit the users who have access to this newly shared resource, you can do so by selecting Permissions. This will bring up the Access Through Share Permissions dialog box, Figure 27.9. It allows you to select from the list of users and groups in the Windows NT domain. When you've selected them, click OK to complete the gateway definitions. At this point, the configuration of the gateway is complete and your Microsoft networking clients need only establish a network connection to the shared resource.

Figure 27.9

The Access Through Share Permissions dialog box.

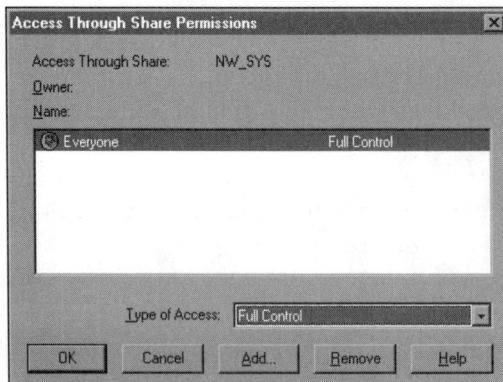

Gateway shares can be restricted to individual users and groups, but in our example here, all users have access.

■ File And Print Services for NetWare

The File and Print Services for NetWare has an extra fee attached to it, but it can save you from having to touch each LAN workstation to add support for the new Windows NT server. It's your best choice for quietly integrating Windows NT Server into your NetWare environment because it makes Windows NT act like a chameleon in NetWare networks; it emulates a NetWare file and print device. This is especially true if your clients are running Novell networking software, such as VLM or Client32. To each and every client running Novell networking software, the Windows NT server looks like a NetWare server. Even many of the standard NetWare utilities such as SYSCON and PCONSOLE work in this environment.

These capabilities can also ease your migration to an all-Windows NT configuration. This option is outlined in Chapter 28, "Moving from NetWare to Windows NT Server."

■ NetWare Directory Services Manager

If you're tired of NDS and really want to move all your NetWare user and server management functions to the Windows NT Server Domain Manager, NetWare Directory Services Manager (NDSM) is likely for you.

The service allows you to centrally manage both Windows NT and NetWare file servers from within a Windows NT domain. There's a single point of logon through one application for both the network client and administration.

At this time, there's one limitation. NDS management utilities can only be run by non-Microsoft network clients. In other words, you'll have to keep a Novell networking client around for running the NDS management utilities.

- *Easing Migration with Gateway Services for NetWare and File and Print Services for NetWare*

- *Running the NetWare Migration Utility*

28

Moving from NetWare to Windows NT Server

WITH THE POPULARITY OF WINDOWS NT SERVER IN APPLICATION serving today, there's little doubt you'll be considering moving some or all of your NetWare services to the Windows NT Server platform. To help you transfer users, their files and access privileges, Microsoft provides the Migration Tool for NetWare.

The Migration Tool for NetWare is a utility application included with Windows NT Server that allows you to move NetWare-based users and groups, applications, and files, to an NT Server, where they can all be contained within an NT domain.

The Migration tool for NetWare isn't an all-or-nothing proposition. You can use it to move users and home directories gradually, even one-by-one, if necessary. You can also move multiple NetWare servers to a single NT server, consolidating users. Prior to actual use, you can test-drive migration specifications. You can view the Results log files to see exactly what should have been transferred.

There are a number of differences between the NetWare bindery and an NT domain. The NetWare bindery is server-centric; users that access resources must have an account on the particular server where those resources are located. If you want to run applications from a number of NetWare 2.x or 3.x servers, you need a user account and access privileges on each one. Additionally, if you maintain a secure environment, with non-repeatable passwords and expiration dates, keeping things synchronized for each user leads to a network administrator's nightmare.

In contrast, the NT domain is designed as a single sign-on solution to the problems associated with bindery-based authentication services. The solution uses one database, the NT domain, for maintaining such items as user access rights and passwords. This approach makes user and resource management in small and medium-sized environments less of a headache and more of a simple administrative task.

If you have a Novell Directory Service (NDS) environment, consider your migration to NT carefully. As a directory service, NT's domain is not hierarchical but instead implements a flat file view of network users and resources.

In small environments, the difference in administrative overhead between managing NT servers versus NetWare servers is minimal. In medium-sized environments with multiple domains, an NDS management scheme offers better directory growth potential. In large, enterprise-level environments, NDS is significantly stronger than NT. This is not to say the situation won't change, so closely evaluate your network's future growth potential.

There are a number of advantages to moving from a mixed NetWare and NT environment to one managed solely by Windows NT. The key benefits to network administrators are a single point of administration, a common user interface with LAN clients, and greater application compatibility.

■ Easing Migration with Gateway Services for NetWare and File and Print Services for NetWare

As we mentioned, you can wean users off NetWare gradually. This may be very useful, especially if you're planning to touch each LAN client but lack the necessary human resources to do so all at once.

There are a couple of ways to gradually migrate users from NetWare to Windows NT Server. If your users are currently running the Microsoft networking client, you can use Gateway Services for NetWare (GSNW) to redirect NetWare search drives to Windows NT shares.

For example, if drive F: points to a user's home directory on a NetWare file server, you can use GSNW to give the user access to the same resource using the Windows NT Server share. Later, you can run the Migration Tool for NetWare to transfer the user bindery information and home directory files to the Windows NT Server. This slow migration process is a balanced method of switching from NT to NetWare.

If your networking clients are currently using either the virtual loadable module (VLM) or earlier NETX variations of Novell's networking client driver set to access a NetWare file server, consider using File and Print Service for NetWare to ease the migration. Because it fakes a Novell client into thinking the Window NT Server is a NetWare server, your users may never be the wiser as to which one they're connecting to. Later, you can remove the Novell client easily at your own pace.

What Is NETX?

NETX is an early version of a Novell networking client driver set. It's actually the executable filename for the main component in the client driver set, NETX.EXE.

The earliest versions of NETX are DOS version-specific, and the X is replaced by the compatible DOS version number. For example, NET3.EXE was specifically for DOS 3.x versions. The final version of this technology was manifested in NETX.EXE, version-compatible with all previous DOS releases.

If you have LAN clients that are using NETX to access NetWare based resources, you may have an application dependency on the use of this technology. Consult with your application vendor for client driver dependency issues.

Windows NT Server automatically installs the Migration Tool for Net-Ware under the Administrative Tools menu, as shown in Figure 28.1.

Figure 28.1

Most management functions are performed using utilities located under the Administrative Tools menu bar.

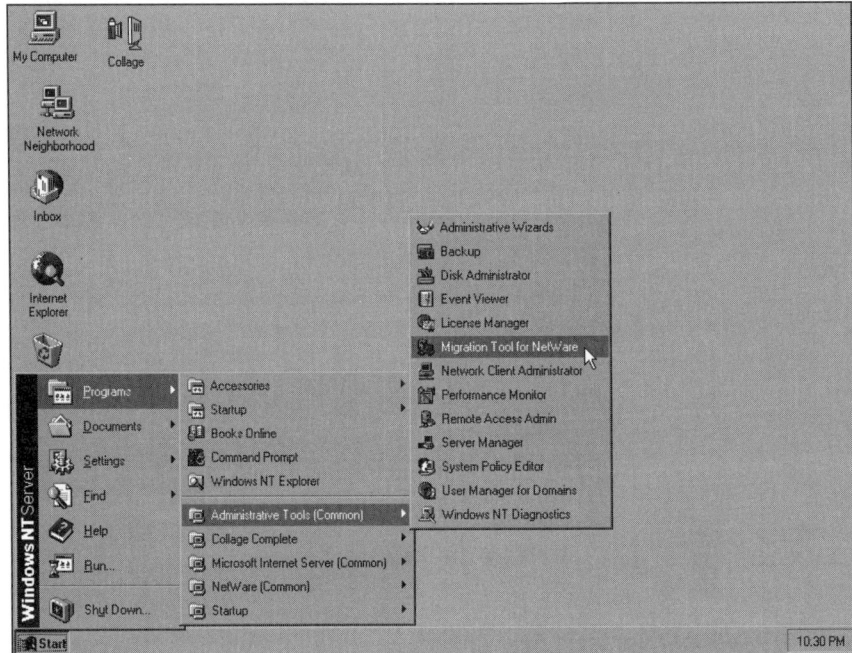

During migration, the following NetWare items are copied to the destination NT server:

- User accounts

- Group accounts

- Security information logon scripts

- Administrator accounts

- Files

- Directories

- File attributes

- File rights

A few key values aren't transferred during migration. They are: Passwords, Limit Concurrent Connections, Grace Logons, and Station Restrictions.

With the exception of the password, the other NetWare values lack a Windows NT-native equivalent. If the destination Windows NT Server is running File and Print Service for NetWare (FPNW), special allowances are made for handling the Limit Concurrent Connections, Grace Logons and Station Restriction parameters. If File and Print Service for NetWare is not running, these parameters are not transferred.

■ Running the NetWare Migration Utility

Running the Migration Tool for NetWare requires that the IPX-compatible transport protocol, NWLink IPX/SPX, as well as Gateway Services for NetWare, be installed and operational on the Windows NT Server you'll be moving to. For information on setting up these services, refer to Chapters 7 and 26, respectively.

From the Windows NT Server console, start the Migration Tool for NetWare by clicking on the menu options shown in Figure 28.1. Then simply follow the following steps.

Select the first NetWare server you want to migrate from. If the server is a NetWare 4.x server, the server's NDS tree will be displayed along with its name, as shown in Figure 28.2.

Figure 28.2

The Migration Tool for NetWare is used to transfer directories and user access information to the Windows NT domain.

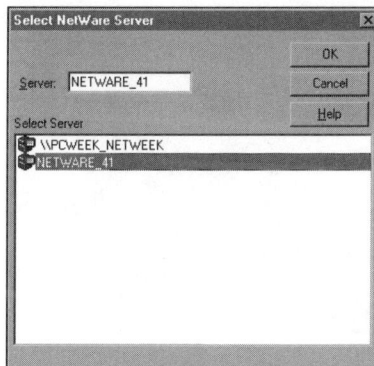

Select the destination Windows NT domain and server for the migration process, as shown in Figure 28.3.

To complete the initial migration specification, click OK in the Select Servers for Migration dialog box shown in Figure 28.4.

When you click OK, the main Migration Tool for NetWare dialog box will come up, displaying the From: and To: servers you've selected. (See Figure 28.5.)

Figure 28.3

Users from multiple NetWare servers can be combined into one Windows NT domain.

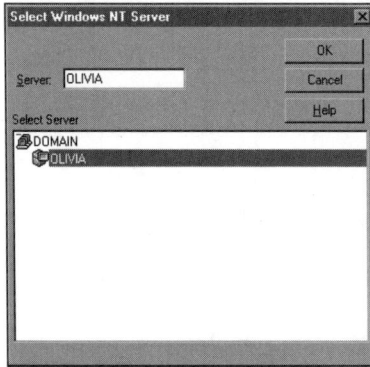

Figure 28.4

Make sure you have administrative or supervisor level access to each NetWare server to be migrated.

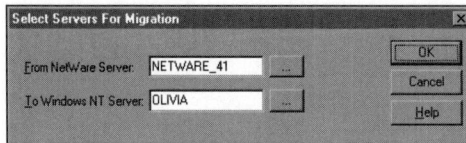

Figure 28.5

The main dialog box in the Migration Tool for NetWare displays each NetWare server with the NT server destination.

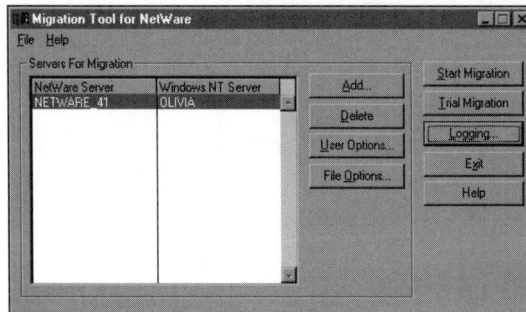

At this point, you can click on Add to add additional From: NetWare servers to the migration specification. The Migration Tool for NetWare only supports one destination server. Now, click on User Options to display the User and Groups Options dialog box shown in Figure 28.6.

Figure 28.6

There are a number of ways to deal with users, passwords, and groups that reside on NetWare servers.

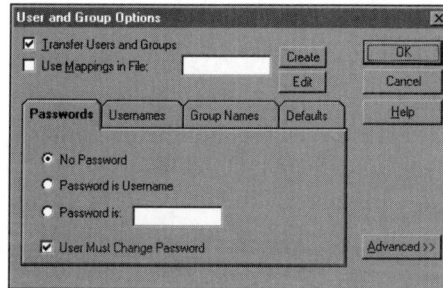

The User and Group Options dialog box contains tabs for controlling how the Migration Tool handles passwords, user names, and group names. Here, you can transfer users and groups or use a user and group mapping file. If you can't generalize your migration plans across a server using the Transfer Users and Group option, you'll need to check Use Mappings in File:, which gives you a scripting-type alternative with which you can perform a more detailed migration.

If you choose to use a mapping file, create the default file by clicking on Create. Then, using a text editor such as NotePad, edit this default file, making necessary changes. Using the Migration Tool in this manner creates a file with the appropriate headings and migration details already included, making further migration definitions just a matter of deleting unwanted information transfers.

Using the broader approach will generally satisfy most migration needs, but in managing this approach, you'll need to consider several elements. One of them is Passwords. If your environment is an open network, you can select No Password. With this selection, however, users transferred from the NetWare server will not have a password. The second selection creates a new password consisting of the user name. The final password option creates an identical password for all users. If you are using the Mapping File alternative, you could change this value for each user and gain a higher level of security immediately following the migration. In all cases, you can check User Must Change Password to force users to change their passwords upon initial logon to the new server.

The Usernames tab, shown in Figure 28.7, is basically for handling duplicate user names. These are users who already exist in the NT domain to which you're migrating. This tab is especially useful if you have already migrated some users to the NT domain.

Figure 28.7

The Usernames tab allows handling of duplicate user names.

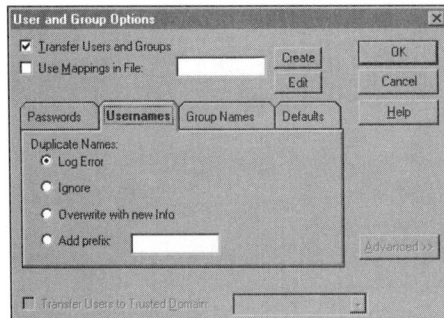

Selecting the Log Error option will not transfer the user, noting the action in the resulting log file. Ignoring duplicate user names will create duplicate users in your NT domain. Correcting this situation could become an administrative hassle. A better choice, Overwrite with new Info, can be used to commit users you had previously tested with. The key in using this option is that it only overwrites new information.

If you're unaware of the current state of users on the NetWare server versus the NT domain, you can add a prefix to each migrated user name. This option, though administratively intensive, almost forces you to manually verify each user account and file access rights.

The Group Names tab, shown in Figure 28.8, works much like the Usernames option, but you won't be able to overwrite existing groups in the NT domain. Use the Add prefix option if you're unsure of the common group names between the NetWare server(s) and the Windows NT domain.

The Defaults tab, Figure 28.9, allows you to automatically create the supervisor account in the Windows NT domain in the Windows NT administrators group.

When you've defined your migration options, click on OK. This will display a File Options dialog box, Figure 28.10, that you can use to specify which files and directories to migrate from the NetWare server(s) and how you want Windows NT Server to treat the migrated directories.

For each destination, the Migration Tool carefully tracks the NetWare source volume and allows you to create a Windows NT share on-the-fly during the migration process. Click on Modify... to bring up the Modify Destination

Figure 28.8

Duplicate groups names can be a headache without proper migration planning. Logging avoids confusion.

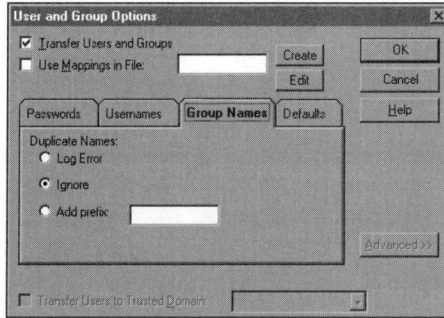

Figure 28.9

The Migration Tool for NetWare can automate the process of using "supervisor" as an administrative account name.

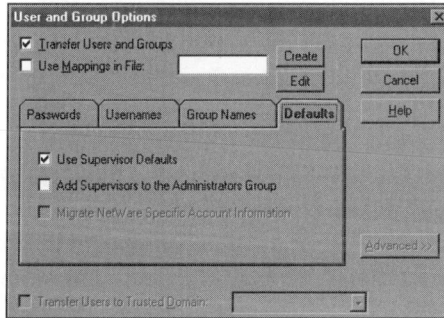

Figure 28.10

Specifying which directories to migrate and how Windows NT Server should treat them is handled through File Options.

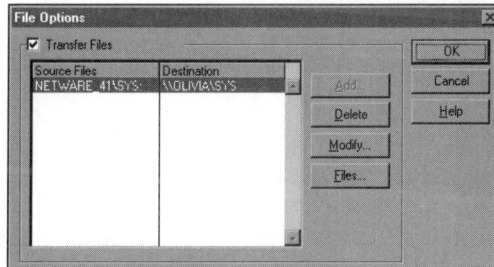

dialog box shown in Figure 28.11. Here, you can specify the new Windows NT share name where the data files will reside and the properties associated with each new share. When you've completed defining the source files and their destination, click on OK to return to the File Options dialog box, then click on OK to display the main Migration Tool dialog box. (See Figure 28.5.)

Figure 28.11

In the Modify Destination dialog box, new Windows NT share names and properties are specified.

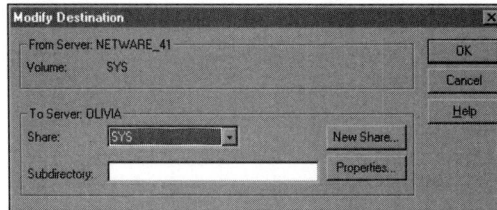

At this point, we strongly recommend that you test the logic of the source and destination parameters you've set up. Click on Trial Migration to start this process.

If you haven't set the migration logging parameters, the Logging dialog box (Figure 28.12) will be displayed, allowing you to do so. If you select the Popup on errors option, you can force the migration process to stop when a transfer error occurs. This can quickly highlight problems so that you can rectify them before running through the entire migration process.

Figure 28.12

Errors can be set to stop the migration process, allowing problems to be rectified at the earliest possible moment.

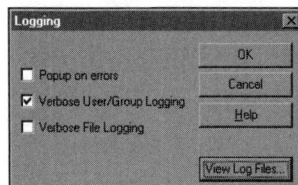

You can select the second option, Verbose File Logging, if you want a detailed listing of each file transferred during migration. Otherwise, only directories will be listed in the log file.

The entire migration process is logged into files with the .LOG extension. If you click on View Log Files... you can see the contents of the three logs that record the migration. The Summary Log File, pictured in Figure 28.13, provides a good overview of the file servers involved in the migration and the numbers of users, groups, and files transferred.

Figure 28.13

The Summary Log File
provides an overview of
the file servers involved
in a migration.

```
+------------------------------------------------------------------+
;| Migration Tool for NetWare Summary Log File                     |
;+------------------------------------------------------------------+
;| Created: Friday, 08/23/1996 (22:38:14)                          |
;| System : OLIVIA                                                 |
;| Admin  : Administrator                                          |
;| Version: 1.1                                                    |
;+------------------------------------------------------------------+

Number of Migrations = 1

[Servers]
From: NETWARE_41       To: OLIVIA


[NETWARE_41 -> OLIVIA]
Total Users Converted: 2
Total Groups Converted: 2

Copying Files From Volume: SYS
To Share: SYS
Total Files Converted: 2,605
Bytes Transferred: 149,011,217


Conversion Finished: Friday, 08/23/1996 (22:44:35)
```

The detailed Log File (Figure 28.14) contains verbose descriptions of users, groups, and resources that were transferred. User account information is clearly recorded showing the original account parameters and the new account parameters (Figure 28.15). If errors were encountered during the migration or test migration, they're captured in the Error Log File (Figure 28.16). Errors due to limited disk space would appear in this log.

Once you're sure that your trial migration has worked smoothly, you can start a full migration. Depending on the sophistication of your environment—the number of users, groups, directories and files, plus the physical disk space involved—the migration could take more than an hour. During the actual migration process, the status window shown in Figure 28.17 will give a good indication of what processes are currently running.

Upon completion, the log files are displayed for your review. As a network administrator, you may want to save off or print these log files for future reference. They can also be useful in building a mapping file for additional migrations.

Caution

As with any major change to your network landscape, make sure you get a good, accurate backup of all devices involved in the change prior to making the change. You never know if you'll decide the previous situation was better than what you have now.

Figure 28.14

The detailed Log File contains descriptions of users, groups, and resources that were transferred.

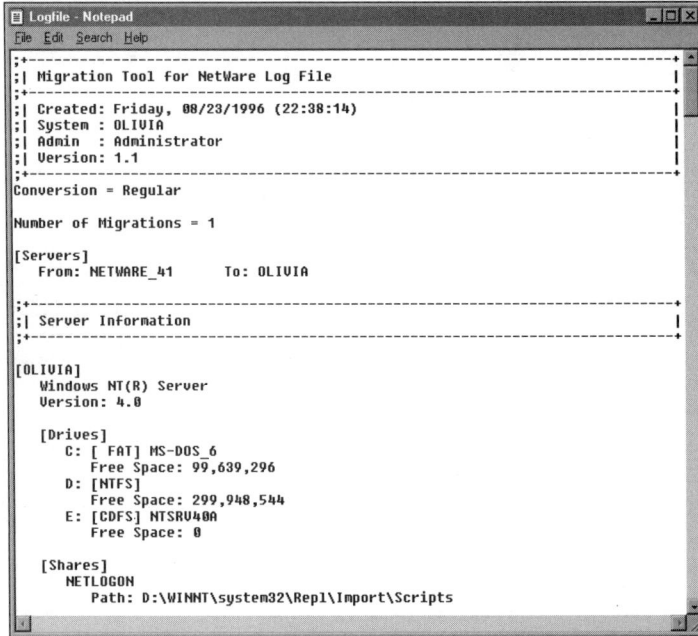

```
Logfile - Notepad
File  Edit  Search  Help
;+-----------------------------------------------------------------------+
;| Migration Tool for NetWare Log File                                   |
;+-----------------------------------------------------------------------+
;| Created: Friday, 08/23/1996 (22:38:14)                                |
;| System : OLIVIA                                                       |
;| Admin  : Administrator                                                |
;| Version: 1.1                                                          |
;+-----------------------------------------------------------------------+
Conversion = Regular

Number of Migrations = 1

[Servers]
   From: NETWARE_41        To: OLIVIA

;+-----------------------------------------------------------------------+
;| Server Information                                                    |
;+-----------------------------------------------------------------------+

[OLIVIA]
   Windows NT(R) Server
   Version: 4.0

   [Drives]
      C: [ FAT] MS-DOS_6
         Free Space: 99,639,296
      D: [NTFS]
         Free Space: 299,948,544
      E: [CDFS] NTSRV40A
         Free Space: 0

   [Shares]
      NETLOGON
         Path: D:\WINNT\system32\Repl\Import\Scripts
```

Figure 28.15

The Error Log File captures errors that occurred during migration.

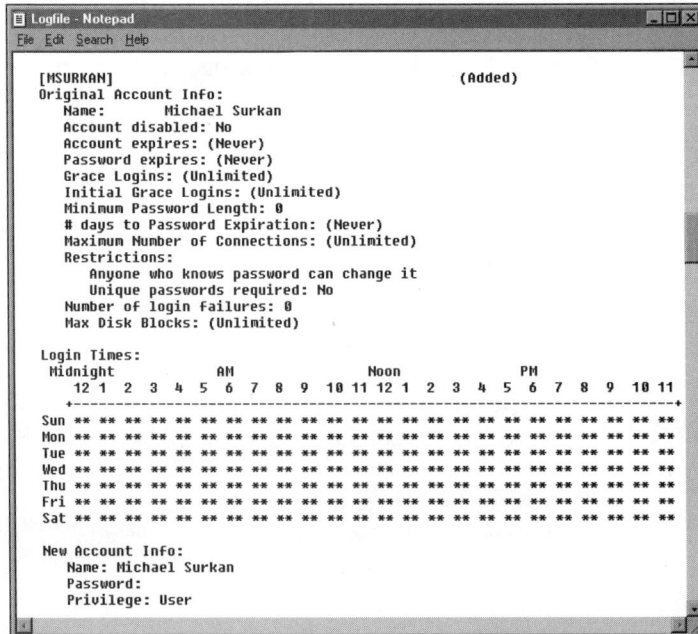

```
Logfile - Notepad
File  Edit  Search  Help

   [MSURKAN]                                        (Added)
   Original Account Info:
      Name:       Michael Surkan
      Account disabled: No
      Account expires: (Never)
      Password expires: (Never)
      Grace Logins: (Unlimited)
      Initial Grace Logins: (Unlimited)
      Minimum Password Length: 0
      # days to Password Expiration: (Never)
      Maximum Number of Connections: (Unlimited)
      Restrictions:
         Anyone who knows password can change it
         Unique passwords required: No
      Number of login failures: 0
      Max Disk Blocks: (Unlimited)

   Login Times:
   Midnight              AM                Noon              PM
      12 1  2  3  4  5  6  7  8  9  10 11 12 1  2  3  4  5  6  7  8  9  10 11
      +-------------------------------------------------------------------+
   Sun ** ** ** ** ** ** ** ** ** ** ** ** ** ** ** ** ** ** ** ** ** ** ** **
   Mon ** ** ** ** ** ** ** ** ** ** ** ** ** ** ** ** ** ** ** ** ** ** ** **
   Tue ** ** ** ** ** ** ** ** ** ** ** ** ** ** ** ** ** ** ** ** ** ** ** **
   Wed ** ** ** ** ** ** ** ** ** ** ** ** ** ** ** ** ** ** ** ** ** ** ** **
   Thu ** ** ** ** ** ** ** ** ** ** ** ** ** ** ** ** ** ** ** ** ** ** ** **
   Fri ** ** ** ** ** ** ** ** ** ** ** ** ** ** ** ** ** ** ** ** ** ** ** **
   Sat ** ** ** ** ** ** ** ** ** ** ** ** ** ** ** ** ** ** ** ** ** ** ** **

   New Account Info:
      Name: Michael Surkan
      Password:
      Privilege: User
```

Figure 28.16

Both original and new account parameters are shown.

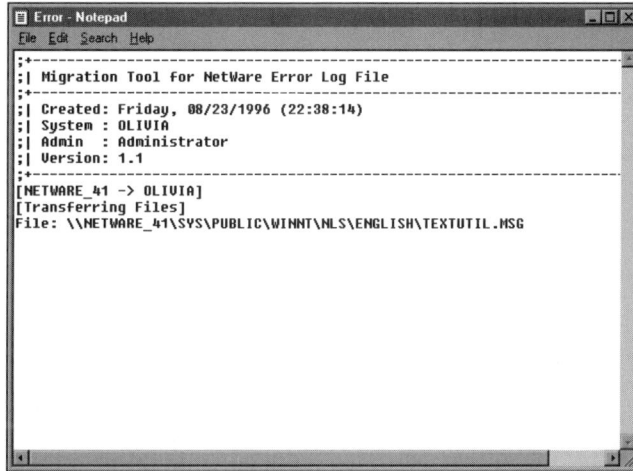

```
;+-------------------------------------------------------------------
;| Migration Tool for NetWare Error Log File
;+-------------------------------------------------------------------
;| Created: Friday, 08/23/1996 (22:38:14)
;| System : OLIVIA
;| Admin  : Administrator
;| Version: 1.1
;+-------------------------------------------------------------------
[NETWARE_41 -> OLIVIA]
[Transferring Files]
File: \\NETWARE_41\SYS\PUBLIC\WINNT\NLS\ENGLISH\TEXTUTIL.MSG
```

Figure 28.17

During the migration, the Converting... window gives a progress report and information on the processes currently running.

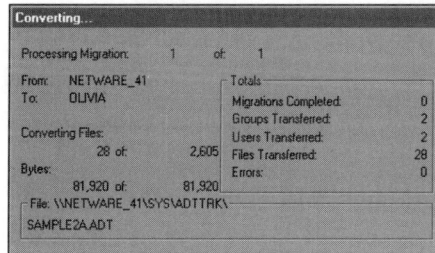

Converting...

Processing Migration: 1   of   1

From: NETWARE_41
To: OLIVIA

Converting Files:
          28 of   2,605

Bytes:
     81,920 of   81,920

Totals
Migrations Completed: 0
Groups Transferred: 2
Users Transferred: 2
Files Transferred: 28
Errors: 0

File: \\NETWARE_41\SYS\ADTTRK\
SAMPLE2A.ADT

6

Remote Computing

29

Remote Access Services

IN THIS CHAPTER, WE'LL EXPLAIN THE REMOTE CAPABILITIES OF Windows NT Server 4 and what decisions are important before plowing ahead. In Chapter 30, we'll take a close look at how to install and configure a RAS communications environment using a non-dedicated Windows NT Server and a multiport adapter. Finally, in Chapter 31, we'll discuss managing and troubleshooting your Windows NT Server RAS.

For inbound and outbound communications, the Windows NT Server 4 includes RAS, which can be installed from the CD-ROM. RAS provides most of the basic dial-in/dial-out functionality you'll need to support mobile users, telecommuters, off-site workers and information systems management staff. It's very flexible, as you can see from Figure 29.1.

Figure 29.1

RAS supports a variety of inbound connection types.

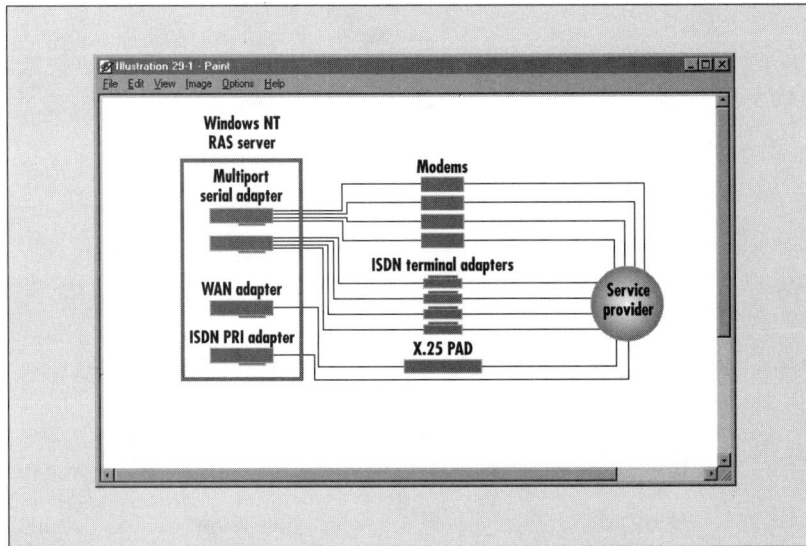

RAS shouldn't be confused with Dial-Up Networking, even though a Windows NT Server 4 will have both applications. RAS is for modem sharing, in which multiple users are accessing several communications ports, both inbound and outbound. Dial-Up Networking is intended as a personal use application for outbound connectivity or a backup access method for remote server management. Modem profiles are shared between both RAS and Dial-Up Networking.

Because RAS is a service of Windows NT Server 4, it can share resources with others of the Server's services, such as file and print service. In general, and under normal conditions, there's little effect on overall server performance when RAS is dealing with multiple remote sessions. This is because the speed at which remote communications occur is far slower than the relative speed of the other components in the complete system.

Depending on the hardware configuration you choose, Windows NT can work with a variety of analog, ISDN, and WAN communications methods. At a minimum, it can support one modem connected to the server's standard serial port. It can also scale up to 256 analog communications ports using specialized multiport serial adapters you'll have to consider if you want to exceed two ports.

For ISDN connection types, both basic rate and primary rate interfaces can be used for increased connection bandwidth.

New in Windows NT Server 4 is support for Multilink Point-to-Point Protocol(PPP) connections. This enables a single remote session to have the increased bandwidth of dual communications links, synchronized by the Multilink protocol standard.

Originally intended for use with ISDN communications, Microsoft has implemented this feature so it can also be used with X.25 packet switching network and analog communications hardware. On the client side, RAS supports DOS plus the Windows siblings, Windows for Workgroups 3.11, Windows 95, and Windows NT Workstation, plus any other PPP-type client. Missing from this list is the AppleTalk Remote Access Protocol (ARAP), long a remote access standard in Apple environments. Many competitive remote access products support this access method natively. But the Microsoft NT Server doesn't support ARAP, so remote access by Macintosh systems has been left up to non-AppleTalk access methods that use the native protocol implementations. These are MacTCP (included with the System 7.5 O/S) and MacIPX (available from Novell, Inc.).

For outbound modem-pooling functions, Windows NT Server has a number of configuration settings, but it stops just short of providing a complete solution that's integrated with RAS. For the final piece of the puzzle, you'll have to look to third-party add-on software to extend the communications capabilities of RAS and gain modem-pooling functions.

■ Decisions, Decisions

Certainly it's important to first get a handle on the number of users that will be accessing the system overall. Then start separating them into groups based on their anticipated use patterns.

Another key aspect of creating a successful and manageable remote access solution involves quantifying the expected use patterns of your road warriors. Each of their situations is different, and in small configurations, the decisions you make today are unlikely to have major ramifications down the road. In large installations, where ports are counted by the dozen and users communicate with your network from a variety of access points and client types, remote access should be carefully planned.

However, no matter what type of installation you're planning, insist on having a small number of users as your remote access guinea pigs. Just because you made a connection in your lab doesn't mean your average user will have the same pleasant experience. Make sure the test group is a good cross-section of your entire user community. Keep these users happy and they'll spread their confidence in your solution to others. They'll be an asset.

When you're ready for general deployment, do it slowly. Let the demands on your system of active remote access increase gradually. Many a remote access project has been crippled at the outset by adding too many users at once.

Before building your remote access solution, you will need to know the following:

1. Do I want dial-in, dial-out, or a combination?

2. What types of remote clients will be accessing the system?

3. What is the highest common denominator of the communications device that will be used for inbound access to the system?

4. How many users will be accessing the system at a single time?

5. How long will the average connection period last for each remote user?

6. What applications will the users be running when they are connected remotely? Are these applications normally run from the network or locally?

After you've determined your need, what can you do to make the process of installation easy? Here are a few tips that will make it as painless as possible:

1. If at all possible, limit the variety of clients and peripherals in your remote access landscape.

2. Keep connection logs for troubleshooting, capacity planning, and security reviews.

3. Implement the security options; don't leave a security hole for the malicious hacker.

4. Bandwidth limitations will always be a problem, so make the best of it by tuning your hardware and software.

5. Deploy slowly. Let the demands on your system increase gradually.

■ Hardware Options

At a hardware level, a single RAS server can scale from one to 256 ports and support a variety of analog, ISDN, and WAN hardware. At the most basic configuration, a RAS server can be set up to use the standard serial ports included with almost all Windows NT Server platforms (COM1 or COM2).

As a minimum solution, using the COM1 or COM2 port will work for applications where a single communications port is required. That said, we don't recommend using them for most remote access applications. Serial ports that are embedded on the server's motherboard have a direct link, called an interrupt, with the CPU. In serial communications, interrupts to the CPU are an annoying interference that result in slowing other CPU activities and therefore overall server performance.

Interrupts can be controlled and processed independently of the main CPU by installing a dedicated serial adapter for asynchronous communications that use external modems.

These adapters come in many flavors as far as number of ports and bus type, but they all have one common goal: to reduce main processor interrupts. They achieve this by allocating large data buffers in on-board memory. Sometimes it's more than 16K per channel. They also have a dedicated processor, which ranges from a Z-80 to a Motorola 68000, and RISC computing to control more than 16 active ports that are transferring data via a single slot in the server. Up to four adapters can be combined in one hardware platform, giving you 64 ports per server.

It's also possible to daisy-chain some multiport serial devices together and exceed even that number to reach a server maximum of 256 ports. There's no real software limitation; it's all a matter of bandwidth. Today's serial communications are transferring data at a maximum of 115.2Kbps, which is a trickle compared to the bus speed and clock cycles of PCI-based server hardware. Even ISDN adapters can run up against a similar limitation.

It's tough to predict accurately the effect that adding RAS will have on your existing Windows NT Server functions. Using a good communications adapter will limit the amount of data-handling the rest of the system will have to do, but there will still be limitations that will be most obvious to your remote users. To draw a line of limits in the sand, probably where others have drawn it before, we advise limiting the number of remote access ports on a non-dedicated server to eight. Beyond eight, seriously consider having a dedicated communications server, not just for performance purposes, but also to avoid creating a concentrated single point of failure by adding another responsibility to a single device.

Here are the remote access hardware adapters that are supported with drivers on the Windows NT Server 4 CD:

- Digi AccelePort 8 Adapter

- Digi C/X Adapter

- Digi DataFire—ISA1S/T Adapter

- Digi DataFire—ISA1U Adapter

- Digi DataFire—ISA4S/T Adapter

- Digi EPC Adapter

- Digi PC/16e Adapter
- Digi PC/16I Adapter
- Digi PC/2e (8K) Adapter
- Digi PC/4e (8K) Adapter
- Digi PC/4e Adapter
- Digi PC/8e (8K) Adapter
- Digi PC/8e Adapter
- Digi PC/8I Adapter
- Digi PC/XEM Adapter
- Digi PCIMAC—ISA Adapter
- Digi PCMAC/4 Adapter
- Digi SyncPort Frame Relay Adapter
- Digi SyncPort X.25 Adapter
- Digi/StarGate ClusterStar Adapter
- Eicon DIVA ISDN ISA Adapter
- Eicon DIVA PRO ISDN Adapter with Advanced DSP
- Eicon Primary Rate ISDN Adapter
- Eicon QUADRO ISDN Adapter
- Eicon SCOM ISDN Adapter
- Eicon Virtual WAN Miniport ISDN Interface
- Eicon WAN Adapters
- IBM 8-Port Async EIA-232 (ISA) Adapter
- Niwot Networks NiwRAS Adapter
- StarGate ACL/Avanstar Family Adapters
- US Robotics Allegra 56 Frame Relay
- US Robotics Allegra T1 Frame Relay
- US Robotics Sportster ISDN Adapter

- *Installing Remote Access Service*
- *Setting Up RAS*
- *RAS Network Configuration*

30

Setting Up Remote Access Services

B EFORE BEGINNING THE INSTALLATION AND CONFIGURATION OF

RAS, the following conditions should exist:

1. Windows NT 4 must be properly installed and operational.

2. All communications adapters should be installed and fully recognized by the operating system.

3. Modems, terminal adapters, and other external communications hardware should be installed and recognized by the operating system.

4. You should be logged on with administrator privileges.

A Note or Two About Modems and Modem Speeds

Modems rated at 14.4 or 28.8Kbps often use hardware data compression methods to increase their overall throughput well beyond their data transfer rate. The compressibility of data sent from one modem to another will vary a great deal. It's largely based on the type of data file being sent. Text files are generally very compressible, while spreadsheet files may not be.

Today's modem compression portion of the V.32 standard, can reach a maximum compression ratio of 4 to 1, meaning that to reach that level of compression, potentially four times the amount of data must be sent to the modem.

If you take the time to zip a file down using a utility such as PKZIP before transferring it over analog lines, we don't guarantee you'll save much time unless the pre-compression and data transfer processes are fully automated. You can download PKZIP and similar utilities through ZDNet, at http://www.zdnet.com.

Modem technologies are now changing about every two years. In 1994 the standard operating speed of an analog modem was 14.4Kbps and its cost about $200. Today the price is still $200 but the speed has doubled to 28.8Kbps.

The 4:1 compression ratio can be improved upon, but it takes more buffer memory to store the raw data prior to compressing it and more CPU to handle the algorithms. New standards could also change this ratio.

Laptops based on Personal Computer Memory Card International Association (PCMIA) standards have modem technology that seems to follow the external or rack mount equivalents by only 6 to 12 months. Plan ahead when purchasing your server communications hardware. Get more bandwidth and throughput than you need now. Users will always eat it up and beg for more.

■ Installing Remote Access Services

You can install RAS during the initial installation of Windows NT or at a later time. If you're installing after-the-fact, you'll need the Windows NT 4 CD for loading various files and drivers. If you're installing RAS on an active production server, at the completion of the installation you'll have to restart the Windows NT server for the changes to take effect. Here's how to do it.

From the Windows NT Server console, select the Control Panel and then the Network icon within the Control Panel. Select the Services tab, shown in Figure 30.1. Click Add to add a new service. A listing of available network services will be displayed.

Figure 30.1

Remote Access Service
is added from the
Network Control
Panel icon.

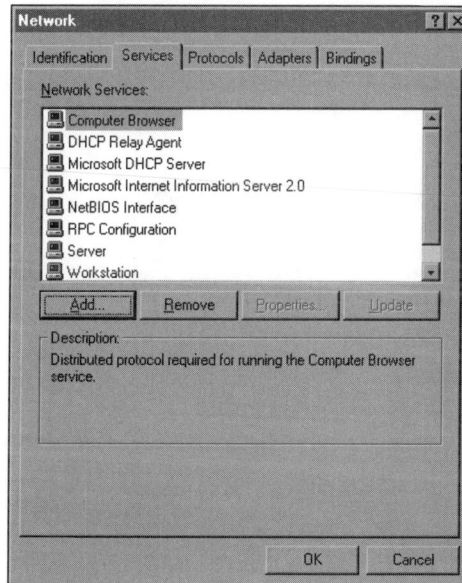

Scroll through the list and select Remote Access Service, as shown in Figure 30.2.

Click OK and the RAS files will be expanded and installed from the Windows NT Server CD. Once this is complete, the Add RAS Device window, Figure 30.3, appears. It shows a list of RAS-capable devices currently installed.

In this drop-down box, select the device(s) the RAS will use for its communications ports. For a minimum configuration, select COM1. Click OK. The Remote Access Setup window will be displayed, as in Figure 30.4.

Figure 30.2

RAS can easily be shared with other services running on the NT Server.

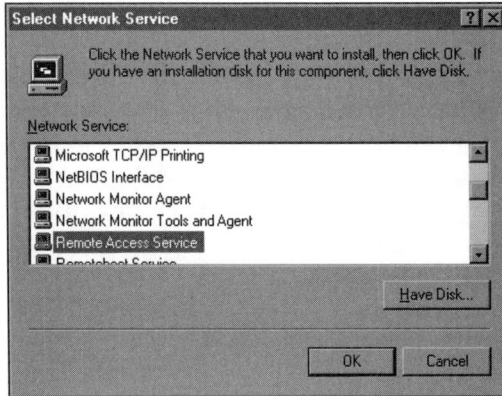

Figure 30.3

RAS allows you to specify the communications devices to be added to the RAS resource.

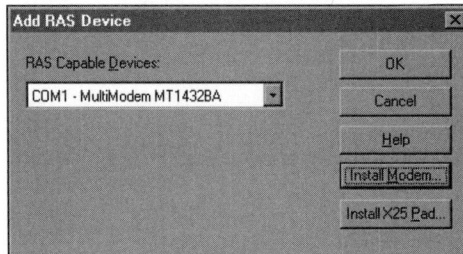

Figure 30.4

The RAS Setup window displays a listing of all RAS-compatible devices, allowing configuration of most aspects of RAS operation.

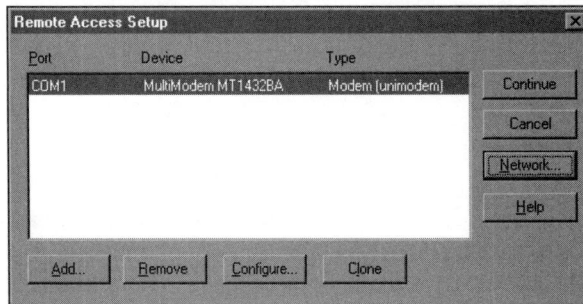

■ Setting Up RAS

The Remote Access Setup window is used mainly to configure port usage and network definitions. However, it can also be used for adding modems to previously installed communications ports and replicating existing port definitions.

During this phase of the installation, this window will be displayed automatically; you'll use it as a launch pad into the various configuration options of RAS. If you need to return to it later, from the Control Panel select Remote Access Service and then from the Network/Services tab, click Properties.

Helpful Tip

For quick installation, click Continue and then OK on each of the three screens that appear, accepting the default values.

Port Usage

Use Configure... to bring up the Configure Port Usage window (Figure 30.5) and define how each port will be allocated: whether for dial-in, dial-out, or both. As we mentioned in Chapter 29, dial-out support requires additional software from a third party. Unless you have that software or intend to use the workstation capabilities of your NT server for dial-out, keep the default setting, Receive calls only. Click OK to save your changes and return to the Remote Access Setup window.

Figure 30.5

RAS allows ports to be allocated for any or all of three options.

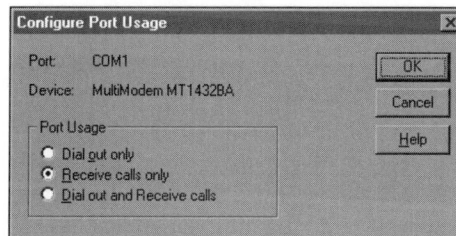

▓ RAS Network Configuration

Selecting Network... displays the Network Configuration window, as shown in Figure 30.6. Here, all settings are port-specific. In most cases, the default options will satisfy your needs. You should have a thorough understanding of protocols and your addressing issues before modifying the default parameters provided by the Configuration Wizard.

Figure 30.6

In most cases, the defaults chosen by the Configuration Wizard will satisfy your network's needs.

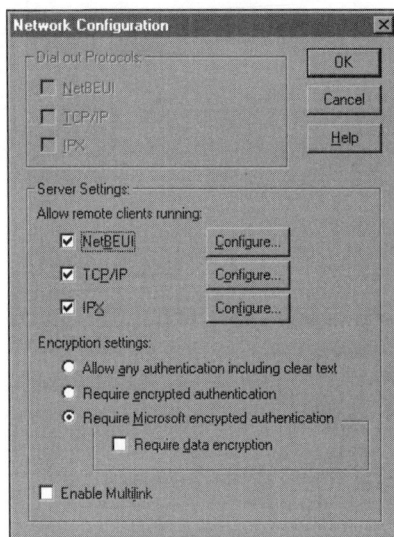

Dial-out Protocols

If you enabled Dial out only or Dial out and Receive calls on the port, the Dial-out Protocols: frame will be active (not inactive, or grayed out, as it is in the figure). Select each protocol you want to support during the dial-out phase—NetBEUI, TCP/IP, or IPX.

You can choose multiple protocols and put them in use at once. For dial-out communications, selecting all three protocols enables communications sessions with the greatest possible variety of remote devices.

Server Settings

The Server Settings: frame contains the server-side protocol parameters. Windows NT 4 RAS supports NetBEUI, TCP/IP, and IPX protocols simultaneously or individually. You can set up any of them to limit inbound access to the RAS server only, or extend access to the entire network. Other configuration options are protocol specific.

NetBEUI

The only option with the NetBEUI protocol is to restrict access beyond the RAS server. When you click on Configure..., the RAS Server NetBEUI Configuration screen is displayed, as shown in Figure 30.7.

Figure 30.7

Remote clients' access can be restricted using the NetBEUI protocol.

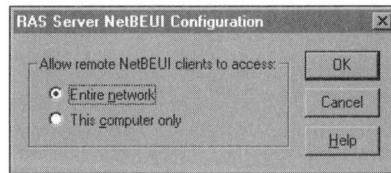

TCP/IP

Clicking on Configure... brings up the RAS Server TCP/IP Configuration window shown in Figure 30.8. For TCP/IP access, client-side addressing is the main issue. Windows NT RAS gives you two main methods: using DHCP to assign a remote address or creating a static address pool.

Figure 30.8

Proper configuration of RAS using TCP/IP requires some knowledge of your network addressing scheme.

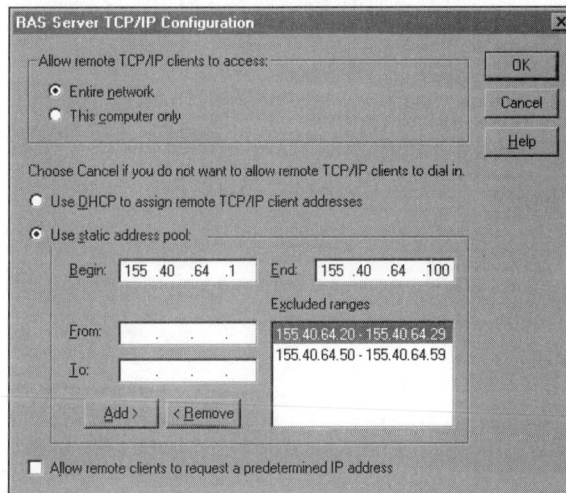

Choose DHCP if you have a host providing this service on the same subnet as the RAS server. The DHCP service can also be installed on the same server that's running RAS. Refer to Chapter 36, "Configuring DHCP, DNS and WINS," for information on configuring the DHCP service.

If you choose the static address pool, you can enter a beginning and ending address range. You can also exclude address ranges.

The final TCP/IP addressing scheme allows the remote client to specify the address of the port. This is for the few applications that are TCP/IP address-specific. Dial-Up Networking supports the entry of a client address.

IPX

Like the NetBEUI and TCP/IP protocol options, in the RAS Server IPX Configuration window (Figure 30.9) you can restrict client access beyond the RAS server under the IPX protocol. IPX addressing is less cumbersome than TCP/IP, and in general IPX addresses can even be randomly generated when needed to allow a specific client access under this protocol. RAS automatically detects address conflicts before providing an address in this manner.

Figure 30.9

For remote clients running the IPX protocol, RAS allocates IPX addresses in a variety of ways.

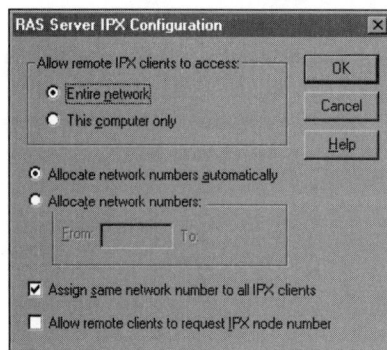

Since RAS is really a software router, you must be careful when allowing a significant number of inbound clients to access the system using unique IPX addresses because each address adds an entry to the router table. To prevent this from becoming a problem in large and complex networks, you can select the check box to have RAS assign the same IPX address to all inbound clients. This option will minimize Routing Information Protocol (RIP) broadcasts generated by a RAS server. For applications that require the inbound client to have a specific IPX address each time it connects, you can also select the check box to have the client specify an IPX address.

Encryption Settings

To ensure that the transmission of data and password is protected, RAS supports several encryption standards.

At the earliest phase of communication between a remote client and a RAS server, a validation process takes place that sifts through a number of authentication methods, attempting to negotiate a common technique between both the client and server. During this negotiation phase, RAS will attempt to communicate at the most secure level using Challenge Handshake Authentication Protocol (CHAP). If the remote client is unable to authenticate using CHAP, RAS tries other encryption schemes, such as Password Authentication Protocol (PAP), Shiva Password Authentication Protocol (SPAP) and MD5, developed by RSA Security, Inc.

The least secure method of validation is PAP, because it transmits the password in clear text, which can be easily compromised. Make sure clients are configured with one of the more sophisticated techniques for authentication into the RAS server.

To give RAS a baseline minimum allowance of who can enter the system, a set of three radio buttons can be used to define a bottom-line encryption method.

Returning to the Network Configuration dialog box of Figure 30.6, select Allow any authentication including clear text if you're sure RAS will be the access point for a variety of non-Windows clients, such as UNIX or Macintosh. This is the least secure option.

We recommend that you select Require encrypted authentication. This option forces any client to provide an encrypted password, disallowing PAP's method of sending it in clear text.

For an even more secure method of user validation, select Require Microsoft encrypted authentication. It's an especially good choice if you're only dealing with Windows clients.

You can also select a secondary option, Require data encryption. This setting encrypts all data transmitted between client and server.

The combination of these last two options creates an extremely secure remote access configuration. This level of security impacts overall system performance because of the complex algorithms that are repeatedly run at the server during data encryption. The client also will experience a performance degradation decrypting and encrypting its share of data.

One Final Note About Security

Certainly the RAS security options and the technology supported is thorough. However, true remote access security employs a number of well-thought-out procedures, not just on the server side but on the client side as well. Even a thoughtfully planned system can be compromised by a fumbling end user.

Although automating the remote access process is a tempting panacea for inexperienced or computer-phobic users, it's a security compromise lying in wait. A stolen remote client often can be more damaging than the loss of the hardware if remote access passwords are saved on the system. Never hard-code a password on a remote client. In not allowing this option, you force the remote user to enter a memorized password for each and every session.

Enable Multilink

The Enable Multilink option actually uses channel aggregation to increase bandwidth for remote users. It's a new feature in Windows NT Server 4. The functionality was originally defined for ISDN communications sharing two B channels for a single session, and it was called Multilink PPP. Since Microsoft implemented this feature, it's been inherited by other the other link methods, analog and X.25.

Analog communications using Multilink require two phone lines at both the client and the server. This is a little unusual for modem links, but it's a standard in ISDN links. Additionally, a Multilink-enabled phonebook at the client side is required.

By now, RAS has been installed and set up on your server. The Network Control Panel lists Remote Access Service among the other services currently installed (see Figure 30.10). Click on Close. Windows NT Server will perform a binding analysis and update the NT registry. Reboot your server when this is complete.

Helpful Tip

For easy access to the Network Properties page, right-mouse click the Network Neighborhood icon found on the NT desktop. At the bottom of the drop-down list you'll find Properties. Select it.

Figure 30.10

When installation is
complete, RAS appears
among the other
available services.

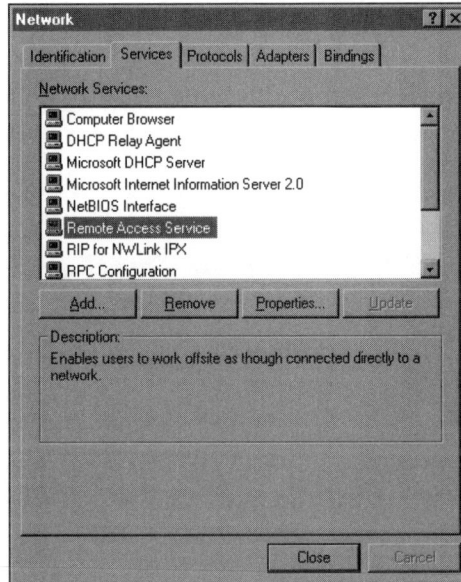

- *Remote Access Administration Console*
- *Using the Event Viewer to Troubleshoot*
- *Troubleshooting Using Dial-Up Networking*

31

RAS Administration

IN THIS CHAPTER, WE'LL COVER THE VARIOUS METHODS OF MANAG-
ing and troubleshooting remote access service (RAS) connections.
We'll also look at security options that can be enabled in RAS. We
assume you have a RAS server up and running now.

■ Remote Access Administration Console

For simple management of the RAS server, the Remote Access Admin application is automatically installed and located under the Windows NT Server Administrative Tools menu among the other utilities, as shown in Figure 31.1.

Figure 31.1

RAS functions are managed using the Remote Access Admin utility.

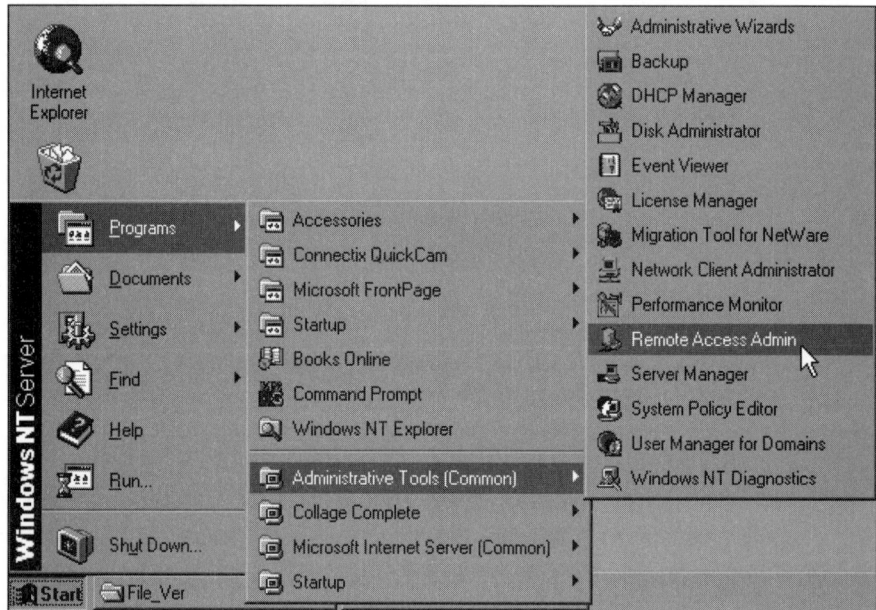

This console displays a brief synopsis of the current conditions of RAS servers within the current domain. Using this screen, you can get a quick snapshot of your remote access activity level, including the number of ports in use, as shown in Figure 31.2.

For a more detailed look, you can double-click the RAS server displayed and view a complete listing of the RAS ports on that server, listed by port, and, if in use, user ID and the date and time the communications session was started. (See Figure 31.3.) This window is useful in getting a quick glimpse of how long users have been connected or whether the load is being balanced between numerous ports.

If it appears that a session has a notably high duration, it could be indicative of a user who has forgotten about his or her remote communications session and left it up and running. When you feel comfortable with what you're doing on the NT Server, you can elect to disconnect the user immediately.

Figure 31.2

When the Remote Access Admin utility is loaded, it will display the current status of all RAS-enabled servers within the domain.

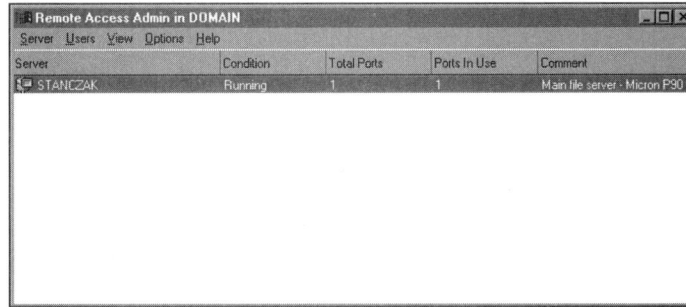

Figure 31.3

You can double-click a RAS server for a more explicit description of the configuration of each server.

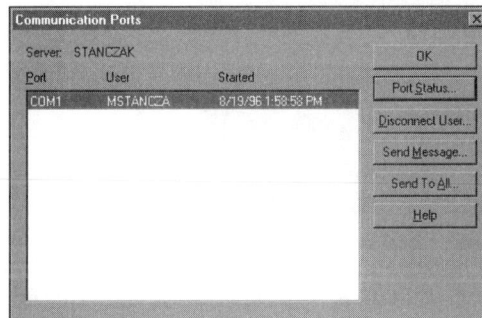

A Disconnect User... window will warn you that you are about to disconnect, giving you one last chance to cancel the disconnect before the connection is dropped, as shown in Figure 31.4. As the administrator, you also have the option of automatically revoking users' access privileges on a permanent basis. This is sure to provoke an irate response from the now outcast user, but from an administrative point of view, you can use the opportunity to gain insight into your customer's use pattern and build a better profile of overall RAS use.

Figure 31.4

When you disconnect a user, you can revoke future access privileges at the same time.

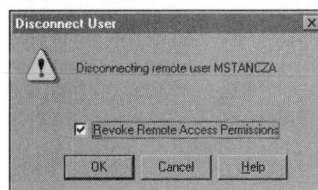

You can drill down further into the connection to view its activity level and connection statistics by selecting Port Status... on the Communication Ports screen. This will bring up the window shown in Figure 31.5.

Figure 31.5

The Port Status window gives important statistics about each active connection. Hardware overruns indicate that the communications port can't keep up with the modem and data is likely being lost.

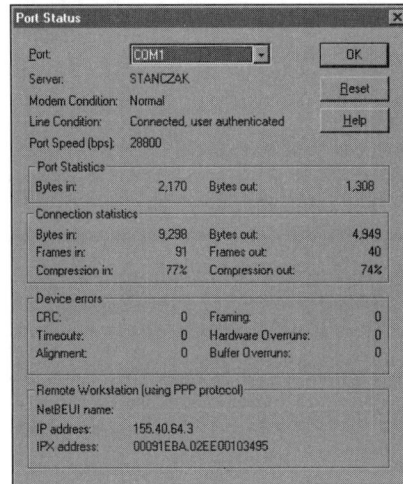

Designed to give you a peek at the inner happenings of a single remote communications session, the Port Status window can only show the server's perspective of the situation, though to its credit, it does break out port statistics from connection statistics and calculates the inbound and outbound data compression rates.

If you've got connections that appear to be overly long, you can tell if they're truly active connections by watching the Port Statistics frame, plus the Bytes in and Bytes out counters. In active connections, these numbers change, though at different rates. Static numbers here could indicate an inactive connection, a hung device or an overtaxed server.

The Port Status window is, among other things, an important tool in troubleshooting remote connection problems. Using this tool, you can watch a user attempt to connect with the system and view the results in a detailed fashion in real time.

The Bytes in and Bytes out counters are connection-specific and will be automatically reset with every new connection. Another useful element here are the Compression in and Compression out counters; they give you an idea of the compression factors that both the client and server are achieving. These numbers will vary but can give an administrator insight into the remote access performance the end user may be experiencing.

In general, remote communications are slow, and any level of compression that can be achieved will improve performance. However, some files, such as large and complex spreadsheets or previously compressed .ZIP files, have a very low compressibility factor, and during their transfer, attempts to compress the data further are unsuccessful. When this occurs, these compression counters will approach a value of zero. If this is a common situation in your remote access environment, you might consider disabling the data compression feature in your modems so they won't even attempt to further reduce the data prior to putting it on the line. High numbers here are remote access nirvana.

The Device errors frame contains counters for a variety of communications error conditions that can prevent connection initially or cause the loss of an existing connection. The most common problem with loss of a session after a given period of time is hardware and buffer overruns.

Hardware overruns are caused by the communications link exceeding the data throughput capacity of the client's hardware. When this occurs, some amount of data is lost, which, at a minimum, forces data to be re-transmitted or worse, the connection to be lost. The major cause of this problem is an insufficient serial universal asynchronous receiver/transmitter (UART) on the client side. When a slow UART is connected to a modem that can exceed the data rate of the UART, a hardware overrun is imminent. As the modem receives and converts the analog phone signal into a digital one, it sends the signal down the pipe through the client's serial port (when external modems are used). If data is arriving at the modem faster than the serial port can forward it onto the bus for further processing, overruns will occur. A client's serial port should allow at least 115.2Kbps of data throughput.

This is not really a problem when working with remote clients that use PC Card slot-based modems or internal modem adapters. Most of these modem solutions are designed to handle the higher throughput requirements.

Also within the Device errors frame is a Framing counter. If you have clients that are unable to connect and this counter is increasing, the client is likely the culprit, sending unrecognizable frames. Sometimes encrypted data can also make this counter increase.

At the bottom of the Port Status window is a listing of protocols under which the client has been authenticated for use. If you have clients that are connecting but can't seem to get to all the services of the network, the likely cause is that you don't have all the necessary protocols loaded and running.

There are other useful elements of this administration console hidden under menu items. Under the Server menu, you can start and stop the RAS service and select a management domain for controlling RAS servers across multiple domains.

Under the Users menu, user access permissions are controlled along with the server-based dial-back rules. On a per-user or global basis, you can define call-back procedures in one of three ways, as shown in Figure 31.6. If you don't want users requesting call-back, you can select No Call Back. You can allow users to request call-back by selecting Set By Caller. To force call-back to a specified number, select Preset To and enter the call-back phone number.

Figure 31.6

For each RAS server, you can specify who has permission to use the service and whether dial-back is supported for that user.

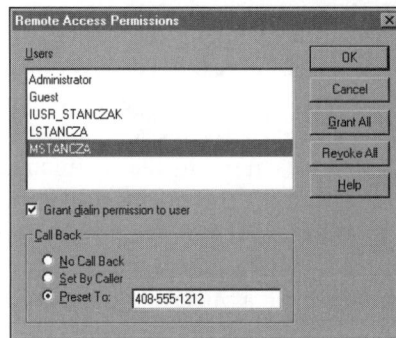

Active RAS users can also be monitored. By selecting Active Users from the View menu, you'll get a Remote Access Users window, shown in Figure 31.7, which lists RAS users by domain and user name, as well as the date and time this particular session was started. For an even more detailed view of the user's access rights, click User Account to display information on the user, as shown in Figure 31.8.

Figure 31.7

Active users are displayed showing the times their connections were established. You can notify them of upcoming downtime or force them off the network.

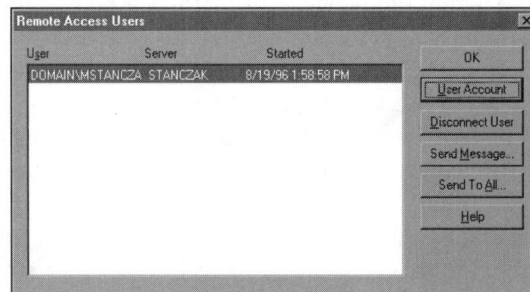

Figure 31.8

The User Account window
provides a quick peek
into security-specific
information about active
remote users.

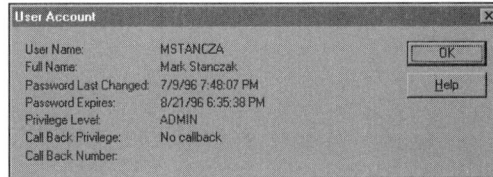

■ Using the Event Viewer to Troubleshoot

Another method of troubleshooting remote connections involves using the
Event Viewer, shown in Figure 31.9, to see the system events that led up to a
problem. RAS-specific events are tagged Remote Access under the window's
Source column.

Figure 31.9

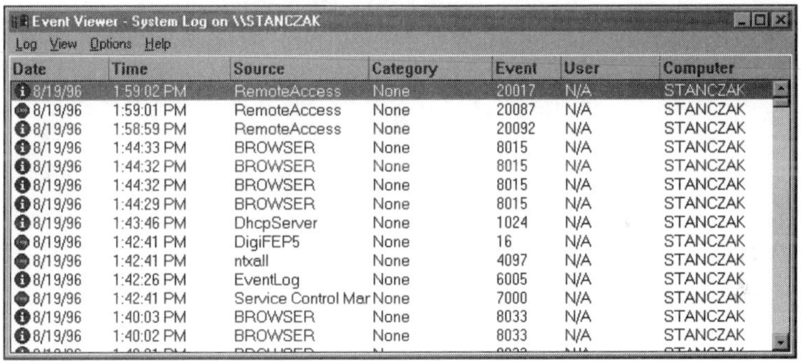

System events that relate
to the RAS can be
tracked with the Event
Viewer. Problems are
flagged with a stop sign
icon on the far left.

The information displayed here is a useful addition to that given by the
real-time monitors of the Port Status window, because it can be archived and
analyzed after the fact, albeit manually. For more information on the general
use of the Event Viewer, refer to Chapter 14, "How to Use the Event Viewer."

The Event Viewer is also useful in auditing remote communications. It
automatically records a wealth of information about each remote session.
One Event ID, number 20050, shown in Figure 31.10, gives a good summary
of a session. It includes user name, port name, domain name, date and time
the connection was established, length of connection, amount of data in
bytes that were sent and received, and the data transfer speed. If the call-
back feature was used, the number that was called back is also recorded in
this Event Detail window.

Figure 31.10

RAS events, as with other service-specific warning and error events, are indicative of server configuration problems and should be addressed locally before attempting to reconfigure remote clients.

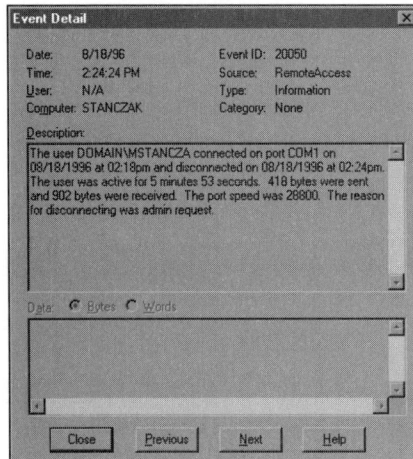

Because the Event Log acts as the audit trail for remote communications, it must be managed. If you want to track your remote access usage, the Audit Log should be periodically exported to disk; otherwise it will be lost when the log file is automatically overwritten. This usually occurs after a preset number of days. The default is seven.

Although RAS doesn't include a utility for processing and summarizing the data collected over any period, you can save the log as a comma-delimited text file, which can then be imported into Excel for graphical summarizing and analysis.

■ Troubleshooting Using Dial-Up Networking

You can do a good deal of troubleshooting at the client side using the Dial-Up Networking Monitor and its Status tab. Figures 31.11 and 31.12 show how to find it. Because of the way Windows NT Server uses communications devices, it can also be used to view session status at the RAS server. This utility controls all aspects of client-side communications, with some elements that can also monitor port status.

The Dial-Up Networking Monitor's three tabs give you a good deal of insight into the communications activities occurring in real time. Similar to the Port Status window in Remote Access Administration, the Status tab clearly shows when data is being transferred from client and server and gives a connection duration. Clicking Details... will display network address settings for the particular session, as shown in Figure 31.13.

Figure 31.11

At the remote client, you can use the status monitoring function of Dial-Up Networking to track your communications session.

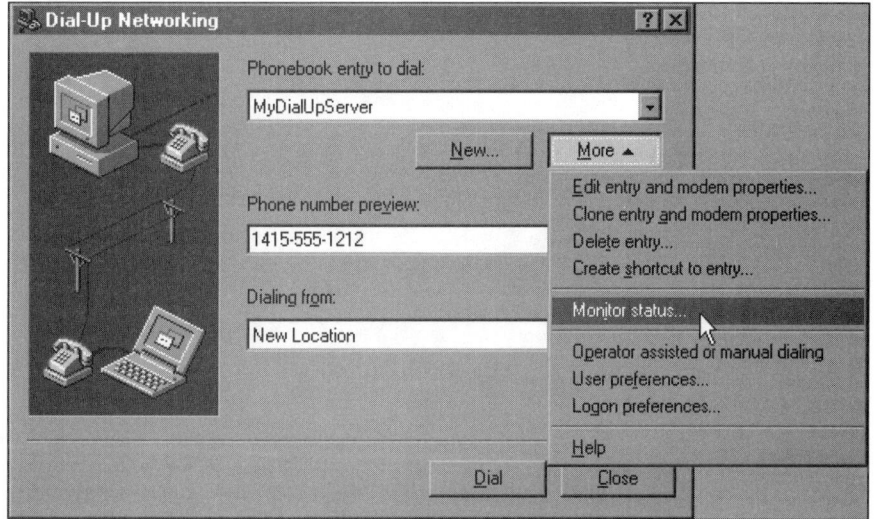

Figure 31.12

The Dial-Up Networking Monitor is especially useful in diagnosing problematic remote sessions at the client side.

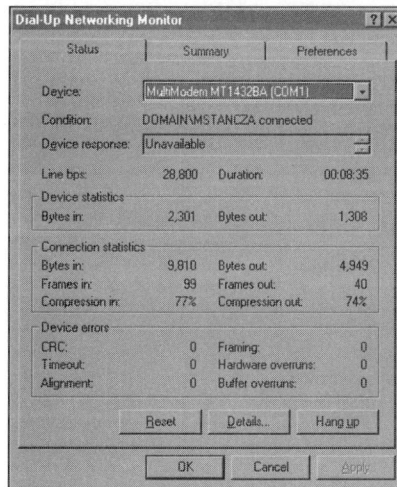

Figure 31.13

The Details window in the Dial-Up Networking Monitor shows the active protocols and their methods of registration.

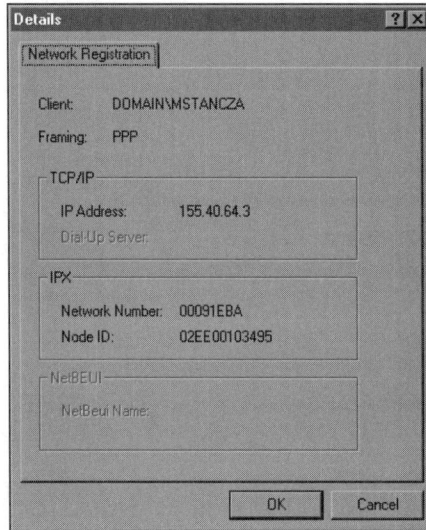

The Summary tab shown in Figure 31.14 is especially useful in RAS environments with multiple serial adapters because of the hierarchical method of accessing each port. Using this tab, on a per port basis, you can view network registration information that is useful in isolating Internet Protocol addressing conflicts.

Figure 31.14

Multilink communications use multiple devices during a single session to improve throughput. The Summary tab shows which devices are in use.

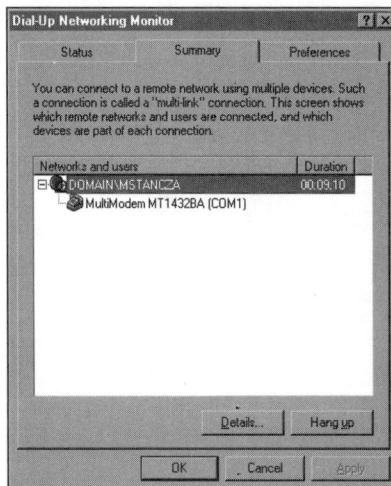

The options on the Preferences tab, shown in Figure 31.15, can be useful in linking sounds to remote communications events, such as when a connection is dropped or when a line error occurs. You can also enable communications lights that operate in semi-real time to give a visual representation of data send and receive activities.

Figure 31.15

Users with internal modems often don't get visual feedback from their communications hardware. Through Preferences tab options, data send and receive lights can be displayed on the desktop or task bar.

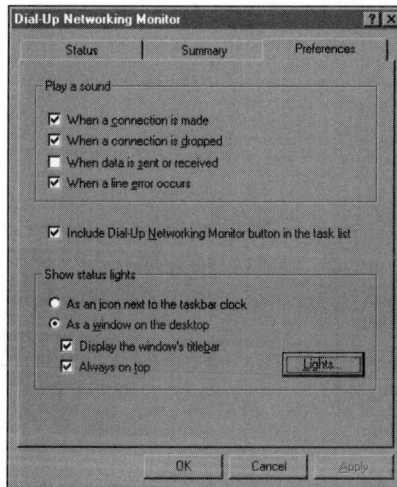

7

Setting Up Windows NT for the Internet

- *Dial-Up Internet Connections*
- *ISDN Internet Connections*
- *Frame Relay or WAN Connections to the Internet*
- *Off-Site or Service Provider-Maintained Web Servers*
- *Security and Firewalls*

32

Windows NT 4 Internet Services

WITHOUT QUESTION, THE FASTEST GROWING SEGMENT OF CORPO-
rate computing today relates to the Internet, a vast connection of
various types of computer systems and devices linked by a common networking protocol, TCP/IP.

One of the most significant aspects of the Internet is its cross-
platform nature. In a broad perspective, the gateway is the Internet, allowing us to share data and computing resources simply by
being attached to it, irrespective of what the back-end systems are.
This inter-linking of systems has created the world's digital store-
house of information, and we are only now starting to really take
advantage of it.

As our dependence on access to data grows, security of the data becomes more and more critical. This has led to the creation of privatized, corporate internets known as intranets.

Intranets work just like the Internet. They use the same plumbing, development tools, and client utilities, and they often have links to the Internet. In many ways, intranets are subsets of the Internet, with the dividing line being the corporate firewall, which usually comes in the form of a hardware router. Figure 32.1 shows a broad view of a corporate intranet and its relationship to the Internet.

Figure 32.1

An intranet resides on the secure side of the corporate firewall. Look at it as your private Internet.

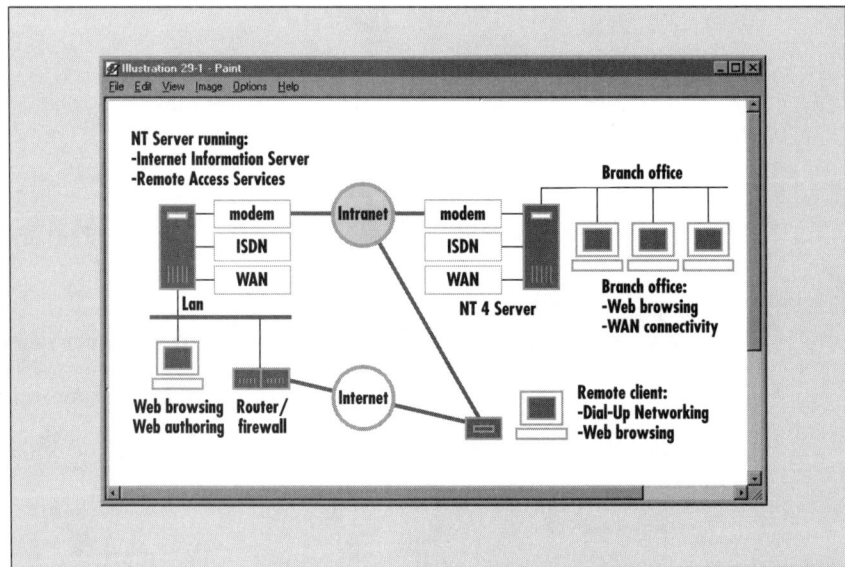

Windows NT Server comes equipped with several Internet-compatible services and applications that allow network administrators to completely set up, design, manage, and access data using intranet-type technologies.

Aside from the Internet work connectivity services, such as RAS and the Multiprovider Router, Windows NT Server 4 includes several applications that round out its Internet-specific functions. They are:

- Internet Information Server (IIS), which adds WWW, FTP, and Gopher functions to Windows NT

- Domain Name Server, which interprets between fully qualified domain names and TCP/IP addresses

- FrontPage, which is an authoring tool for building and maintaining Web pages

- Index Server, which is a Web content indexing engine

The chief component in Windows NT Server is the IIS. At its most basic level, IIS can be a dedicated one-man show, the sole intranet/Internet server for a small business by providing users with online access to a product catalog and contact information through a standard Web browser. Or, at a corporate level, it can scale to be one of many servers supporting a large number of users that constantly accesses frequently-changing corporate data, such as sales figures and product inventory status.

The following capabilities are provided by the IIS:

1. World Wide Web service. IIS provides Web functions using the HTTP engine. To enable use of the fully qualified domain name (for example: zdp.mcp.com), a DNS server is required. Otherwise, clients must use the TCP/IP address of the Web server (for example: 192.64.47.205) to access the default Web page.

2. File Transfer Protocol service. FTP is a common method of downloading files directly from an Internet server. Web pages can be scripted to automatically invoke FTP for transferring a file to a Web client. During the installation of IIS, the FTP server is added by default.

3. Gopher service. This is a directory-based method of navigating to specific files for downloading. It's really just a slightly more intuitive method than FTP to drill down directory levels in search of files.

As you would expect, there are a variety of methods to consider in connecting your IIS server to the Internet. In in all cases, you'll need to bring an Internet service provider into the picture to provide the actual back-end Internet link.

Each connection method has its advantages and disadvantages. Here are our summaries.

■ Dial-Up Internet Connections

The advantages are that it's inexpensive and relatively easy to configure. Dial-Up Networking requires only a modem and an analog phone line.

The biggest disadvantage is that it's excruciatingly slow. The best dial-up connection rarely offers more than a 24Kbps data transfer rate. To make matters worse, the call setup time for a connection can easily be more than 30 seconds. Finally, using analog connections means that reliability suffers.

Most users will be unsatisfied with this type of connection to your Web server, but if you're just experimenting, it's a starting point.

■ ISDN Internet Connections

This is still a relatively inexpensive and easy way to configure connectivity to the Internet that uses Dial-Up Networking. It offers better throughput than dial-up lines (up to 128Kbps) and much faster call setup time (usually less than five seconds), making the connection process almost instantaneous to the end user. This very scaleable solution is best suited for small business and active personal Web servers.

A disadvantage is that support varies with your geographic region, and orchestrating the installation with your local phone company can be a nightmare. The data throughput, though significantly better than dial-up, won't be satisfactory for active Web sites.

■ Frame Relay or WAN Connections to the Internet

The king of the hill in Internet connectivity, Frame Relay offers high-speed access using bandwidths that can vary up to 1.55Mbps, known as T-1, or to 45Mbps using T-3. This is the solution for big-time Internet access, and a single server can support multiple links. This type of connection is always live. Many organizations bring the Internet to networked clients using this technology.

The disadvantage is that monthly connection charges can frequently run into thousands of dollars. Also, there's a more complex setup involving additional third-party hardware for T-1 and T-3 connectivity.

■ Off-Site or Service Provider-Maintained Web Servers

Many Internet service providers offer complete Web server maintenance functions through hardware and software that are housed at their site. They often provide a high-speed data pipeline to your business location if you plan to maintain the Web content yourself.

For companies not prepared to make the investment in equipment and maintenance staff for an Internet presence, this may be the best solution. Why not take advantage of the expertise offered by your Internet service provider? This resource can put a new Web site online quickly, saving you many hours in planning and setup time.

The downside is that monthly costs can be somewhat uncontrolled because they're often based on hit counts and content volume. Keeping your Web site's content up-to-date can be more difficult if you don't control the Web server.

NT's scalability gives it the potential to work at very high volume levels of service as a Web server. This means that if your server hardware has reached its maximum capacity, you can fairly easily add disk drives, memory, or CPUs to increase overall system throughput and support a higher hit count rate. For even greater capacity, multiple IIS servers can be set up on a network and the load can be balanced.

In a horse race, so to speak, it would be hard to put a limit on NT's performance as a Web server. This is because it's so scalable. You only need to determine where your bottleneck in performance is and take the time to upgrade that component. In Web serving functions, link speed will almost always be your number one performance limiting factor.

In general, unless you're an Internet service provider or a corporation supporting a very high volume of hit counts per minute, NT should be able to fit your needs.

Just as a point of reference, it's generally accepted that most Internet service providers have implemented UNIX-based Web servers as their platform of choice for leased Web server functions. The Microsoft Web site (http://www.microsoft.com) is one of the most frequently accessed sites. It is actually run on several NT-based servers.

NOTE. *When considering your need for disk space, consider the fact that most Web servers house a large amount of data that grows at an alarming rate. One storage vendor indicated that storage is the most frequently upgraded component of a Web server, often doubling in size every six months. Experience has shown us that you just can't have enough raw storage capacity for Web-based content. If your data has a large degree of graphical content, it will consume disk space faster than pure text-based content.*

■ Security and Firewalls

For NT networks that have a connection to the Internet, security should be on your mind. Several configuration methods and third-party applications termed firewalls exist to enable the system administrator to closely limit inbound access over the Internet.

This is one of the strengths of hardware-based routers such as those from Cisco Systems, Inc. and Bay Networks, Inc. Because they act as the gateway to the Internet, linking your network to the world's network, configurations can be defined that ignore network packets outside the parameters set forth by the network administrator. Limiting factors can be as detailed as the client address during specific times of day. There's a great deal of flexibility allowed though configuring a hardware router usually requires a good deal of training combined with first-hand experience.

Depending on how your Windows NT is configured to link to the Internet, the location of your firewall will vary. (For more information on this subject, see *Intranet and Internet Firewall Strategies*, by Edward Amoroso and Ronald Sharp, ZD Press, 1996.)

You can use these simple security rules as a general set of guidelines:

1. Rename Administrator account. Administrator is a default user name in Windows NT for controlling and configuring all aspects of the NT server and the NT domain. Hackers get a good start if you still use this user name as your main management entry into the system. Change it, but don't forget it.

2. Remove Guest and Anonymous user accounts. Windows NT Server automatically installs a guest user account for general network access. In your efforts to group users and access privileges, you may be unintentionally providing guest user access to privileged data. Delete the guest account.

3. Enable password lock-out to prevent hackers from guessing passwords. Once a hacker has a valid user name (these are usually easily guessed by someone in possession of a company phone list), he will eventually attempt to guess user passwords. Password lock-out disables user accounts after a given number of failed password attempts. Although this solution may mean a few more phone calls by forgetful users into IS, it's well worth the effort when compared to the added level of security it provides. A good default value is three failed logon attempts before disabling the user account.

4. Use encryption for dial-in authentication. In some cases, passwords sent across the LAN medium are done so in plain text format. Protocol analyzers or *network sniffers* can capture and display these passwords. Make sure to use some form of password encryption, even for LAN-attached client workstations.

5. Expire all passwords every 30 days. When first implemented in our workplace, this was an annoyance that led to at least a couple of calls into IS to re-enable user accounts. But once we got accustomed to the frequency of change, we grew to expect it and appreciate its usefulness; it guaranteed that if anyone did get our passwords, they were only valid for a limited time.

6. Passwords should have a minimum length of six to eight characters. The longer the better when it comes to passwords.

7. Use unique, not easily guessed passwords. Many passwords can be hacked by using terms or names that are common to the user, the company or the environment. It is best to use non-English combinations of letters and numbers as your password.

Caution

Unique passwords can be quickly forgotten, which can result in users keeping a written record of each password, thus creating yet another potential security risk.

Networks that use TCP/IP as the standard access protocol for internal network clients can be more susceptible to security breaches. Some configurations use TCP/IP to gain access to the Internet but take advantage of gateway-type applications that provide protocol encapsulation using IPX or NetBEUI to distribute the Internet access to non-TCP/IP network clients.

NOTE. *About hit counts...Each time a client requests a response from IIS and it responds, the result is called a hit. In general terms, as a user, when you request a hypertext document or page, you generate a hit count on that page. These hit counts are tracked and used to measure the frequency of access to a particular page. This information is often used for billing purposes in Web-based advertising. A single user can generate multiple hits by repeatedly requesting the same Web page, so this measurement of true interest level is not accurate. Survey forms are another method of measuring interest level. Users completing a form are likely to be truly interested and worth more effort. But toss out unfinished forms. They are seldom valid, oftentimes containing false, inaccurate and incomplete data.*

■ Summary

To publish documents on the Internet, you'll need to contact an Internet service provider. In addition to the back-end connectivity they provide to the Internet, they can also provide you with domain name registration services that allow users accessing your system to use common, or friendly, names, such as www.pcweek.com, as opposed to your server's physical IP address.

For intranet access, working with an Internet service provider may not be necessary. Using the NT Server tools and services such as DHCP and WINS, you can create your own private Internet (or intranet) with the domain naming conventions you determine. Later, you can add access to the Internet by using a router with a leased line to the Internet service provider.

33

Installing the Internet
Information Server

A<small>S WE MENTIONED IN THE LAST CHAPTER</small>, IIS CAN BE THE
information center of your intranet or Internet. Its behavior in either environment can be determined by the level of outside connectivity you've already established. Before beginning IIS
installation, make sure the following configuration elements are in
place.

TCP/IP must be configured and fully operational. If you're building true Internet access, your Internet service provider should have given you a server IP address, subnet mask, at least one default gateway IP address, and the address of at least one domain name server.

To implement friendly names for access into your server, you will need access to a DNS server or you can install and configure the Microsoft Domain Naming Server. For Internet access, as we just mentioned, you'll need to register your server's domain name, also known as the host name, through your service provider. In this case, you won't need your own DNS server—the provider will give you one in the form of a DNS address, usually more than one.

Installing IIS requires the NT CD-ROM and uses the Network Control Panel method of adding new services. At completion, you aren't required to reboot the server for the changes to take effect. As you'd expect for this level of server configuration, you'll need to be logged on with administrative privileges.

Open the Network Control Panel. Select the Services tab, shown in Figure 33.1. Click Add to display a list of supported services. Scroll down and select the Microsoft Internet Information Server shown in Figure 33.2. Click OK to start the Installation Wizard.

Figure 33.1

Usually, the IIS is part of the default Windows NT Server installation. If it's not present in the Network Services list, you can easily add it.

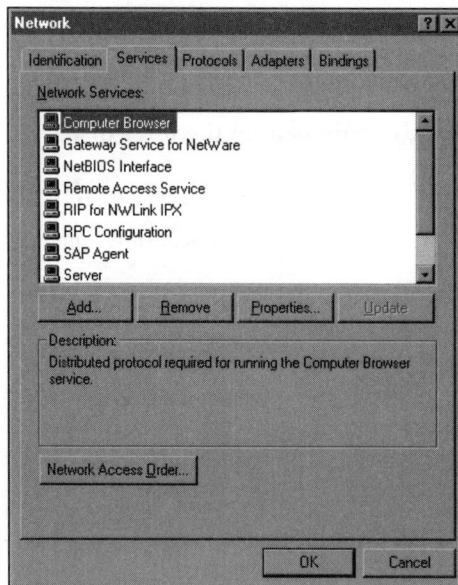

Figure 33.2

IIS is among the several new Internet-related services now included with Windows NT Server, all of which share a common installation procedure.

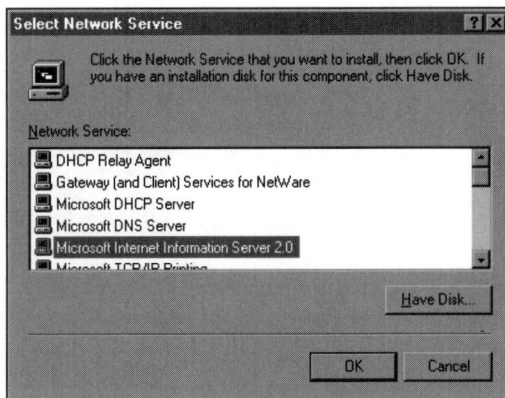

The initial setup window displays the various components of IIS and their installation directories. If you don't intend to support FTP or Gopher services, you can deselect those options here before continuing the installation process. (See Figure 33.3.) Hackers will sometimes attempt to gain access to your system using these services because they can be more difficult to secure with the potential for backdoor access in a poorly implemented network environment. Note that the directory displayed in this window is only for the purpose of installation; it doesn't determine in which directories you will be locating your HTML documents or downloadable files. Click OK to copy the files and start IIS Setup.

As you can see in Figure 33.4, the Publishing Directories window allows you to define where WWW, FTP, and Gopher directories will be physically located on your Windows NT Server. The default locations for these directories are:

D:\InetPub\wwwroot
D:\InetPub\ftproot
D:\InetPub\gophroot

You may wish to publish information located in another directory. If so, you can point to it here. Later, you can set up a virtual server to separately access and publish data in other directories. Accept the default directory assignments by clicking OK.

For each IIS service you're installing, the files will be copied and the appropriate directories created. Additionally, each service is automatically started.

If your networking configuration is in error, messages to that effect are displayed now. Later, you can go back and view the Event Monitor to get a better handle on what configuration elements need more attention.

Figure 33.3

Although it takes only 3.8MB of disk space to install the entire suite of Internet serving applications; HTML data files can take a lot more.

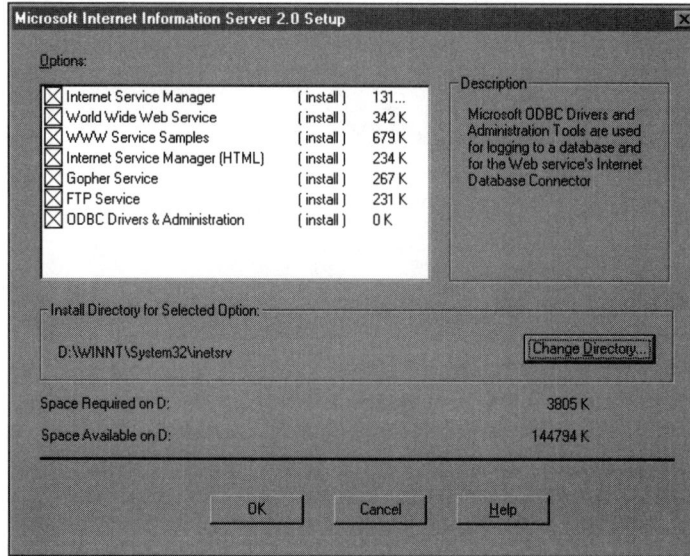

Microsoft Internet Information Server 2.0 Setup

Options:

☒ Internet Service Manager	(install)	131...
☒ World Wide Web Service	(install)	342 K
☒ WWW Service Samples	(install)	679 K
☒ Internet Service Manager (HTML)	(install)	234 K
☒ Gopher Service	(install)	267 K
☒ FTP Service	(install)	231 K
☒ ODBC Drivers & Administration	(install)	0 K

Description

Microsoft ODBC Drivers and Administration Tools are used for logging to a database and for the Web service's Internet Database Connector

Install Directory for Selected Option:

D:\WINNT\System32\inetsrv   [Change Directory...]

Space Required on D: 3805 K

Space Available on D: 144794 K

[OK]   [Cancel]   [Help]

Figure 33.4

The default directories for each service can be easily changed, though the directory structure provided makes navigation for maintenance purposes a snap.

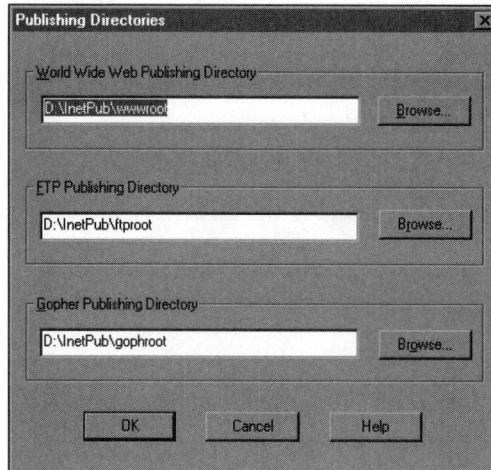

Publishing Directories

World Wide Web Publishing Directory

D:\InetPub\wwwroot   [Browse...]

FTP Publishing Directory

D:\InetPub\ftproot   [Browse...]

Gopher Publishing Directory

D:\InetPub\gophroot   [Browse...]

[OK]   [Cancel]   [Help]

IIS can deposit usage information directly into a database. Support for this feature is provided by specifying which connectivity method you want to employ. For each open database connectivity (ODBC) link you want IIS to support, select the corresponding driver from the list of drivers that are currently set up and running on your server. (See the Install Drivers window, Figure 33.5.)

Figure 33.5

The Install Drivers window.

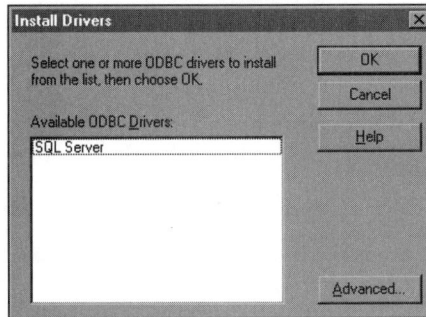

The Install Drivers window allows you to select a driver for open database connectivity links to your IIS.

If you selected ODBC Drivers and Administration in the initial IIS Setup screen, you'll be prompted now to install the details of that option. The default is SQL Server. Clicking on Advanced... brings up Advanced Installation Options, Figure 33.6, where you can check versions for each driver and translator that will be set up.

Figure 33.6

In the Advanced Installation Options window, you can check versions for drivers and translators.

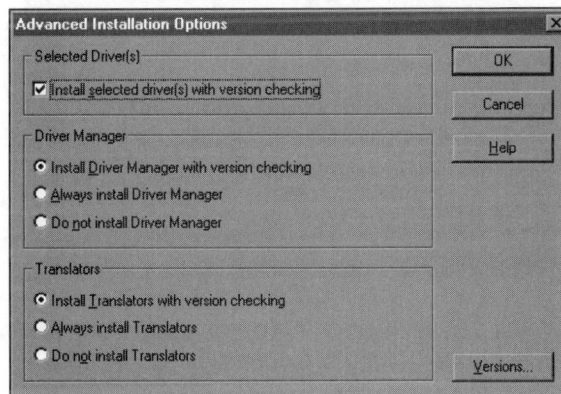

This completes the installation of your IIS. At this point, each service you selected—WWW, FTP and Gopher—are up and running. The default directories for each service are also set up on the volume you've specified under the root:

\InetPub\wwwroot
\InetPub\ftproot
\InetPub\gophroot

For verification purposes, a default HTML data file has been copied to the WWWROOT directory. Titled DEFAULT.HTML, the IIS will automatically respond to client requests at the root using this file. This allows you to immediately test access to your Web server with any standard browser either on your NT Server or a LAN-based client. Simply load the browser and enter the universal naming convention (UNC) or specific address of the NT Server running IIS. If IIS is up and operating properly, you should get the Introduction to IIS Web page shown in Figure 33.7 displayed on your browser.

Figure 33.7

When IIS is successfully installed, you can access the default HTML file by simply entering the URL of the server in the Internet Explorer.

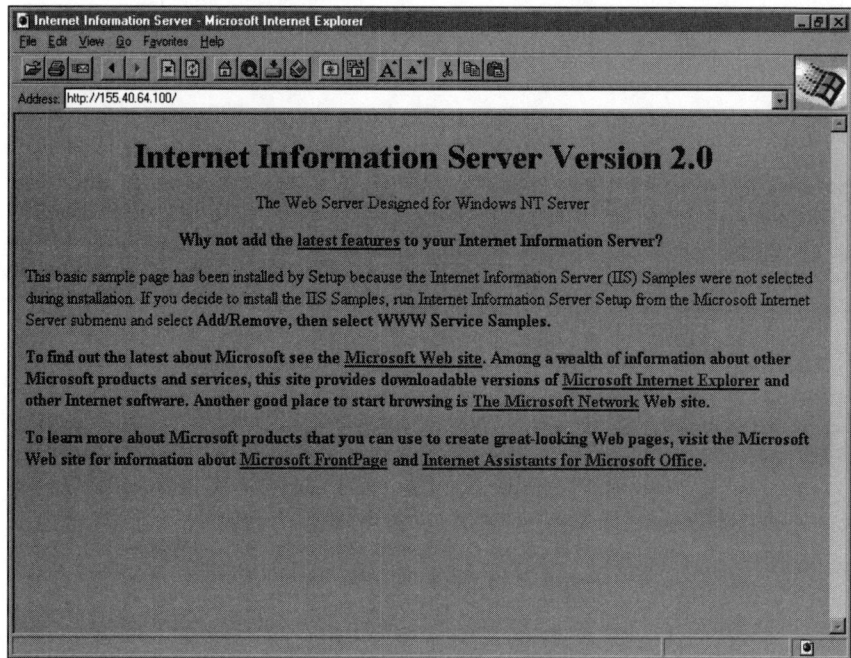

If you already have HTML files, they can be placed into the WWWROOT directory. Additionally, files you have for download can be placed into the appropriate FTP and Gopher directories.

To manage your IIS, you can use the Internet Service Manager, available under the Administrative Tools menu. For a detailed explanation of managing your IIS, refer to Chapter 35, "Managing Your Web Site."

For new Web servers, you can use Microsoft's FrontPage, included with Windows NT Server to design your own Web pages. See Chapter 34, "Building a Web Site with FrontPage" for more information.

- *What You Need to Know about HTML*
- *Installing FrontPage*
- *Using the Templates and Wizards*
- *Images in FrontPage*
- *Using Bots*
- *Putting It All Together*

34

Building a Web Site with FrontPage

Microsoft's frontpage world wide web authoring tools are included on the Windows NT Server 4 CD. FrontPage can be installed as a separate application on any Windows 95 or Windows NT client workstation. FrontPage can be used to create and manage self-standing Web sites. Learning how to take advantage of its rich set of features will earn you the title of Webmaster without forcing you to learn Hypertext Markup Language (HTML).

FrontPage was originally developed by Vermeer Technologies, Inc. as a non-technical Web development tool. Late in 1995, Microsoft acquired Vermeer, its engineering staff, and their Web authoring software. The full range of features offered by FrontPage includes authoring and post-development management of Web sites.

In addition to supporting Microsoft's Internet Information Server, files created with FrontPage are also compatible with many other Web servers that interpret HTML.

To ensure a high level of compatibility with these Web servers, Microsoft includes the FrontPage Server Extensions. When applied to your Internet server platform, such as IIS, translation functions are performed between your FrontPage-created Web site and your Web server. We will cover installing the FrontPage Server Extensions later in this chapter.

The FrontPage development environment is made up of two main components: FrontPage Explorer and FrontPage Editor. Together, these two applications allow you to create new Web sites and modify existing ones.

FrontPage Explorer is a higher level application designed to outline the organization of your Web site and implement the linking relationship between Web pages. FrontPage Explorer includes several wizards for creating a new Web site that automate many site creation procedures. There are wizards for creating a personal Web page, a corporate Internet presence, and a survey form, among others. Using these wizards, you get a fill-in-the-blanks approach, which results in a complete Web site that performs its intended function, though the sites themselves may end up looking a little mundane. The only remaining task is to personalize the appropriate sections with your company-specific data.

FrontPage Editor is used for the actual creation or modification of specific pages within a Web site, and allows you define the appearance of your Web site.

FrontPage Personal Web Server, which also ships with FrontPage, is used for testing and, as the name suggests, running a personal Web site. This is a relatively unsophisticated Windows application that should really only be used for development purposes or on a very small scale, say two or three users at most. This is because this system can not create activity logs or provide much in the way of tracking status information.

Tracking the ongoing development and maintenance of your Web site can be an enormous task, especially as the richness of your Web content increases. This function and others can be maintained on a site-specific To Do List which is useful for assigning and prioritizing content management tasks within a workgroup.

■ What You Need to Know about HTML

HTML is a text-based programming language that presents Web page content in a format understandable by Web browsers such as Microsoft Internet Explorer. All Web pages are made up of HTML objects that contain various elements of a Web page such as graphics, pull-down menus, text boxes, and hyperlinks.

Viewing a complex Web page in its native HTML format is difficult, and working with it can be anywhere from merely cumbersome to virtually impossible. There are now a number of Web page authoring tools that use different methods to generate native HTML code. These products dramatically reduce Web page construction time and make updating Web pages more intuitive.

For large sites, some authoring tools also offer Web site management functions where the chore of manually maintaining multitudes of pages and links will quickly become a logistical nightmare. FrontPage includes both of these functions.

HTML is constantly adding new features. Supporting new HTML functions usually requires a software update of the Internet service, the authoring tool, and the client browser.

Recently, a new feature called *tables* was added to HTML. This function makes it easier to build and display data in a row and column format such as you might want for a product list. Many Web sites have been quick to encompass this new feature because it makes presentation of spreadsheet data much less painful to code for accurate display. But clients with browsers that lack support for tables are unable to view the data. Though tables are generally considered a standard today, other incompatibilities between a Web site and client browsers are still a concern. Current incompatibilities are in the varied support for Java applets and in the use of frames that split the browser window into sections.

Planning Your Web Site

With HTML enhancements, the rapid implementation of new features has led to a remarkably short period of time between the release of new versions of client browser applications.

In fact, this technology is changing so fast that the only way to keep up with it is to frequently check for updates at the vendor's Web site. Compatibility with a new feature in a Web site may even require the use of beta software from the manufacturer of your browser.

The pace of this product release cycle has led to the term *Internet year*, generally accepted to be the length of time between new browser versions that originate from the same manufacturer, usually 60 to 90 days. For perspective, prior to the explosive growth of the Internet, a period of 12 to 18 months or more between new product releases was common.

The only way to move a product that quickly is to distribute it electronically, and the Web is a natural for that. Significant production time can be saved by avoiding delays inherent in the duplication of program disks and documentation when they can all be delivered electronically instead. This is probably the main reason computer software companies make up a large portion of Web sites: You just can't get updates to the end-user any faster.

The two most popular browsers for Windows clients are Netscape Navigator and Microsoft Internet Explorer. Windows NT and Windows 95 include Version 3 of the Internet Explorer. It can also be downloaded free of charge from Microsoft's Web site and numerous other places. It's also included on the Windows NT Server and Workstation CD's.

Today, the dominant player in the client browser market is Netscape Navigator. It too can be downloaded at no charge from a variety of Web sites, including Netscape's. But it's not really free. Unless you purchase a client license (approximately $50), you'll be forced to download a fresh copy every 30 days or so.

With the rapid changes in the technology, it is strongly recommended that you regularly check for updates to FrontPage and Internet Explorer for new feature support. Before implementing an update, consider whether or not use of the update will have an effect on client browsing capabilities.

In any Web construction project, the planning phase is critical to the overall success of the site. Items that have been overlooked have a tendency to become major bottlenecks in later phases and could seriously set back a deployment schedule.

At the outset of the planning phase for your Web site, ask yourself these questions:

1. What is the intended purpose of this Web site?

2. Who will use it?

3. Who will maintain it?

Rules of a Good Web Site

Below are six basic rules for good Web site design. These were compiled from complaints that *PC Week* collected over several months. In most cases, these complaints could have been avoided by more careful planning.

Outdated Data

By far the greatest number of complaints about a Web site have to do with lack of maintenance. One of the biggest strengths of Web publishing lies in its ability to deliver current information. Unfortunately, many authors are quick to get information into HTML format, but they neglect to update it when the information changes. Where possible, avoid the process of duplicating data before adding it to your Web page. Find ways to access the data directly, without having to create a second copy.

For example, to create a department phone list, I might start with the printed version on my desk, entering each name and extension. When a new list comes out, it will have to be closely scrutinized for changes and then those changes made to the HTML document on the Web.

A better process would be to directly link the Web page to the author's stored data file. Any changes saved in the file would be automatically reflected in the Web site. Although this may be more time consuming at first, the process you've established will ensure that the most current data is delivered. Rule Number 1: Update your content.

Gobs of Graphic Elements

Some Web authors have gone overboard with the graphical capabilities of Web publishing. Many of these Web authors are former graphic artists that have plunged into the leading edge of computer publishing, the World Wide Web. They create beautiful, artistic, and eye pleasing Web pages that have only one major flaw: When bandwidth is limited, these pages are painfully slow to load.

If you are planning an intranet that will only be accessed internally by using Ethernet-attached clients on a LAN, then the amount of graphical content in your Web site won't be much of a concern. In most cases, there is plenty of bandwidth for everybody.

In contrast, publishing graphically saturated Web pages on the Internet has an extremely adverse result when your connection bandwidth is limited by busy networks or a low capacity connection like an analog phone line. Rule Number 2: Be conservative with graphics.

Unlinks

I always laugh when I see a book that is advertised as a complete list of Web sites. Not possible. The Internet is always changing. New sites appear and others disappear all the time.

Creators of Web sites with Internet links should be careful when trying to operate it like a launching pad by displaying a list of other Web sites, often called "My Favorite Links." Keeping these links accurate requires constant attention.

Intranets can suffer a similar fate when links to documents are lost. This can be due to changes in a company's computing infrastructure. Many organizations move or alter network resources periodically, and these changes can have a ripple effect on your Web content. Rule Number 3: Keep links linked.

Offending Appearance

Your Web site's home page creates a first impression about your company and its services. Make it a good one by using common sense when laying out your Web pages. FrontPage's wizards and templates use basically sound graphical design elements that will help you achieve a satisfactory result. Though they have an ordinary look, the information displayed on a page is easily readable and doesn't strain the eye. This will help you avoid getting your site on one of the many Ugliest Web Site lists.

If necessary, hire a graphic artist to help design your home page. Use that page as the foundation for the look and "feel" of your other pages. Try to minimize the number of separate elements you use in a Web page to reduce the busy feeling that some pages have.

Remember, today's standard minimum graphic resolution is 640x480 pixels in 256 colors. Many users have systems that are set to 800x600 pixels, and graphics created on these systems will appear much larger when displayed on the 640x480 system. Rule Number 4: Make it look professional.

Useless Data Hiding Useful Data

I've seen Web sites that I know have important information on them, but locating what I'm looking for is sheer drudgery: point and click, point and click. Make sure you create links to content that will require a minimum amount of navigation between links. Put links to important data directly on your home page.

The Corporate Presence Wizard creates a What's New link and an associated page. Use this type of link to enable users to get right to the most recent information.

With FrontPage, a search engine can be set up that supports user queries across the entire content of your Web page. This can be another useful method of quickly locating information. Rule Number 5: Create multiple methods of accessing your content.

Give Me Bandwidth

A frequent cry heard from Webmasters and Web browsing clients is for faster delivery of data. Many Web development projects fail to prepare for growth. Several Web sites we've dealt with experience a higher volume of use than their developers had anticipated. The result is slow performance.

The biggest factor affecting performance is your link to the Internet via your Internet Service Provider (ISP). Other factors include the limitations of the hardware your Web server is running on. Fortunately, a Web server based on Windows NT can leverage the operating system's wonderful support for hardware scalability. Need more bandwidth? Add another link to the ISP or fatten the one you've got. Need more CPU cycles? Add another processor. Need more cache? Add more memory.

If one hardware platform can't meet your needs, upgrade to a newer system and copy your Web site to the new server using the FrontPage copy menu option. Rule Number 6: Proactively implement performance improvements.

■ Installing FrontPage

Microsoft FrontPage is included on the Windows NT Server CD. Because it's really a client application, the installation is performed separately from the installation of the server components.

Follow these steps to install FrontPage:

1. Insert the Windows NT Server CD into the client's CD-ROM drive.

2. Using the Windows Explorer, navigate to the FRONTPG\FRONTPG directory on the CD.

3. Double-click the Setup icon to start the installation wizard.

When installation is complete, you'll find a new Microsoft FrontPage task bar menu item containing the FrontPage Explorer, FrontPage Editor, FrontPage TCP/IP Test, Personal Web Server, and Server Administrator. You're now ready to create a Web site.

If you are planning to implement your Web site on IIS, you should also install the FrontPage Server Extensions for IIS. This must be done from the Windows NT Server that is running the IIS.

Follow these steps to install the server extensions for IIS:

1. Insert the Windows NT Server CD into the server's CD-ROM drive.

2. Using the Explorer, locate the directory \FRONTPG\ISEXT.

3. Double-click the Setup icon to start the Server Extensions installation wizard.

■ Using the Templates and Wizards

To keep Web site development at a non-technical level, the FrontPage Explorer includes several application-specific Web templates and wizards. Templates are static Web pages that contain a default set of elements. For example, the Personal Web Page template has predefined links for current projects and contact information (such as names, e-mail addresses, phone and fax numbers, and snail mail addresses).

Wizards offer another method of creating a new Web site that involves stepping through a decision tree of content topics, allowing you to select the topics which best meet your requirements. For example, in the Corporate

Presence Wizard, you can specify whether or not you want a link to press releases on your page.

The following templates and wizards are good tools to use to start constructing your Web site. Many elements will still need to be completed before a Web site created in this manner is ready for actual deployment. But with a little forethought, you should be able to complete these tasks in just a couple of hours.

FrontPage Web templates and wizards include:

- Normal Web—New Web template consisting of a single blank page.

- Corporate Presence Wizard—Contains all the basic elements for creating a business Web site. Have your company's mission statement and products and services lists handy.

- Customer Support Web—A small Web template with the main elements for dealing with product support and the distribution of product updates.

- Discussion Web Wizard—This wizard can be used for building a discussion forum where users can add their own content.

- Empty Web—A blank Web page, devoid of elements.

- Personal Web—This template is designed for client-level deployment in corporate intranets.

- Project Web—Use this template for project-specific Web content. It includes links to schedule, status, and discussion archive pages.

FrontPage Explorer is an excellent tool for defining the logic of a Web site. To drill down further into the elements of specific pages, you'll need to invoke the FrontPage Editor, a browser-like application for working with individual Web pages in your Web site.

During the creation process, you'll probably move frequently between the Explorer and the Editor, fill in content and add graphical elements, then move to another section of your Web site and repeat the process. Both the FrontPage Explorer and FrontPage Editor have toolbar icons for moving quickly between these two applications. In addition, double-clicking a Web page icon in Explorer will automatically invoke Editor in that page.

FrontPage Editor includes several page-oriented wizards and templates that help to make adding specific features to your Web site an easy, step-by-step process. Many of these sample pages are used when you create a new Web site using FrontPage Explorer. The following sample pages have been included with FrontPage Editor:

- Normal Page
- Biography

- Confirmation Form
- Directory of Press Releases
- Employee Directory
- Employment Opportunities
- Feedback Form
- Form Page Wizard
- Frames Wizard
- Frequently Asked Questions
- Glossary of Terms
- Guest Book
- Hyper Document Page
- Lecture Abstract
- Meeting Agenda
- Office Directory
- Personal Home Page Wizard
- Press Release
- Product Description
- Product or Event Registration
- Search Page
- Seminar Schedule
- Software Data Sheet
- Survey Form
- Table of Contents
- User Registration
- What's New

■ Images in FrontPage

Including images within your Web pages adds a great deal of visual appeal to your site. You can use images to display static data, such as a digitized photo of an employee or a historical sales performance chart. Many images act as graphical representations for links to other content. These types of images are saved within your Web site. A single element, such as your corporate logo, may be displayed on several pages in your site, but only one file is physically stored in the Web site's source directory.

Dynamic images may also be a required part of your Web site. These images are added to a Web page on the fly, only when a client browser requests the document from your Internet server. For example, Web sites that perform a traffic monitoring function are able to provide basically live images by pointing an image link to the URL of the device which does the image capture. These image files are not stored within a Web site, but require external connections to the places where the images are stored.

The following image formats can be imported into FrontPage Web pages.

Image File Type	Image File Extension
GIF	*.gif
JPEG	*.jpg
Windows and OS/2 BMP	*.bmp
TIFF	*.tif
Microsoft Paint	*.msp
Windows Metafile	*.wmf
SUN Raster	*.ras
WordPerfect	*.wpg
PostScript	*.eps
PCX	*.pcx
Targa	*.tga

Images that are imported are saved by FrontPage in either Graphical Interchange Format (GIF) or Joint Photographic Expert Group (JPEG) file formats within the Web site.

■ Using Bots

Bots are predefined mini-applications that perform a specific function in a Web page. The use of bots can save a Webmaster an immense amount of time by reducing the effort involved in adding capability to a Web page.

For example, FrontPage includes a search bot that can easily be dropped onto a page that will display a text entry field with buttons for initiating and resetting the search. A fairly complex search application runs behind the scenes to display the search results when the Start Search button is clicked. Without this bot, a specific application would have to be written by a programmer to perform a similar function.

The following bots are included in FrontPage:

- Annotation

- Confirmation Field

- HTML Markup

- Include

- Scheduled Image

- Scheduled Include

- Search

- Substitution

- Table of Contents

- Time Stamp

Settings for each bot are handled by a properties page. In the above example, the search bot's properties page contains the parameters for controlling various aspects of the search process and displaying the search results.

Gathering user-entered data through your Web site is a valuable method of collecting information from your site's visitors. FrontPage includes a powerful Forms Page Wizard that uses bots to automate much of the process of creating a data entry form page. It also incorporates methods for storing the collected data in either HTML or text formats for later analysis.

■ Putting It All Together

The best way to build a new Web site using the Windows NT Server is to use the FrontPage Explorer to create the basic structure, and then use the FrontPage Editor to modify each page, adding content, images, and bots where appropriate. We recommend using FrontPage's Personal Web Server to test and debug your Web site during the development process. Once your site is completed, you should move it to IIS for actual deployment.

Before beginning construction on your Web site, make sure that the images and content you plan to incorporate into your Web pages are readily accessible. It can be frustrating to find out that the image you plan to use doesn't exist or is stored in the wrong format.

To Build a New Web Site:

1. Start FrontPage Explorer. The screen will appear as shown in Figure 34.1.

Figure 34.1

Use the FrontPage Explorer to define the type of Web site you want to create.

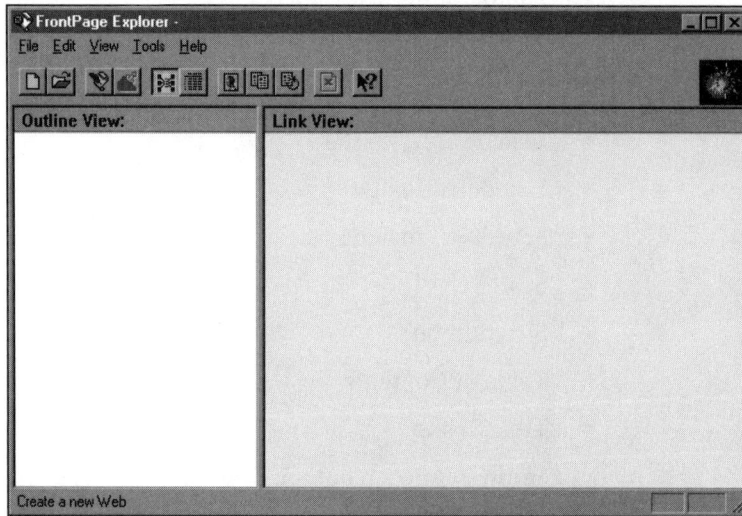

2. Select File/New. The New Web window will be displayed containing the list of templates and wizards that can help in creating a basic Web site, as shown in Figure 34.2.

Figure 34.2

A number of templates and wizards included with FrontPage simplify the Web construction process.

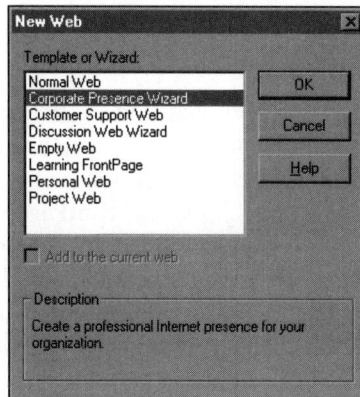

3. Select a template or wizard that will best fulfill the functions you have in mind for your Web site.

4. Click OK.

5. Select the Web Server you want to create the new Web on and specify the name for the new Web. Figure 34.3 shows the Web Server specification screen.

Figure 34.3

The Web name is used only for creating and modifying your Web site, not for browser access.

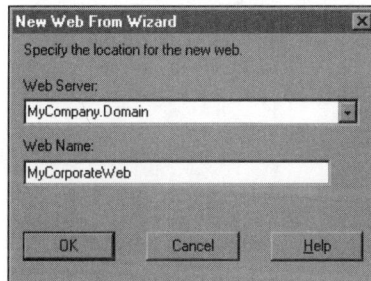

6. Click OK.

7. Enter the name and password for the Web server (see Figure 34.4). These values are case-sensitive.

Figure 34.4

The Name and Password screen.

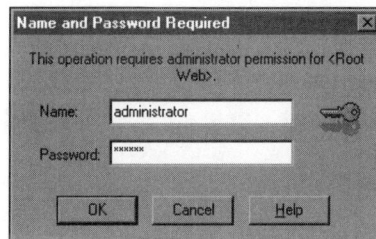

FrontPage will now attempt to create the directory structure and initial files for your new Web. This may take a couple of minutes. If you selected one of the new Web wizards, you'll be asked to make several choices that pertain to the organization of the Web and its general content.

When this process is complete, the Outline View frame will display the main elements of your Web page. At the top of the Outline View is an icon of a small house that represents your home page. Along with the icon, the Web name you previously defined will be displayed, followed by the words *Home Page*. Figure 34.5 shows the outline view of a home page along with the elements that are called from that page.

Figure 34.5

The FrontPage Explorer displays two views of a single HTML document and its components.

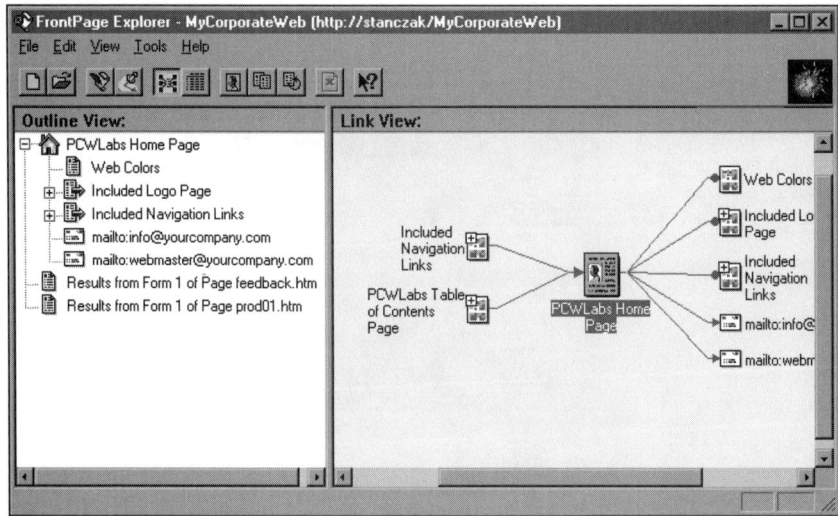

Using the Windows outline conventions, click the "+" icon to the left of the Web site's home page. This will expand the outline and display the various elements that are part of your new home page. These include color settings, image links, and other navigational links.

To the right of the Outline View frame is the Link View frame. If your Home Page is selected in the Outline View, the Link View will display a diagram of the structure of your Home Page with arrows indicating links between each element. This view of your Web site makes it much easier to understand how links and content are connected and what resources are used.

As you navigate through Link View you'll find all the elements of your Web site that are listed in the Outline View. Each element can be highlighted with a single mouse click. Once selected, use the right mouse button to display a quick menu. Choose the Properties menu option to display the settings for that particular element.

To modify a Web page, simply double-click its representation in the Link View. For example, double-click on the Home Page icon in your new Web site. This will invoke the FrontPage Editor and load the Home Page file. From here you can modify the sample text, add images, and specify URL links to content materials. Figure 34.6 shows a freshly created Corporate Presence home page.

Figure 34.6

Just fill in the text and graphic elements that are unique to your company and your Web site is nearly complete.

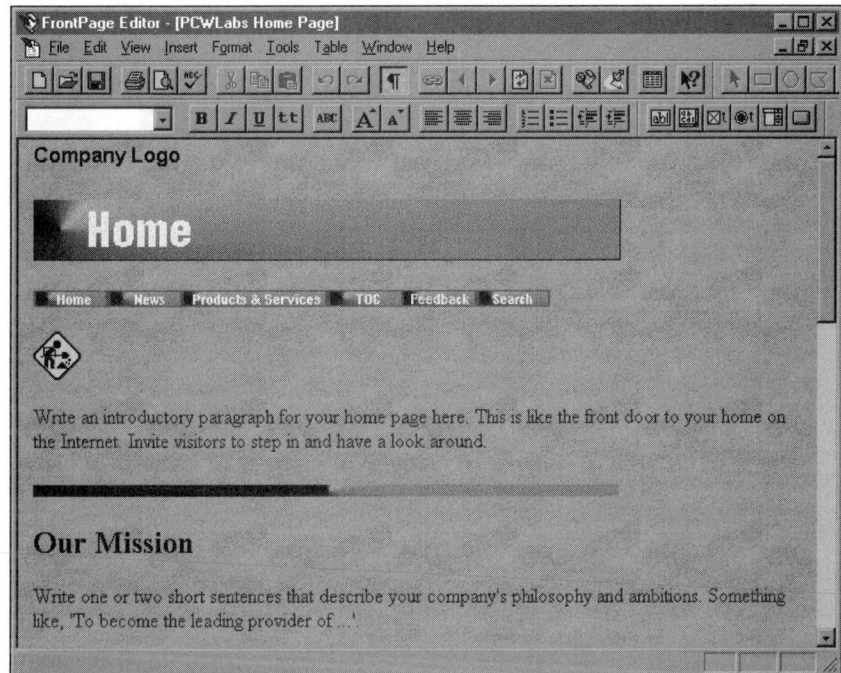

FrontPage Explorer also includes a Summary View to quickly locate source files and documents in large Web sites. This view lists the contents of a particular site, file by file. Clicking on a column title such as File Name will quickly reorder the list alphabetically based on your selection. Figure 34.7 shows the Summary View of a sample Web site.

FrontPage's To Do List can be a real help for keeping track of the tasks involved in completing a new Web site. The To Do list can be opened from the Explorer's Tools menu option. If you've created your Web site with a wizard such as the Corporate Presence Wizard, many tasks will automatically be entered in the To Do List. Figure 34.8 shows the To Do List for a newly created Web site.

To jump quickly into completing a task, highlight a task displayed in the To Do List and click the Do Task button.

Figure 34.7

The Summary View in the FrontPage Explorer gives a detailed listing of all source files used in a Web site.

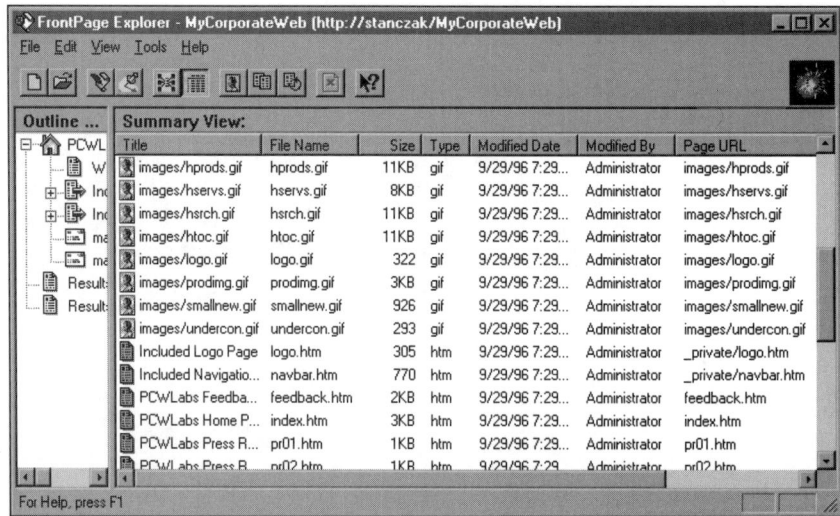

Figure 34.8

A To Do List is automatically generated when you use a wizard to create your Web site. Use this feature to plan and prioritize modifications.

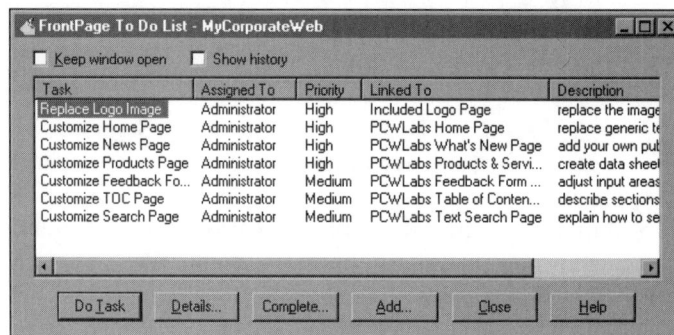

- *Service Properties*
- *Directories Properties*
- *Logging Properties*
- *Advanced Properties*

35

Managing Your Web Site

T HE IIS IS MANAGED USING A UTILITY CALLED THE INTERNET SERVICE
Manager (ISM). It's used for controlling the behavior of your IIS,
including access permissions, service logs, and directory locations
for your Web files. This application is added to the task bar menu
next to the Administrative Tools menu during the installation of
IIS. It's one of the few management applications for Windows NT
Server that has its own submenu, called the Microsoft Internet
Server. Figure 35.1 shows the task bar access tree to the ISM.
Most of the tasks performed using this utility don't require the
server to be rebooted, and the new settings become effective
immediately.

Figure 35.1

The Internet Service Manager comes in two flavors: a Windows-based application and one that supports HTML access.

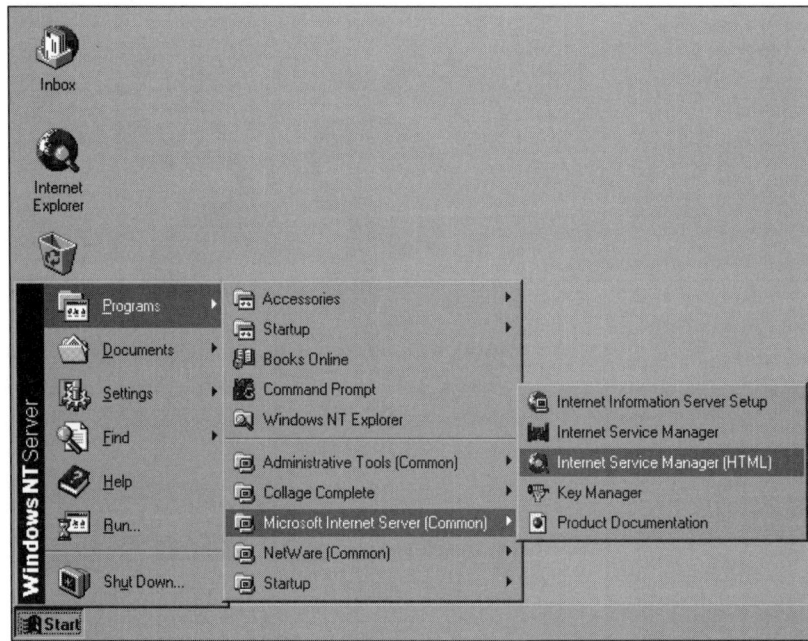

Within the Microsoft Internet Server menu are two versions of the ISM: one is a Windows-based application, the other is an HTML version of the application. The ISM displays all known IIS servers that are broadcasting on your network. For each IIS server, the current state of each of the three Windows NT Server Internet services—World Wide Web, Gopher, and FTP—is displayed. The screen in Figure 35.2 shows the current status of each service.

Under normal operating conditions, the state of each service is listed as "running." Unfortunately, that's the extent of the real-time status provided by this utility.

At this top-most level, you can stop, start, or pause services individually using icons located on the tool bar or via menu options. Stop drops all users from the halted service immediately, while Pause only disables the IIS response to client requests. These functions might be invoked when you upgrade your Web site or to help in diagnosing a problem. To restart a service, simply click the Start icon or select Start from the ISM menu. Make sure you have the appropriate service highlighted before stopping, starting, or pausing it.

Figure 35.2

The status of each
Internet service is clearly
displayed when you start
up the Internet
Service Manager.

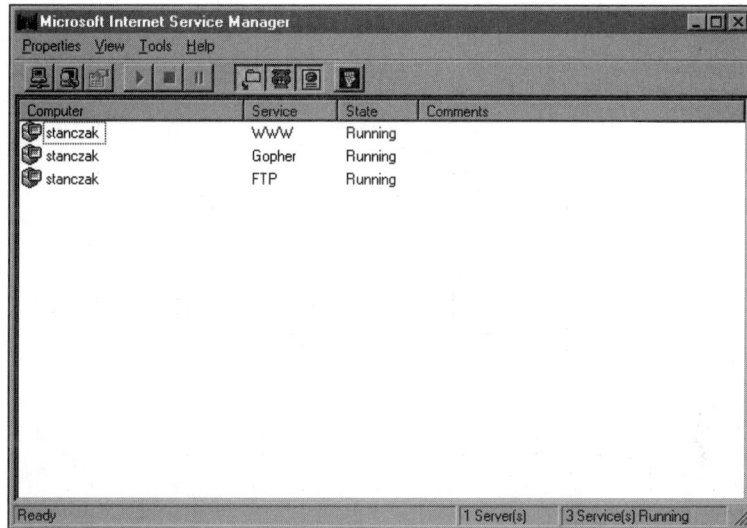

The real meat of the ISM is accessed when you highlight a service and select the Properties menu. (An icon in the tool bar is also available for this option.) As shown in Figure 35.3, there are four tabs accessible from the Properties window: Service, Directories, Logging, and Advanced. The FTP and Gopher services have separate, though similar, property tabs.

■ Service Properties

At the top of the Services tab is the TCP/IP port setting. This value is used to control the port on which the particular service will be run. For the WWW service, the default port is 80. You can change this value, though doing so may affect the ease at which clients access this service. When you change a port value, you must reboot the server for the change to take effect. Changing the port value can also make it more difficult for others to hack into your Internet server.

Among the other settings available on the Services tab are parameters for controlling Connection Timeout and the maximum number of connections supported by this service. Depending on your experiences running your Internet services on a given hardware platform with a limited amount of network bandwidth to support client access, you may choose to restrict the total number of clients accessing your server at one time. This can be used to provide a default level of responsiveness by limiting the number of simultaneous users on a given service. There are no hard and fast rules to achieve this,

Figure 35.3

Each service has its own
Properties window. Here,
you can change the
default TCP/IP port that
the WWW service is
accessed through.

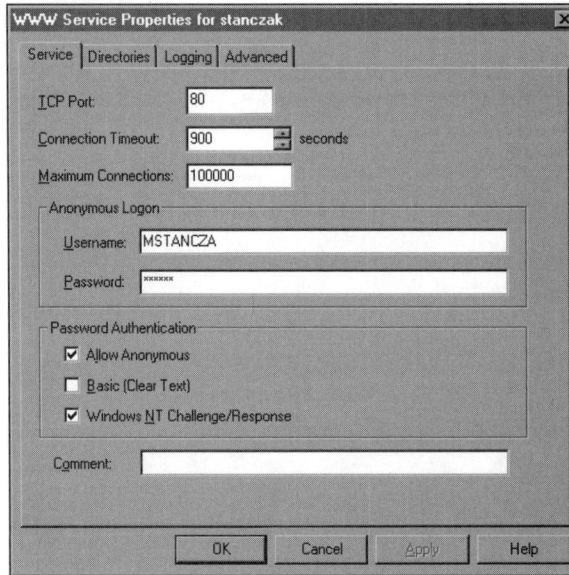

though, and only experience and tinkering will give you the information you
need to determine the proper setting for your environment and use pattern.

When IIS is installed, an anonymous logon account with a random password is added to the Windows NT Domain. The default value is
IUSR_*computername*. This password is only used within Windows NT. It's
important to note that if you change this password in the User Manager for
Domains, it must also be changed in the ISM.

Password Authentication allows you to set the authentication process to
use. If you've disabled the anonymous access method, the Basic (Clear Text)
authentication method is designed for use with Secure Sockets Layer (SSL).
Working with SSL, the Basic authentication method encrypts user names
and passwords prior to their transmission. If SSL is not used, both the user
name and password are transmitted in clear text.

Another authentication option is Windows NT Challenge/Response. To
take advantage of this level of security, the client must use the Microsoft
Internet Explorer browser.

The final option in the tab allows you to enter a comment that's displayed at the top level of the ISM.

■ Directories Properties

The Directories properties sheet is generally used for controlling the directory path for the files used by the selected service. For each directory listed, the alias IP address and any error conditions associated with the directory are displayed. Figure 35.4 shows this tab.

Figure 35.4

The Directories tab allows you to add new data sources and set the default document to deliver to a client browser.

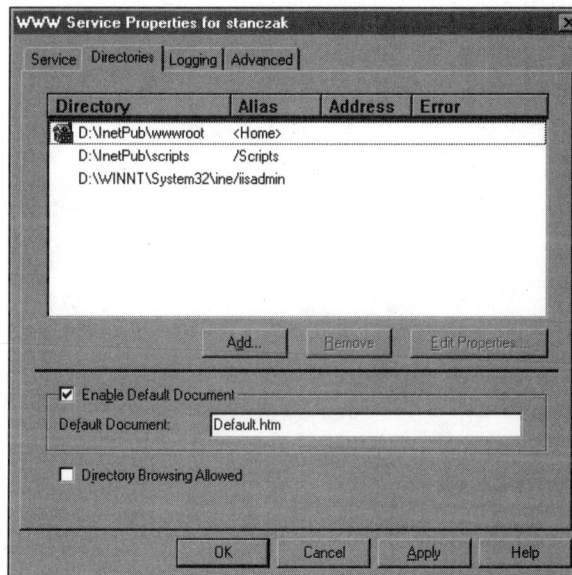

You can control the default document name here. The default value is default.htm. This is the file that will be automatically displayed to a client browser when they enter the URL of your Web site. Usually a Web site's home page has been renamed to match this value.

■ Logging Properties

IIS supports a number of logging options that offer a worthy method of evaluating the usefulness of your Web site and its level of activity. Use the Logging tab to specify how you want the service's activities tracked. In Figure 35.5, we show a configuration set up to create a new log file on a daily basis.

An important number to track is a log's size and how fast it's increasing. Left unmanaged, log files can unnecessarily consume more than their fair share of disk space. The Logging tab allows you to determine how often a log is archived. Depending on the level of activity of your IIS, you can specify

Figure 35.5

Log files can be kept locally or placed in an ODBC compliant database. New log files can be created at any of several intervals.

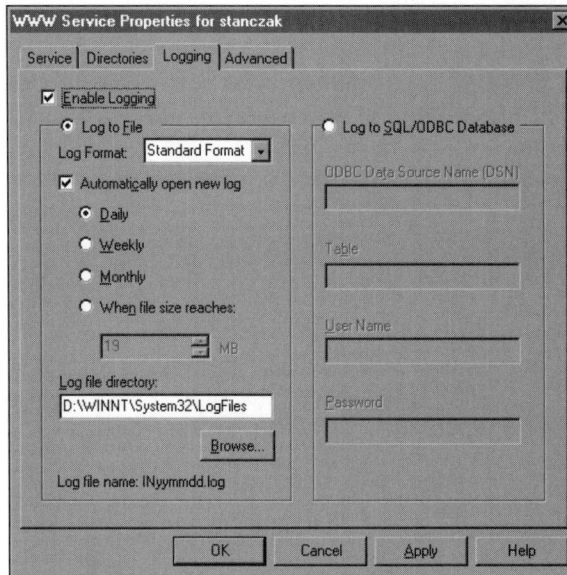

regular archives on a daily, weekly, or monthly basis. You can also set the archive interval for the log file based on its size in kilobytes. The default directory for log files is \WINNT\System32\logfiles.

Service activity can alternatively be set to store data in a Structured Query Language (SQL) database using the ODBC drivers that are part of the Windows NT Server default installation. Doing so requires that you enter the ODBC source name and table name, plus a qualified user name and password.

■ Advanced Properties

The Advanced tab provides a method of restricting user access based on IP address and subnet mask. You have the option of creating a list of users to whom you either grant or deny access. To grant access to all users, select Denied Access and leave the user list blank. You then have the option of adding users of questionable merit to the list on an individual basis. This option also works conversely. Refer to Figure 35.6 to see this feature.

You can use the Maximum network use option to tune the perceived performance of your system, almost guaranteeing a minimum level of service to clients. Enabling this option allows you to specify limits on the maximum network bandwidth for outgoing network traffic. This parameter requires some investigation into usage patterns and server hardware performance bottlenecks.

Figure 35.6

The Advanced tab allows you to grant and deny access to the service based on a client's physical IP address.

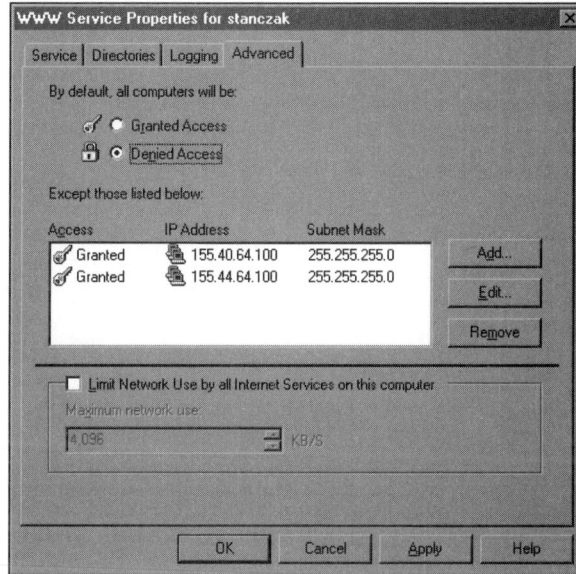

NOTE. *In general terms, at a hardware level the bandwidth of your WAN link will likely be the first factor limiting performance of your IIS server. After opening up that pipe, Windows NT Server seems to always have an appetite for more RAM and an additional CPU or two. But it's important to look closely at any potential bottlenecks in the whole system, inside and out.*

- *Overview of DHCP*
- *Overview of DNS*
- *Overview of WINS*

36

Configuring DHCP, DNS, and WINS

THIS CHAPTER EXPLAINS HOW TO INSTALL AND CONFIGURE WINDOWS NT Server to allocate IP addresses and resolve UNC names using the services provided with the operating system. For a thorough explanation of the networking theory and detail of the inner workings of these services, consult the Microsoft Windows NT Server 4 Networking Supplement and the Microsoft Windows NT Resource Kit Networking Guide.

NOTE. *Depending on the complexity and sophistication of your present networking environment, there's likely to be a vast number of issues you should consider before enabling and configuring DHCP, DNS, or WINS functions. Each of these services has been designed to fit well into mixed environments. Through experience, you'll find various ways to optimize each service to work best in your network.*

The DNS, WINS, and DHCP functions are provided via a set of services that can be optionally loaded on any existing NT server. These three are the services Windows NT Server uses to resolve IP addressing and host naming issues. They've been intelligently designed by Microsoft to communicate with one another, offering a complete solution.

Because of the importance of these services, TCP/IP clients, such as Windows 95, also support the assignment of backup servers to provide similar functionality should the primary service provider fail. We strongly recommend that you implement backup server assignments where possible.

When combined within a LAN environment and properly implemented, these services enable clients to freely access local intranet and external Internet resources using friendly names without being concerned with IP addressing issues. Unfortunately, a significant amount of time can be spent configuring and reconfiguring these services until you get the right fit. Unfortunately, in many cases the configuration changes you make will require a server reboot for the new changes to take effect.

■ Overview of DHCP

Because of the complexity in controlling individual client IP addresses, a number of methods have been devised for divvying them up on an as-needed basis. These solutions generally offer a centralized point of control over address ranges and can make a positive impact in reducing overall LAN administration in a TCP/IP environment. The only limitation to DHCP is that forcing the allocation of a fixed client IP address can be difficult.

Depending on the environment into which you're installing Windows NT Server, you may already have a host system supplying IP addresses. In completely private intranets or other controlled environments, however, Windows NT can act as the central IP address provider using the DHCP service. This is the recommended method for controlling client IP addressing in an intranet.

The Microsoft DHCP server is a service brought over from the fully service-packed NT Server 3.51. When the DHCP service is loaded, Windows NT processes client IP lease requests, using a static pool of addresses you provide. When a client releases an address by shutting down, for instance, the address can then be made available for other requesting clients. This address pool is highly configurable, allowing for specific address range inclusions and exclusions. Refer to Figure 36.1 for a diagram of how DHCP allocates IP addresses.

Figure 36.1

Use DHCP to alleviate IP address maintenance at the client level.

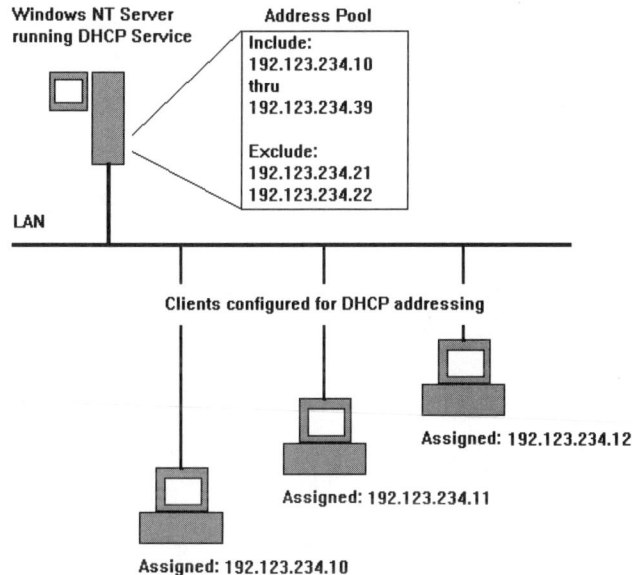

You can define allowances for clients that require a fixed address for application-specific dependencies. This provision uses addresses that are tied to the unique Ethernet number (or MAC address) of each client's network adapter (assuming you're using Ethernet). Applications that require fixed client IP addresses tend to quickly become an administrative nightmare as new clients are added into the network scheme.

One of the biggest advantages of DHCP is that new clients can simply be plugged into the network and configured to obtain an IP address from the DHCP server. A bare minimum of tinkering with a client's network settings is required to make it fully functional.

Installation of DHCP

The DHCP Server is installed from the Network Control Panel Services tab. Open the Network Control Panel and select the Services tab. Click Add to bring up the Select Network Service window and display a list of supported services. Scroll down and select the Microsoft DHCP Server, as shown in

Figure 36.2. Click OK to start the installation wizard. When the installation is complete, you must click OK to accept all changes and reboot for the changes to take effect.

Figure 36.2

The Microsoft DHCP Server included with Windows NT Server is easily added through the Network Control Panel.

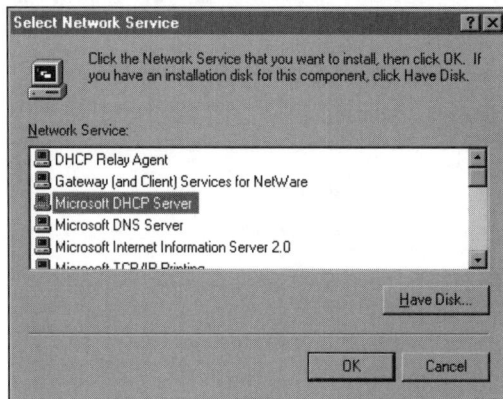

After reboot, the Microsoft DHCP Server will be listed among the installed services under the Network Control Panel's Services Properties window. Additionally, you'll find a new application, the DHCP Manager, in the Administration Tools.

NOTE. *If you had previously configured your system for use with a DHCP server, you'll be required to change the setting by specifying a fixed IP address. Refer to Figure 36.3 for an example of the TCP/IP Properties window.*

Configuration of DHCP

The configuration and management of the DHCP service is controlled by the DHCP Manager. During installation this utility is added to the Administrative Tools task bar menu as shown in Figure 36.4.

The modifications made in the DHCP Manager are immediately effective and don't require a server reboot. When you start DHCP Manager for the first time, the local computer is displayed in the DHCP Manager window. Figure 36.5 shows a single DHCP server and the address range it controls. If other DHCP servers exist on your network, they along with their scopes will also be displayed.

To begin providing DHCP services, you'll need to create one or more DHCP scopes. A DHCP scope is a group of client computers that obtain their IP address using the DHCP client service. Scopes should be created for each subnet on your network. You can have only one scope for each subnet.

Figure 36.3

The IP address of the server providing the DHCP functions must be hard coded and not set by another DHCP server.

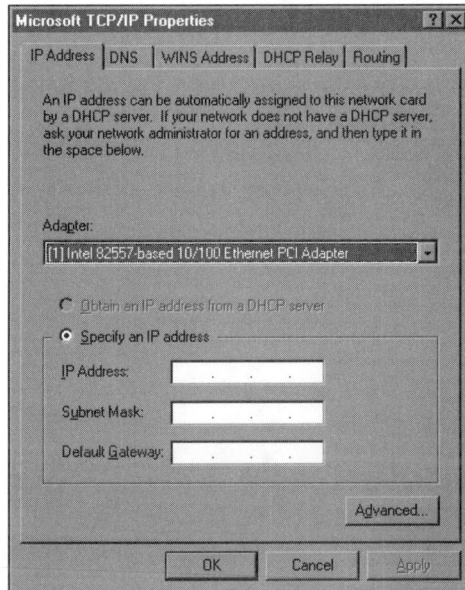

Figure 36.4

Use the DHCP Manager to define the pool of IP addresses that can be allocated to clients and other servers.

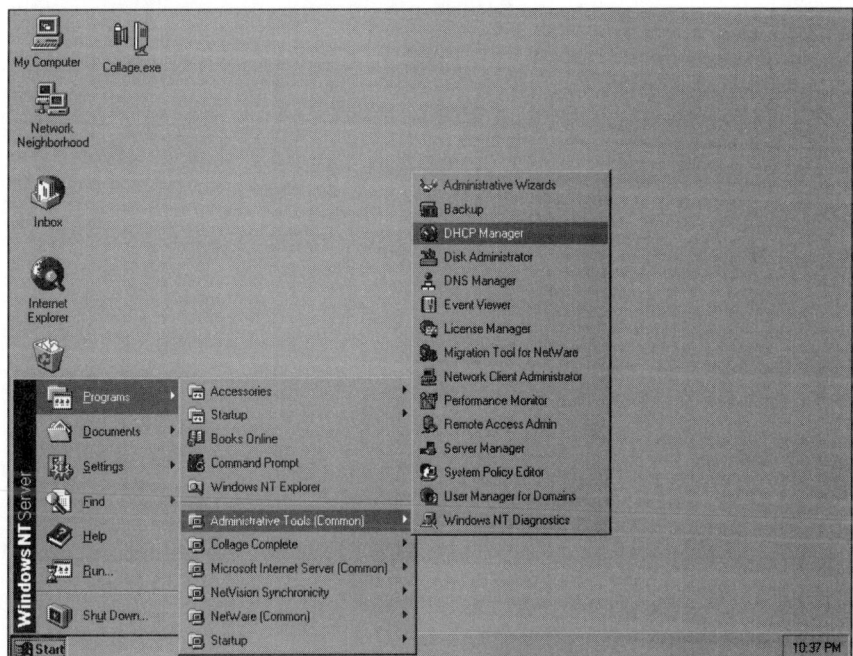

The "Local Machine"
displayed here is the
Windows NT Server
running the DHCP
service. A single scope
has already been defined.

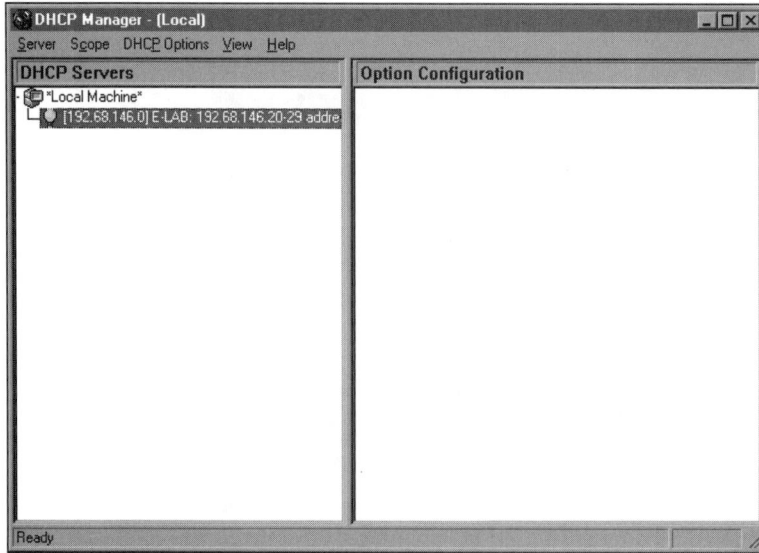

To create a DHCP scope, using the DHCP Manager, select the server for
which you want to create a scope. From the Scope menu, select Create. This
will display the Create Scope window shown in Figure 36.6.

Figure 36.6

Scopes are used to
create each pool of IP
addresses and the
restrictions that govern
their use.

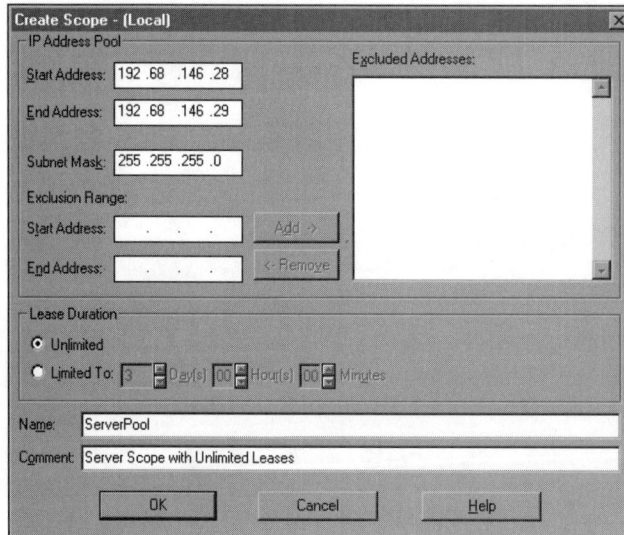

Enter the Start Address and End Address ranges for this scope. A default subnet mask will be created. In most cases, this subnet mask should be used. Enter any excluded address ranges that fall within the starting and ending address ranges you've defined. Click on Add to place these ranges into the Excluded Address list box. Individual IP address exclusions can be added only by completing the Start Address value and clicking Add.

Now specify the lease duration for IP address in the new scope by activating either Unlimited or Limited To. Leases within a scope can be limited to days, hours, or minutes. Finally, specify the name of the new scope. This name should describe the subnet or uniqueness about the address range. You have the option to enter a comment for giving a more detailed description of the new scope. Click OK to add the new scope.

A message, shown in Figure 36.7, will be displayed indicating that the new scope has not been activated. Select Yes to activate the new scope or No to hold off until you complete the DHCP Options section of your configuration. Clients won't be able to access the address ranges in the scope until it's activated. To activate a scope, highlight it and select Activate from the Scope menu.

Figure 36.7

Newly created scopes must be activated before they can be implemented. Make sure the addresses in a scope are not in use before you activate it.

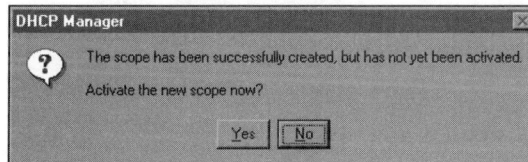

In addition to the IP address allocation settings, other DHCP parameters that are passed to DHCP clients should be configured for each scope. These settings, called the DHCP Options, can be set to apply globally to all scopes managed by the server, to a single scope, or on an individual client basis. For a detailed description of the use and implementation of these options, refer to the Networking Guide in the Microsoft Windows NT Resource Kit.

To configure client leases, from the DHCP Manager highlight the scope that contains the clients you want to configure. Select Active Leases from the Scope menu to display the Active Leases window shown in Figure 36.8. Active DHCP clients will be displayed by current IP address and Windows name. In larger environments, you can choose to sort this list by the name as opposed to the IP address.

Highlight the client you want to modify and select Properties. This will display the Client Properties window shown in Figure 36.9. To assign a fixed IP address to this client, enter the client's hardware media access control (MAC) address in the Unique Identifier field. You can optionally specify a client name and comment. Click OK to accept these settings.

Figure 36.8

The Active Leases window gives a good overview of which IP addresses are in use within the scope.

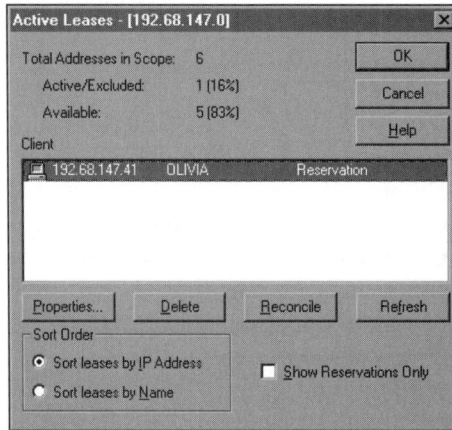

Figure 36.9

To force the allocation of an IP address to a specific client (or server), you need to know the MAC address of the network adapter in the client.

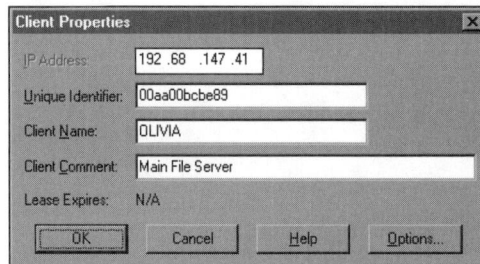

Configuring Client Reservations

Based on the larger configuration of your network, you may need to reserve a specific IP address for certain clients. This is typically done where other devices are present that also assign IP addresses.

To configure client reservations, using the DHCP Manager, select Add Reservation from the Scope menu. This will display the Add Reserved Client window, shown in Figure 36.10. Enter the IP address from the reserved address pool. Obtain and enter the MAC address for the client's network adapter in the Unique Identifier field. You can optionally enter values for the client name and comment fields. Click Add to complete the definition of the new reservation and add the entry to the DHCP data file. Finally, restart each client you've defined a reservation for. This will free up the older address and process a lease renewal request.

Figure 36.10

IP addresses within a
scope can be reserved
for specific clients. These
are tied to each client's
MAC address, a value
that's unique for all
network adapters.

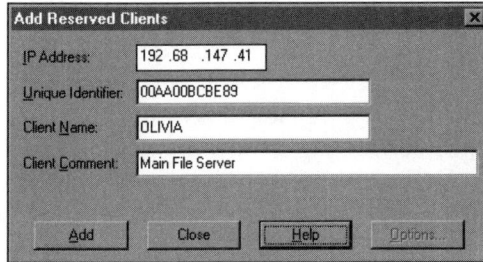

Add Reserved Clients	☒

IP Address: 192 .68 .147 .41

Unique Identifier: 00AA00BCBE89

Client Name: OLIVIA

Client Comment: Main File Server

| Add | Close | Help | Options... |

■ Overview of DNS

The Microsoft DNS Server, also a new feature of NT Server 4, is an application that maintains the table of standard IP addresses and their related fully qualified domain names (FQDN). Figure 36.11 is a diagram of how the DNS table links IP addresses to the FQDN. In a nutshell, it interprets conventional Web addresses like www.pcweek.com and translates them into IP addresses such as 192.244.116. In doing so, it communicates with other DNS servers and responds to client browser queries.

Figure 36.11

The Microsoft DNS
Server resolves friendly
names into IP addresses
by querying a static table.

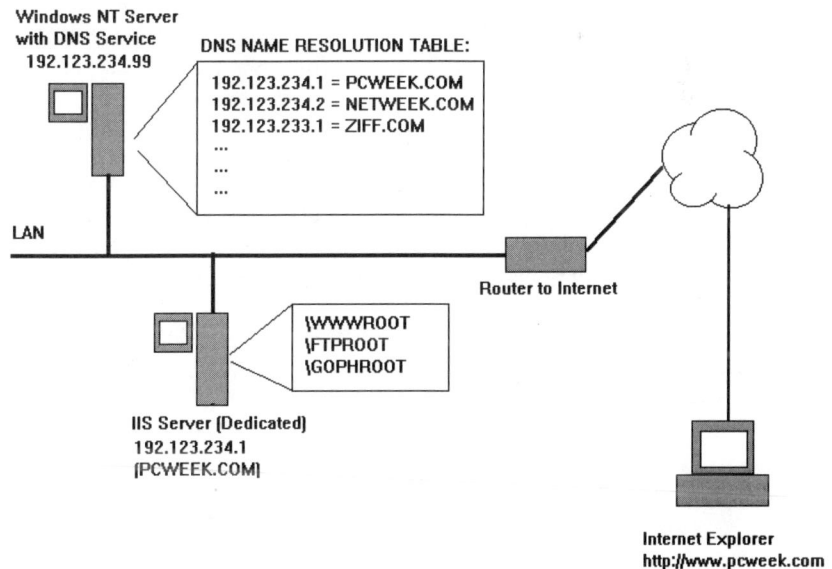

**Windows NT Server
with DNS Service
192.123.234.99**

DNS NAME RESOLUTION TABLE:

192.123.234.1 = PCWEEK.COM
192.123.234.2 = NETWEEK.COM
192.123.233.1 = ZIFF.COM
...
...
...

LAN

Router to Internet

\WWWROOT
\FTPROOT
\GOPHROOT

**IIS Server (Dedicated)
192.123.234.1
[PCWEEK.COM]**

**Internet Explorer
http://www.pcweek.com**

Because of the importance of this function, larger sites may have more than one server providing DNS functions, each communicating with the other for information concerning the contents of its DNS database. Breaking up your DNS into zones like this can resolve issues that become evident in wide-area connectivity where synchronizing the changes to your DNS can be hampered by slow or unreliable links.

Within the networking configuration properties for each client, the specific address of your primary DNS server must be specified. Fortunately, the networking portion of client operating systems like Windows 95 support more than one entry for the DNS server, adding a level of redundancy for protection in case one should go out of service.

If you've already set up your NT server to obtain an IP address via DHCP or WINS, you'll need to alter the configuration by hard coding the server's IP address before completing the installation of DHCP or WINS.

The DNS domain name is often designated as a company or organization name with a period that denotes the type of organization. For example in the FQDN named PCWEEK.NETWEEK.COM, the company name is PCWEEK and the domain name is NETWEEK.COM. This can be expanded to create a hierarchical structure of departments and workgroups within an organization. For example, MyCompany with one of many regional centers in Seattle could refer to the inside sales group in that location as mycompany.seattle.sales.inside.

NOTE. *The DNS domain name isn't the same as the Windows NT domain name. TCP/IP domains can be assigned by other systems on the LAN or by an ISP, whereas the Windows NT domain name is server-centric, easily changed by the server administrator.*

Client and server queries to the DNS can be excessive and overly tax the capacity of your network, so we advise implementing secondary name servers. These should be located intelligently, perhaps on both sides of a router or WAN. This has the added benefits of load balancing and fault tolerance in addition to the reduction of network traffic.

NOTE. *Microsoft's DNS Server automatically builds a cache for speeding up recursive client requests. As new domain addresses and names are resolved, the cache becomes a repository for the most common requests. At this point, frequent queries are satisfied from cache, improving the performance of the name service.*

Installation of DNS

To install the DNS Server, open the Network Control Panel and select the Services tab. Click Add to display the window shown in Figure 36.12 and a list of supported services. Select the Microsoft DNS Server. Click OK to start the installation wizard. When the wizard is done, select OK to reboot the server and put changes into effect.

Figure 36.12

The Microsoft DNS Server, included with Windows NT Server, can be easily installed from the Network Control Panel.

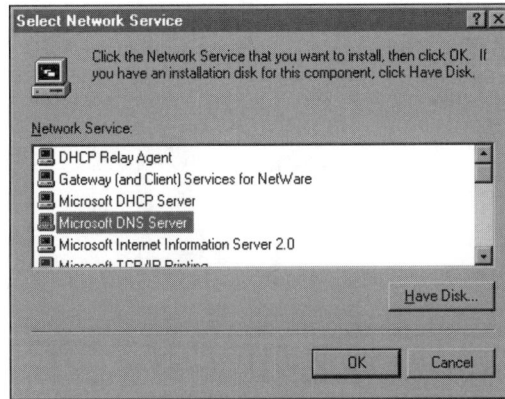

When the installation and post-installation reboots are complete, the Microsoft DNS Server will be listed among the installed services under the Network Control Panel's Services tab, as shown in Figure 36.13. Additionally, you'll find a new management utility, the DNS Manager, under the Administration Tools task bar menu, shown in Figure 36.14.

Configuration of the DNS Server

The configuration and management of the DNS Server is controlled by an administrative tool called the DNS Manager. During installation this utility is automatically added within the Administrative Tools task bar menu. You can use it to manage the local DNS database or remote DNS Server databases.

Once installed, modifications made in the DNS Manager are immediately effective and don't require a server reboot or the service to be reloaded. To manage your server's DNS table, within the Administrative Tools task bar menu, click on the DNS Manager. This will load the Domain Name Service Manager utility, as seen in Figure 36.15.

Initially, the DNS table is empty. Under the DNS menu, select New Server. This will display the dialog box shown in Figure 36.16. To register a new DNS server in the DNS table, enter its Windows name, or its IP address. Click OK to add the new server to the DNS table.

Figure 36.13

When installed, the
Microsoft DNS Server will
be listed among the other
services you've set up.

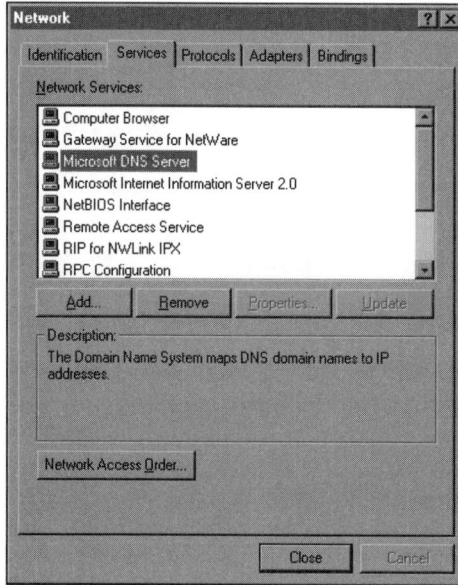

Figure 36.14

Use the DNS Manager to
define and maintain the
local DNS table.

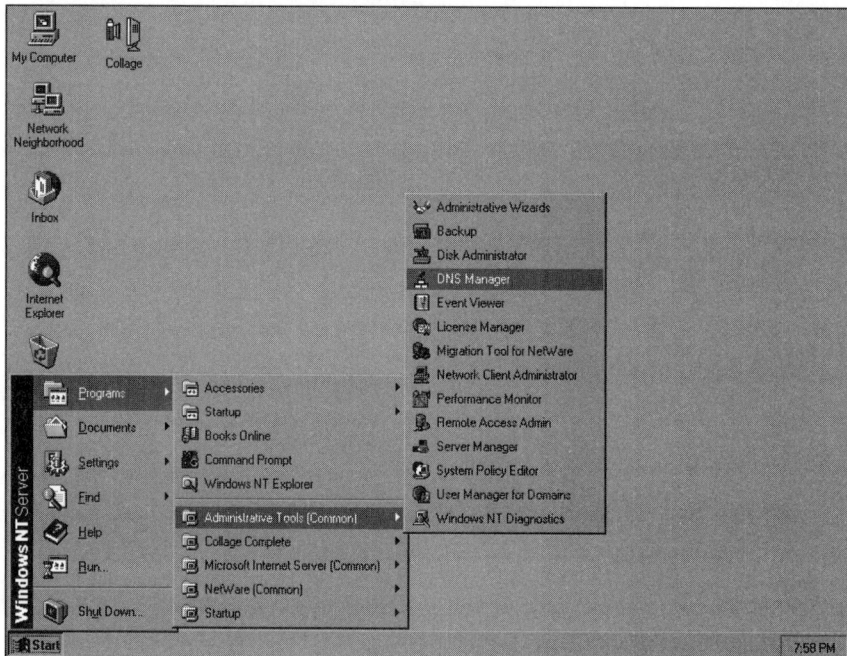

Figure 36.15

When the DNS Server is
installed, the DNS table
is empty. You assign the
relationship between an
IP address and
host name.

Figure 36.16

A DNS Server is added to
the table by entering
either the IP address or
the NetBIOS name of
the server.

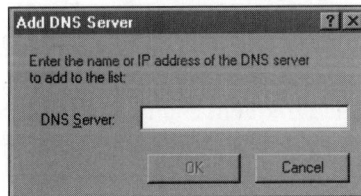

NOTE. *Although the DNS Manager will allow you to create duplicate entries of the same server—one using the NT name and another with the IP address—it's a good idea to be consistent when entering this value. The Windows NT name may appear to be the more intuitive choice, but in many environments, the physical IP address may be required.*

For the creation of DNS zones, Windows NT Server uses a small wizard that is invoked from the DNS Manager menu. To create a new DNS zone: Highlight the server you want the new zone created for. Under the DNS menu option, select New Zone. This will start the new zone wizard shown in Figure 36.17. Using this wizard, you can create a primary or secondary zone by entering a zone name and server, or you can drag the hand icon to a previously defined zone and the value will be automatically filled in.

Figure 36.17

For administrative purposes, the DNS table can be subdivided into primary and secondary zones.

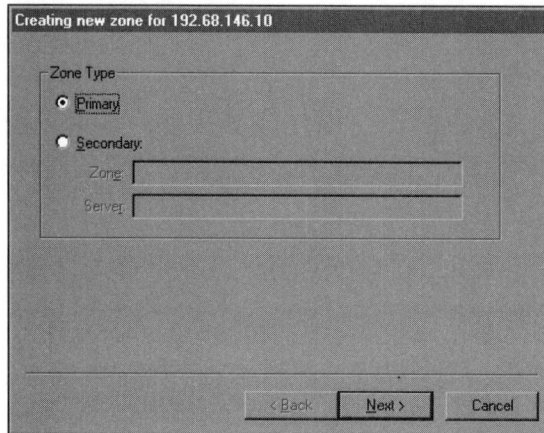

NOTE. *A secondary zone is a read-only copy of the primary zone and therefore cannot be modified except by changes in the primary zone.*

■ Overview of WINS

WINS was designed to solve one major limitation of DNS: its dependency on fixed IP addresses when they're obtained via DHCP. This is especially true for LANs that experience frequent changes in the DNS host table, which ends up requiring manual reconfiguration because DNS uses a static table for name resolution. Figure 36.18 shows a diagram of the interaction between DNS and WINS. We strongly recommend that when you enable the Microsoft DNS Server, you also enable WINS. Working together, these two services can make client access to your server a smooth process.

DNS resolves host names, such as pcweek.netweek.com, and WINS resolves computer (NetBIOS) names such as \\myserver. Using a feature called dynamic addressing, when a host requests a new address using DHCP, it automatically registers the address at the WINS server.

In Windows NT Server, WINS works closely with DHCP and is automatically installed and enabled when DHCP is configured with WINS server information.

Installation of WINS

You'll need administrative privileges to the server you'll be installing WINS on. Open the Network Control Panel and select the Services tab. Click the Add button to display a list of supported services. Scroll down toward the

Figure 36.18

WINS is a dynamic table of NetBIOS names and IP addresses that interacts with DNS.

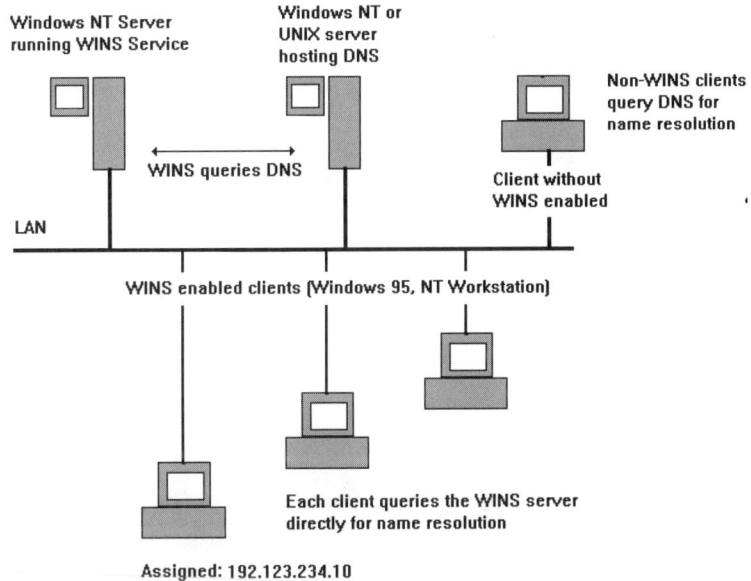

Windows NT Server running WINS Service

Windows NT or UNIX server hosting DNS

Non-WINS clients query DNS for name resolution

WINS queries DNS

Client without WINS enabled

LAN

WINS enabled clients (Windows 95, NT Workstation)

Each client queries the WINS server directly for name resolution

Assigned: 192.123.234.10

end of the list and select the Windows Internet Name Service, as shown in Figure 36.19. Click OK to start the installation wizard. During the installation process, the wizard may determine that your TCP/IP configuration requires modification. If so, the Network Control Panel's TCP/IP properties window will be displayed for you to make adjustments.

Figure 36.19

Like many other network services, WINS is included with Windows NT Server and is installed using the Network Control Panel.

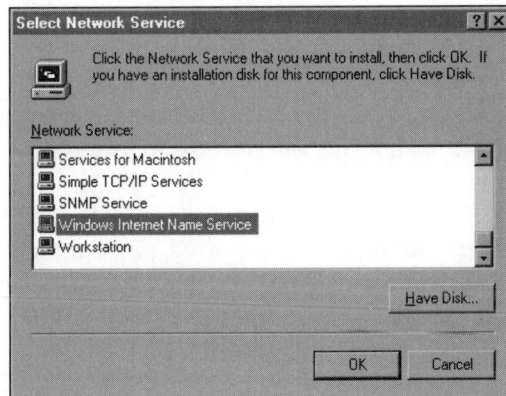

Select Network Service

Click the Network Service that you want to install, then click OK. If you have an installation disk for this component, click Have Disk.

Network Service:
- Services for Macintosh
- Simple TCP/IP Services
- SNMP Service
- Windows Internet Name Service
- Workstation

Have Disk...

OK   Cancel

When the installation is complete, the Windows Internet Name Service is displayed among the other network services, as shown in Figure 36.20. You can close the window and reboot the server for the changes to take effect.

Figure 36.20

When the WINS installation is complete, it will be listed among the other network services that have been setup.

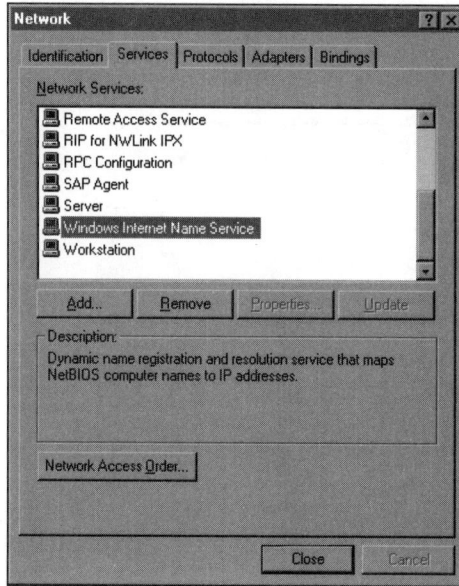

Configuring WINS

The configuration and management of the WINS is controlled by an administrative tool called the WINS Manager. During installation this utility is automatically added within the Administrative Tools task bar menu as shown in Figure 36.21. It can be used to manage the local WINS server or remote WINS servers.

To configure WINS, select the WINS Manager from the Administrative Tools task bar menu. This will start the WINS Manager application as shown in Figure 36.22.

The WINS Manager displays two panes. The left pane shows the known WINS servers that have been reported. The right pane gives basic statistics about each WINS server listed in the left pane. At least one WINS server IP address will be displayed. To manage a specific WINS server, highlight the server in the left pane.

Figure 36.21

The WINS Manager utility
is used to administrate
the WINS database.

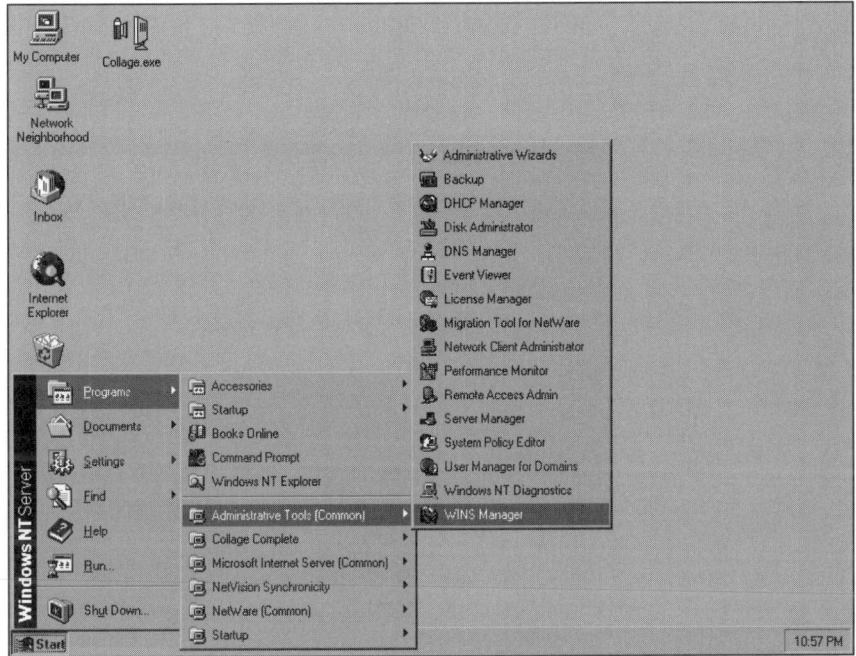

Figure 36.22

The statistics displayed
in the WINS Manager
show how often the
database is queried
and replicated.

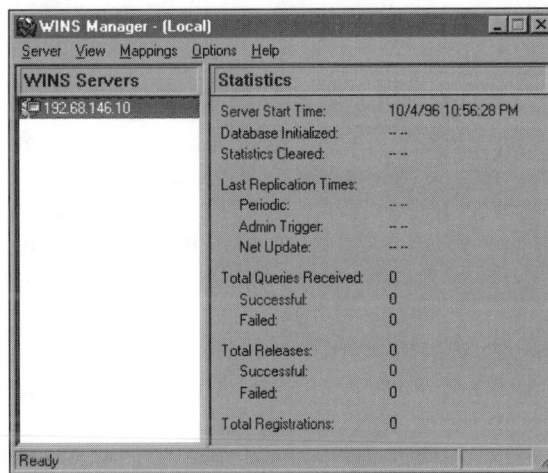

Select Configuration from the Server menu. This will display the WINS Server Configuration window shown in Figure 36.23. This window is used for managing intervals and defining replication partner relations. The interval settings are used to trigger database replication based on time and the number of changes that have occurred to the database.

Figure 36.23

Use the WINS Server Configuration window to define how the database gets replicated to other WINS servers.

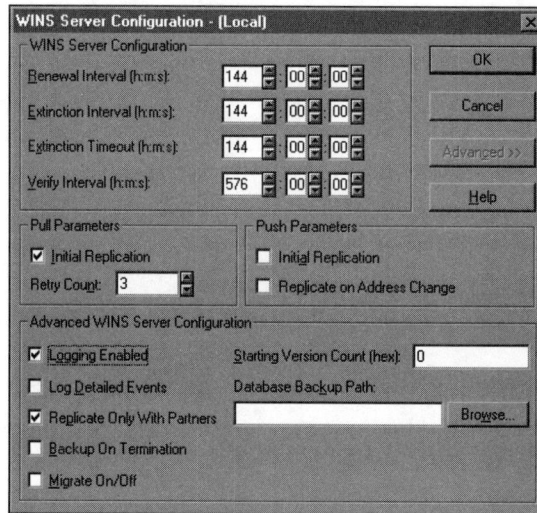

The renewal interval defines how often a client must re-register its name in the WINS database. The extinction interval defines the length of time between entries that are released and when they become extinct. Extinction timeout sets the amount of time before an extinct entry is removed from the WINS database. Verify Interval controls the interval at which the WINS server verifies other names that it does not own.

The Server Configuration window is also used to set the frequency of the server's push and pull parameters. Push replicates to other WINS databases. Pull is used to gather data from other WINS databases.

WINS Replication

Replication of the WINS database is a major function of WINS servers. Configuring multiple WINS servers ensures the accessibility to hosts on your TCP/IP network and can provide a good level of load balancing. There can be a great deal of theory behind setting up a reliable replication scheme involving numerous servers, but at a basic level, changes made to one server, the primary, will eventually be communicated to the other WINS servers, or

backups, on the network. As the administrator of this service, you control
when this process occurs and the communications hierarchy.

The specific servers involved in these relationships are defined using the
Replication Partners window, as shown in Figure 36.24.

Figure 36.24

Replication of the WINS
database is critical. This
window is used to define
partnering relationships
between WINS servers.

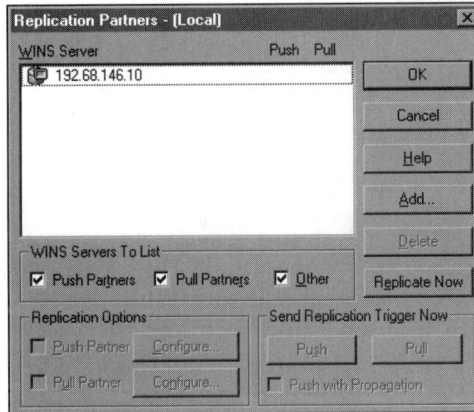

Using this window, you can add new replication partners and define the relationship they have with each other. You can also trigger an immediate replication between all WINS databases currently being maintained on your network.

NOTE. *To maintain consistency between primary and backup WINS
databases, each should be configured as the push and pull partner of the other.
We also recommend this bi-directional relationship for replication partners.*

The default settings for your WINS server are set using the Preferences
window. You can find this under the Options menu in the WINS Manager
utility, as shown in Figure 36.25.

To define the frequency of the pull process between this WINS server
and its partners, click Partners to display the partner configuration options.
For push partners, you can set a threshold for the number of changes that
can occur to the local database before a replication is triggered.

To view the WINS database, select Show Database from the Mappings
menu in the WINS Manager. This will display the Show Database window
shown in Figure 36.26.

There are a number of options provided that allow you to sort and filter
the displayed data to more easily locate specific computers that have registered with the database. The display also shows which entries are active (denoted with a check mark in the A column), and which are static (denoted
with a check mark in the S column). The expiration date indicates when the
current record is set to expire.

Figure 36.25

The Preferences window is used to set the default display settings and how new partners are handled.

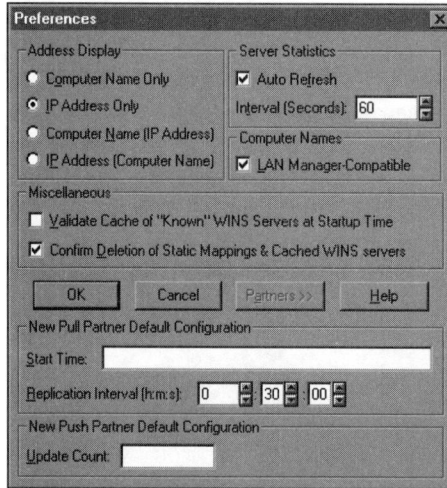

Figure 36.26

At times you may need to search the WINS database. As your database grows, you can define filters to more easily locate a specific mapping.

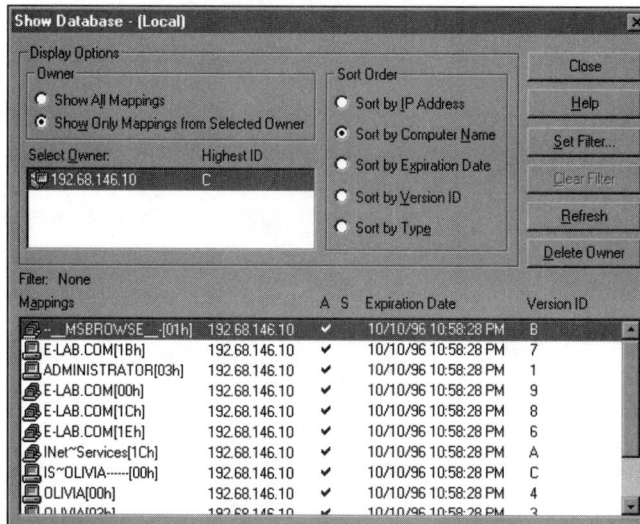

8

Tuning Windows NT for Performance

- *Starting Performance Monitor*
- *The Performance Monitor Architecture*
- *Setting Up Performance Monitor Charts*
- *Logging and Reporting*
- *Key Counters*
- *Alerts*

CHAPTER
37

How to Monitor Server Performance

W INDOWS NT IS KNOWN AS A SELF-TUNING OPERATING SYSTEM. This means it has a number of algorithms that check application memory requirements, available memory, disk space, and a host of other items to make sure the operating system is always running at peak performance. So if Windows NT does such a good job at tuning itself, you may question, why do we have so many pages dedicated to performance optimization? The reason is not that Windows NT does an inadequate job at tuning. In fact, quite to the contrary, Windows NT puts forth a superb effort, and we can think of no other operating system that does such a good job. The fact is, there's no way Windows NT can know exactly how your organization works, what applications are running or how they're used. It's in these areas that we'll show you how you can tune your configuration to tweak out a few more processing cycles from your hardware.

The first step in optimizing Windows NT is to isolate performance bottlenecks. Fortunately, the system includes several monitoring and diagnostic tools that make it possible to peek into the internals and discover how best to fine-tune your system. The most important of these utilities is Performance Monitor, which is geared for measuring real-time system activity, though it can also be used to record—or take a snapshot—of system performance to gather a performance history. This history includes, but is not limited, to processor, disk, and even application performance, albeit only for those applications that support it.

■ Starting Performance Monitor

To start Performance Monitor, locate it in the Windows NT Administrator Tools group and launch the program. You'll be presented with a graphical screen with a toolbar and grid and a data window used to display performance statistics. One thing you'll notice is that Performance Monitor is not measuring any performance activity. You'll have to manually configure the program to measure the statistics you want by clicking on the button with the + icon shown in Figure 37.1.

■ The Performance Monitor Architecture

The items Performance Monitor measures are divided into a hierarchical structure beginning with the specific computer system, then the object, counter, and finally the instance. Each of these branches in the hierarchical tree is related to the other. For example, the computer name contains objects, objects contain counters, and instances are representations of more than one object. If this system seems complicated, take a deep breath. It gets more so when there are numerous systems involved—especially multiprocessor systems—and when there are many applications installed on the server. The next section describes a way to navigate through the muddle.

The Computer

When you click on the + icon on the toolbar, the Add to Chart dialog box opens to allow you to track the performance of your network or system. At the top of the screen is the computer name. By default, this is the name of your computer preceded by the standard Windows NT resource designation of two back-slashes (\\).

Performance Monitor
doesn't show anything by
default. You'll need to
add the items you want
to track.

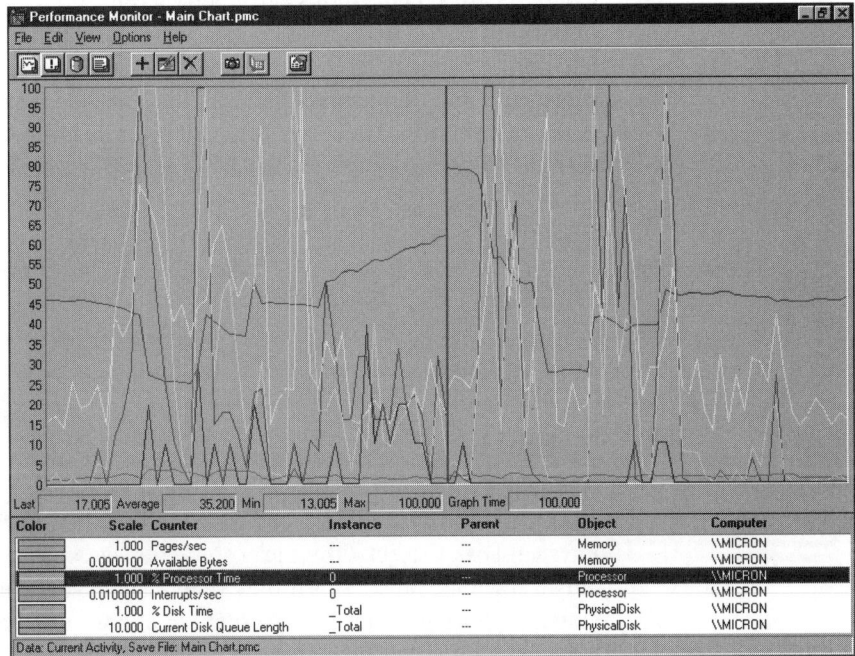

Performance Monitor, however, also allows you to monitor any computer on your network. To do so, click More..., and Performance Monitor will list all the computers accessible by the network. Choose a computer by selecting it and clicking OK.

Performance Monitor Objects

Objects are one of the core pieces of Windows NT and go far beyond the narrow scope of Performance Monitor. Objects consist of physical devices, such as disk drives or memory, and processes that make up applications. When tracking performance, you're actually monitoring these objects. Since Windows NT creates these objects according to what applications are installed, what processes are running, and the configurations selected, there can be dozens of variations between one system and the next, even if they're configured identically. Most systems will have, at least, objects for the processor, memory, cache, disk drive, cache, system, server, threads, and processes.

Counters

Counters are specific items (grouped by objects) for poking into the details of Windows NT's performance. It's by tracking counters that you'll truly isolate performance bottlenecks. However, counters are not solely atomic measurements, and there some counters that provide more or less a summary detail of an object. There are often 20 or more counters for each object, thus making it difficult to tell exactly what you're tracking.

Helpful Tip

Performance Monitor tracks hundreds of items, and their descriptions are often confusing. Click on Explain for a brief description of each item.

Instances

As the name implies, instances are representations of more than one object. For example, a system with two disk drives will have two instances of the Physical Disk Object. Obviously some objects, such as memory, can have only a single instance. But if they're available, you can track instances individually, plot two or more on screen, or choose a summary counter that displays an average of the instances.

■ Setting Up Performance Monitor Charts

Once you've chosen the computer system you want to monitor, click on the Object list and choose the appropriate item. For example, click on Processor, and then choose %Processor Time to see if your processor is being overloaded. For now, choose Instance 0, the only instance in a single processor system and the first in a multiprocessor system. Finally, choose a color, scale (it's best to leave the default scale if you're measuring only one statistic), and line width for your chart, and click Add. You'll immediately see a graph of your processor performance and a vertical pace bar indicating real-time measurements.

Helpful Tip

To delete a counter from Performance Monitor, select it and click the x icon on the toolbar.

Performance Monitor's default graphs can get difficult to interpret if there are too many counters being measured at one time. You can select Edit Chart from the Edit menu to adjust the scale or line width of the counter.

But this won't get you far if there are simply too many elements on screen. Instead, change to a bar graph representation (shown in Figure 37.2) that's a little easier to understand. Select, Chart from the Options menu, and check Histogram.

Unlike the name implies, histograms only measure true real-time performance. Graphs show several minutes of activity, which can give you a better idea of the spikes and troughs of performance in your system. Note that you can also turn off Legends and Value Bars and further configure your chart grid by clearing the appropriate options.

Figure 37.2

Performance Monitor's histogram can be easier to read than charts, with their cumbersome multiple counters.

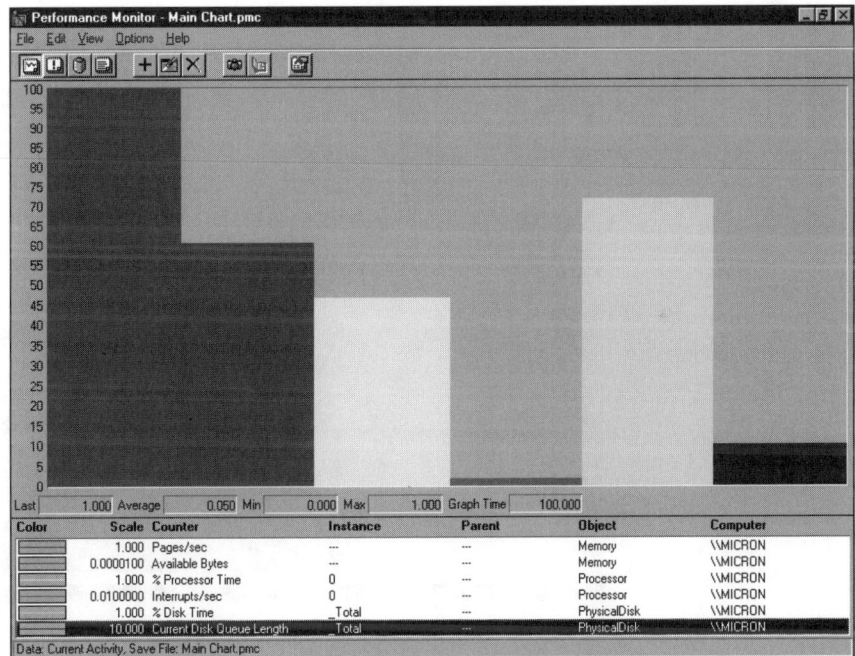

■ Logging and Reporting

While you'll often only need to track real-time activity, we highly recommend creating a history of performance that can be used as a baseline against current activity. Performance Monitor has two built-in features that make it easy to save measurements: logs and reports. Logs are for collecting activity for viewing later. It's especially helpful for capacity planning because you can view trends over longer periods of time. Reports, like charts, only keep track of real-time activity, but they display the data in columnar format. All data from charts, reports, and logs is interchangeable among the various formats, and the data can be exported into a spreadsheet-compatible format.

Logs

To create a log, click the log icon (the hard disk symbol) on the toolbar or select Log from the View menu. A blank screen opens. Click the + icon on the toolbar to add objects to your log—these are the elements that will be tracked—making sure to select the appropriate computer. Notice in Figure 37.3 that no specific counters appear in the dialog box. This is because Performance Monitor tracks all counters from each object selected; you can pick and choose the appropriate counters later.

Figure 37.3

Performance Monitor tracks all counters for each object in log mode, providing detailed historical system activity.

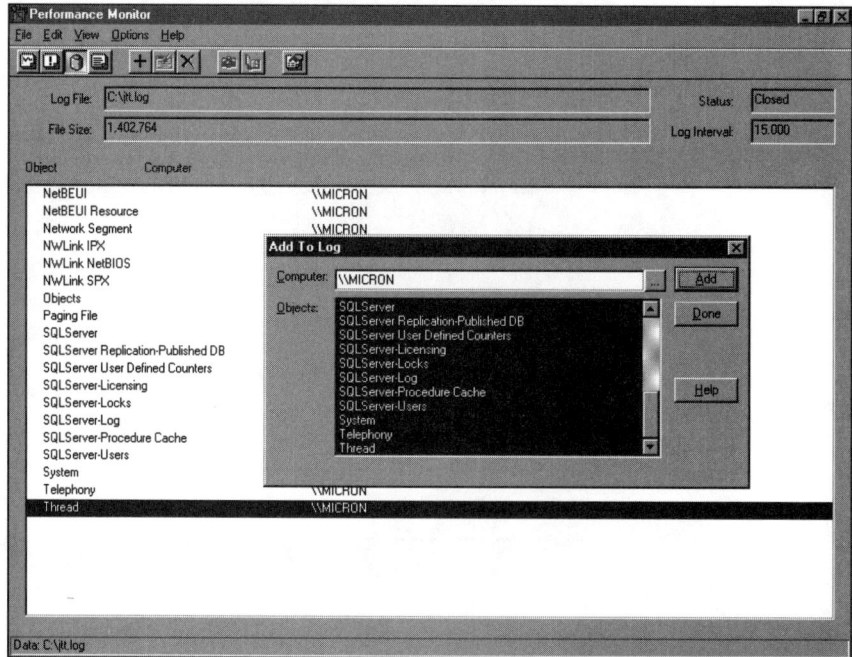

The log does not start automatically. You must start it by selecting Options, then Log, and then specifying a file name to store the data. Next select a periodic update time to control how often Performance Monitor updates the statistics or choose a manual update, and click Start Log, shown in Figure 37.4, to begin recording.

Figure 37.4

Log Options is where you
start the logging process
and configure the
frequency of updates.

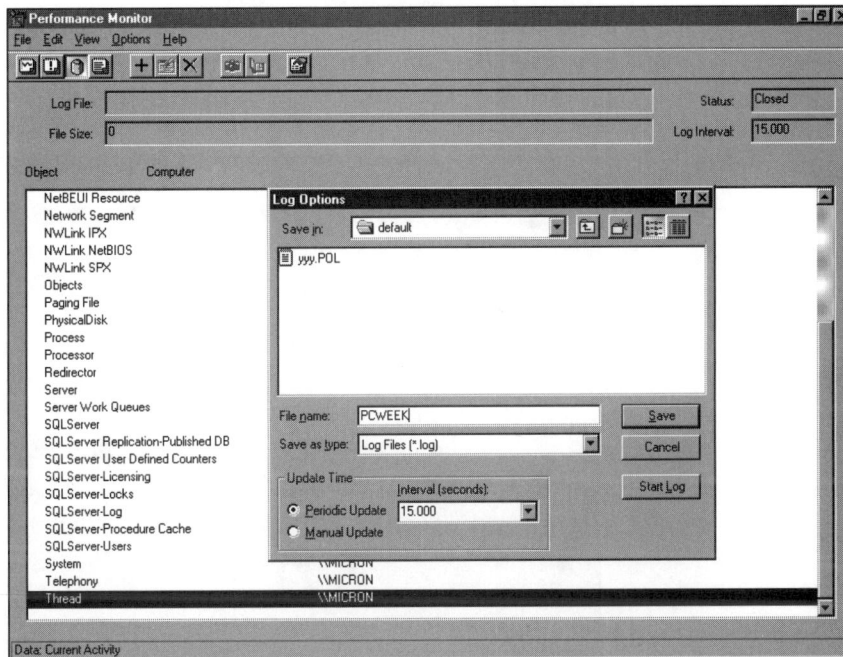

Helpful Tip

*Logs can get quite hefty in size. Make sure you choose only the objects
you want to track and increase the periodic update to reduce the size of
the file. Storing the log file on a large disk drive not part of your server
will also reduce the chance of a performance bottleneck.*

Once you think Performance Monitor has gathered enough information
for you to analyze your network, you'll want to view some of the results.
After saving your log settings, by pressing Shift-F12 (or using the File menu),
open the Chart window as previously described. Next, select Options, Data
From..., click Log File, and use the Windows NT file browser to locate your
log file. Instead of tracking real-time system activity as before, Performance
Monitor will now use the data points saved in your log file. However, the
steps to add objects and counters to your chart are exactly the same. Choose
any of the elements you tracked earlier (elements you didn't track won't
show up), and add the appropriate counters. An historical graph will appear.

To export this data into spreadsheet format, select File, Export Chart...,
and enter a name and a file format. Performance Monitor includes two export

file types, the Tab-Separated Value (TSV) format and the Comma Separate Value (CSV). Most spreadsheets can handle both formats, but the CSV format is more commonly used, especially when with spreadsheets such as Microsoft Excel. Next launch your favorite spreadsheet and open the file. For an idea of how these results appear, see Figure 37.5.

Figure 37.5

Exporting Performance Monitor data into a spreadsheet can make it easier to analyze data.

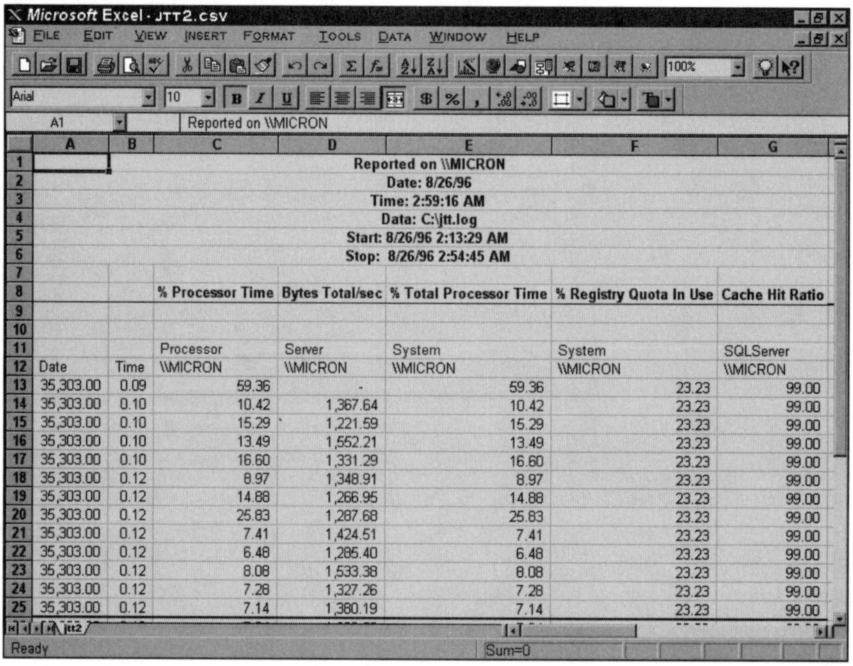

	A	B	C	D	E	F	G
8			% Processor Time	Bytes Total/sec	% Total Processor Time	% Registry Quota In Use	Cache Hit Ratio
11			Processor	Server	System	System	SQLServer
12	Date	Time	\\MICRON	\\MICRON	\\MICRON	\\MICRON	\\MICRON
13	35,303.00	0.09	59.36	-	59.36	23.23	99.00
14	35,303.00	0.10	10.42	1,367.64	10.42	23.23	99.00
15	35,303.00	0.10	15.29	1,221.59	15.29	23.23	99.00
16	35,303.00	0.10	13.49	1,552.21	13.49	23.23	99.00
17	35,303.00	0.10	16.60	1,331.29	16.60	23.23	99.00
18	35,303.00	0.12	8.97	1,348.91	8.97	23.23	99.00
19	35,303.00	0.12	14.88	1,266.95	14.88	23.23	99.00
20	35,303.00	0.12	25.83	1,287.68	25.83	23.23	99.00
21	35,303.00	0.12	7.41	1,424.51	7.41	23.23	99.00
22	35,303.00	0.12	6.48	1,285.40	6.48	23.23	99.00
23	35,303.00	0.12	8.08	1,533.38	8.08	23.23	99.00
24	35,303.00	0.12	7.28	1,327.26	7.28	23.23	99.00
25	35,303.00	0.12	7.14	1,380.19	7.14	23.23	99.00

Reports

Reports are set up much in the same way as charts and logs. Select View, then Report, and click the + icon on the toolbar to add objects and counters to your report. Unlike Charts and Logs, Reports organizes the counters logically by object and displays only real-time data.

Unfortunately, report data can't be printed; however, it can be exported into spreadsheet format by following the steps for exporting under the Log option.

■ Key Counters

Because of Windows NT's adaptive tuning capabilities, there aren't that many knobs and buttons to adjust to get faster performance. However, there are several key areas that should be measured frequently or even continuously to make sure you head off bottlenecks before they occur. Even with all the available counters and objects, you'll most likely want to focus on several key areas to judge overall system bottlenecks. These areas deal with memory, processor, and the disk subsystem. (See Table 37.1.)

Table 37.1

Key Performance Monitor counters

OBJECT	COUNTER	WARNING FLAG	NOTE
Memory	Pages/sec	Consistently Greater than 5	Pages/sec measures the number of pages Windows NT reads or writes to the disk in order to resolve low-memory issues. If the counter goes consistently above 5, you need to add RAM to your system.
Memory	Available bytes	Consistently below 1MB	This counter measures the amount of physical memory available to your applications and processes. If it goes below 0MB available, your system is paging to the disk, resulting in dramatically slower performance.
Process	% Processor time	Nearing 100 percent	If your system is continually nearing 100 percent processor use, your CPU is the bottleneck. Isolate what applications are taking up CPU cycles and move them to another system. If that's not possible, you may need to upgrade your system.
Processor	Interrupts/ Sec	Over 1000	If your processor is continually being interrupted to service requests, you probably need to look at a bottleneck in the disk subsystem or network interface cards.
Physical Disk	% Disk Time	Nearing 100 percent	This counter measures the latency between disk requests and the subsystem's servicing of the requests. If this counter nears 100 percent, it means your disk subsystem can't handle the load and should be upgraded.
Physical disk	Avg. Disk queue length	Greater than 2	This counter measures pending disk requests. A measurement of 2 means there are two disk requests not being serviced because of a slow disk subsystem.

Microsoft has these additional recommendations (see Table 37.2) for counters to watch:

Table 37.2

Thresholds of counters

OBJECT	COUNTER	THRESHOLD
Processor	Processor time	85 percent
Server	Sessions errored out	5
	Work item shortages	3
Logical disk	Free space	85 percent
Paging file	Usage	99 percent
Redirector	Network errors/sec	5
	Reads denied/sec	5
	Writes denied/sec	5
	Server sessions hung	5
	Current commands	Number of network adapter cards plus 2
Server work queues	Queue length	4
System	Processor queue length	2

■ Alerts

A good way to tell if your system is underperforming is to set alerts that warn you when preset thresholds have been exceeded. Alerts work the same way as charts, logs, and reports. To set alerts, from the View menu, select Alerts and click the + icon to add a list of objects and counters. The Add to Alert dialog box will appear. Before clicking Add in this dialog box, enter a threshold in the Alert If frame, as shown in Figure 37.6. Alert settings will appear in the bottom of the Alert screen, while warnings of exceeded thresholds appear in the top window.

Figure 37.6

Alerts offer an excellent
way to track performance
bottlenecks.

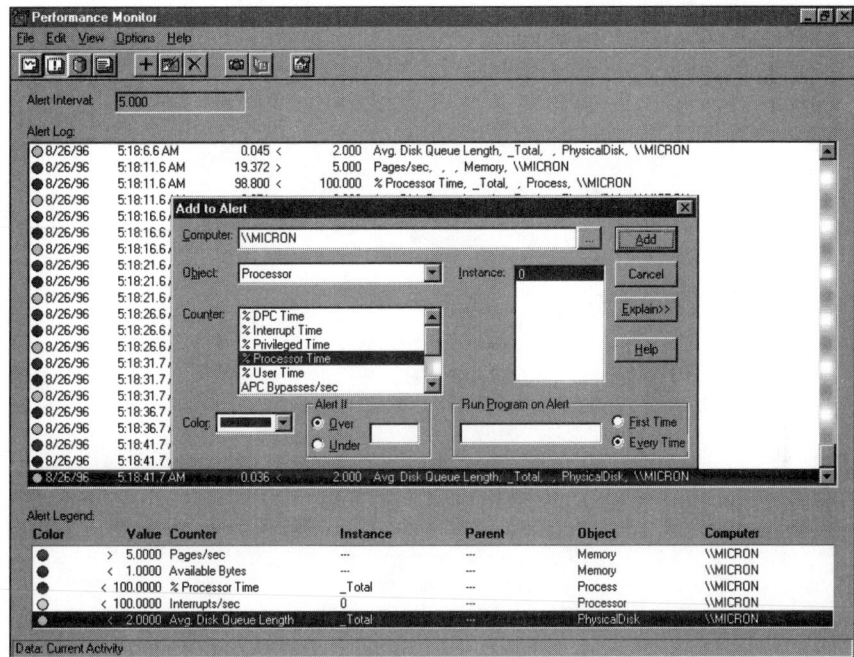

Performance Monitor's Alerts also allow you to run customized programs when an alert is exceeded. For example, you can place an alert that calls a program that pages you when there is zero network throughput (possibly indicating that the network is down). Alerts don't come with any pre-built applications, and there's no scripting language to allow you to build conditional statements into your warnings, but the simplicity of the tool makes it a time-saver.

- *Processes and Threads*

38

How to Set Thread and Processor Priorities

As most people know, Windows NT is a multitasking operating system that can run multiple programs simultaneously using whatever resources are available. Windows NT also automatically converts itself to a multiprocessing multitasking operating system when the system it's installed on has more than one processor. These features are especially useful for a network operating system because the operating system is invariably servicing more than one request at a time. These services range from managing multiple users' file and print requests to ensuring that the operating system fulfills its role as an application server. If Windows NT didn't have this capability, it would be dramatically slower because it would have to run all processes serially.

By default, Windows NT automatically prioritizes the applications it runs to make sure that all of them are serviced and run efficiently. To do this, a part of Windows NT is constantly evaluating applications and assigning and reassigning these priorities. While Windows NT does a spectacular job of prioritizing, the performance of some applications may be compromised. This is why Windows NT features a command-line switch that allows you, as the administrator, to set the priorities of applications you feel should get either more or less CPU time. While we don't recommend implementing the priority switches to start applications in most cases, doing so may yield some performance improvements in critical applications.

To appropriately discuss this thread and process prioritization, it's necessary to explain in summary form Windows NT's layered architecture. Windows NT is a complex operating system, though, and even a summary explanation of how it works can fill a book. Therefore, we'll stick to covering the basics. We'll also stray slightly from our typical format of plowing through procedures on implementing individual features. Instead, we'll start with the background information and definitions of terms and concepts and then proceed with step-by-step instructions.

■ Processes and Threads

Most of us install an application and expect it to work without considering what's happening in the background. This is whole idea of the operating system, and it's far easier to do this than it is to flip switches and watch LEDs, as programmers had to do in the era before the operating system. When the switch flippers of the old Altair computers and the like ran programs, they had to go through a pre-defined process in order for the program to run.

The idea of this process is the same today with Windows NT, but now the programs are far more complex, the systems are thousands of times faster, and the operating system takes care of most of the switch-flipping (make that bit-flipping) chores. The applications you install and run on Windows NT are more than just executable programs. They're a set of processes that includes a private space in operating system memory that allows the program to run, and the processes include all of the system resources required by the application during run-time. Processes also are made up of threads, which are the actual execution units in Windows NT. This means that when you launch an application, it's not the executable that is being launched—at least it's not to Windows NT. It's one or more threads that Windows NT schedules to run. Because a program can consist of one or more threads and Windows NT is able to run one or more applications simultaneously, Windows NT is called a multi-threaded operating system.

All processes that run under Windows NT are assigned a priority level from 0 to 31, with the higher numbers taking on higher priorities and getting access to the processor before those with lower priorities. (See Figure 38.1.) Most user applications fall between 0 and 16. All processes with the same priorities share the processor until application execution is completed. You may wonder what happens to low priority applications when a series of high priority applications are running. Windows NT has built-in fail-safes to make sure that all applications run. For example, it will bump up (promote) or demote priorities to ensure that all applications run.

Figure 38.1

Windows NT Server process and thread priorities are assigned priority levels, with most user applications receiving priorities between 0 and 16.

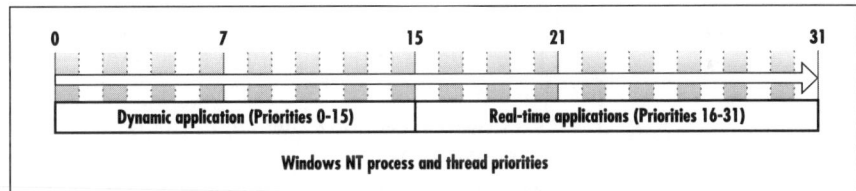

The first 15 priorities are assigned to dynamic applications, including most programs installed by users and those processes used by Windows NT that are not critical to the operating system's functionality. Priorities 15-31 are assigned to real-time applications. These are almost solely limited to processes that are critical to the operating system, including the kernel (kernel.exe). By default, all user application processes are assigned a normal priority of 7, but this value is not set in stone, as developers often increase the priority through code. Users can even tweak the priority settings of their applications with the switches we touched on in the first section or by modifying the foreground and background performance of their applications.

User Definable Priorities

This section deals solely with 32-bit applications designed for Windows NT. While Windows NT can run DOS and 16-bit Windows programs, these applications are not, in most cases, designed for the server environment. Both 16-bit Windows applications and DOS applications were, in most cases, developed as single-threaded applications, whereas this section focuses solely on the processes and threads that comprise applications. Those older applications also highlight a fundamental difference between programs and processes: programs operate as single entities while processes are dynamic and can launch a series of threads that actually perform the application execution.

As we mentioned above, priority scheduling is a complex issue that should be undertaken with cautious hands. A variety of factors affect performance, including the way an application performs, the size of the page file, the application that's running, and whether or not the application is in the foreground or background. Before setting the priorities of an application, make sure to first experiment with setting the foreground and background properties of your applications, and always set up a test run before implementing a switch for widespread use. Also remember that the threads spawned by processes in Windows NT don't always inherit the same priority that you've assigned to the parent.

Instead, child threads are assigned a priority relative to the parent. Table 38.1, pulled from the Microsoft Knowledgebase, shows the relative priorities for Real-time, High, and Low switches. To read the table, locate the Real-time base priority at the top of the table and scan down the column. You'll see that even when Windows NT assigns the current priority to Idle, it still receives a priority level of 16, which in this case is greater than the any thread in the High priority. The implication is that any process you assign to a Real-time priority is given all the resources it requires, regardless of the other applications running on your system.

NOTE. *Windows NT does not modify the priorities of real-time threads—only of the threads spawned from real-time processes.*

Table 38.1

Relative priorities for switches

PRIORITY	REAL TIME	HIGH	IDLE
Time critical	31	15	15
Highest	26	15	6
Above normal	25	14	5
Normal	24	13	4
Below normal	23	12	3
Lowest	22	11	2
Idle	16	1	1

Despite the complexity of the Windows NT architecture, setting priorities in Windows NT is fairly easy. It merely involves launching an application from the command line with one of four special switches. First, open a command prompt by running the program CMD.EXE or by starting a command prompt. The syntax for setting priorities is:

START /[switch] [program name]

NOTE. *You need administrator privileges or the administrative right to increase scheduling priority to use the start switch.*

Although there are 32 priority levels, there are only four switches: Low, Normal, High, and Real Time. The base priority level of the Low switch is four, Normal is 7 as mentioned before, High is 13, and Real Time is 24. For example, to change the priority of a Performance Monitor application to High, enter the following line at the command prompt:

START /HIGH PERFMON

Helpful Tip

> *Although it's possible to run applications in REALTIME mode, we strongly recommend against it, as a CPU-intensive application may adversely affect performance.*

Performance Monitor is not typically a CPU-intensive application, so running it in the High priority level should not adversely impact your system. However, it will take up CPU cycles, as shown in Figure 38.2. The figure shows two instances of Performance Monitor running: one with a high priority and the other with a low priority. Notice how the high priority instance takes over most of the resources, while the low priority version receives almost none. Note that this was done with the default settings, and foreground programs (such as the instance of Performance Monitor shows) were set to run faster than background tasks. However, even when we ran the low priority version of Performance Monitor in the foreground, the high priority version still took significantly more CPU cycles.

There are several occasions when setting a high priority application will cause a decrease in performance or even make it appear that your system has locked up. As a test, for example, open Performance Monitor, and then in a DOS window start the DOS editor program with a Real-time priority switch on a system that is not running any critical applications by typing:

START /REALTIME EDIT

Figure 38.2

Performance Monitor
shows that applications
set to run with a High
priority are dedicated
significantly more CPU
cycles than those with a
Low priority.

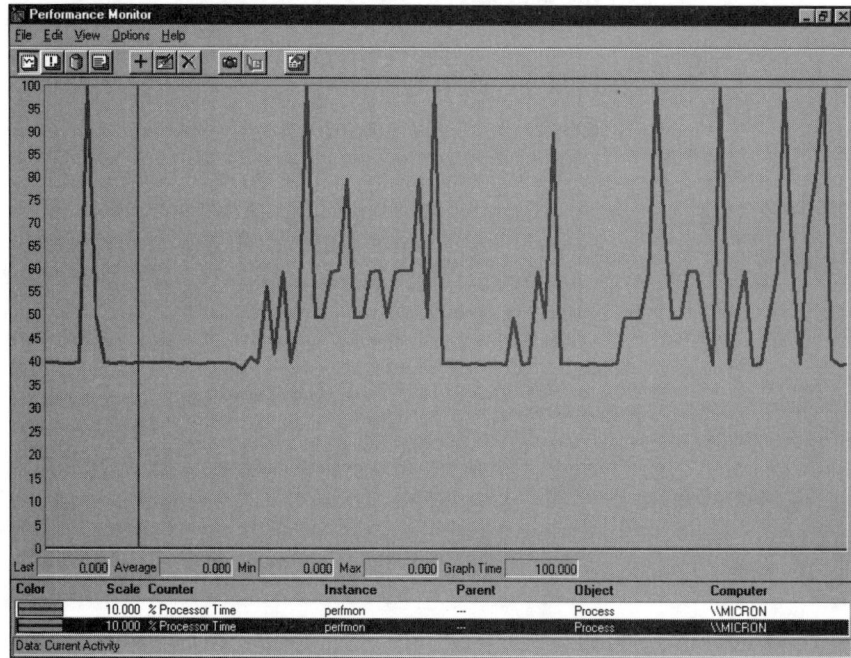

Now check Performance Monitor's Process counter and look at Processor Time. Select the NTVDM instance. This will measure the processor resources consumed by the NT virtual DOS machine, which in this case is running the MS-DOS Editor. You'll see that Editor is consuming few if any resources, which is what you'd expect from an idle program. Now, to initiate an action from the Editor, select the File menu, and leave it open. If you can, switch back to the Performance Monitor and check the process statistics. You should see that the DOS Editor, as shown in Figure 38.3, is now consuming nearly 100 percent of the system resources even though it's running in the background.

If your system appears to have crashed, it's because the application consumed so many resources that none were available for other operating system processes—including the keyboard and mouse! You can attempt to gracefully exit the application in one of two ways. You can try to task switch over to it and close it normally or you can close it the easier way by pressing Ctrl+Alt+Delete to bring up the Windows NT Task Manager. In the Task list select MS-DOS Editor and click End Task, as shown in Figure 38.4.

Notice the three tabs at the top of the Task Manager screen. By default, you should be in the Applications tab which shows a list of running

Figure 38.3

Even a simple program, such as the MS-DOS Editor can overtake system resources when set to run with the Real Time start switch.

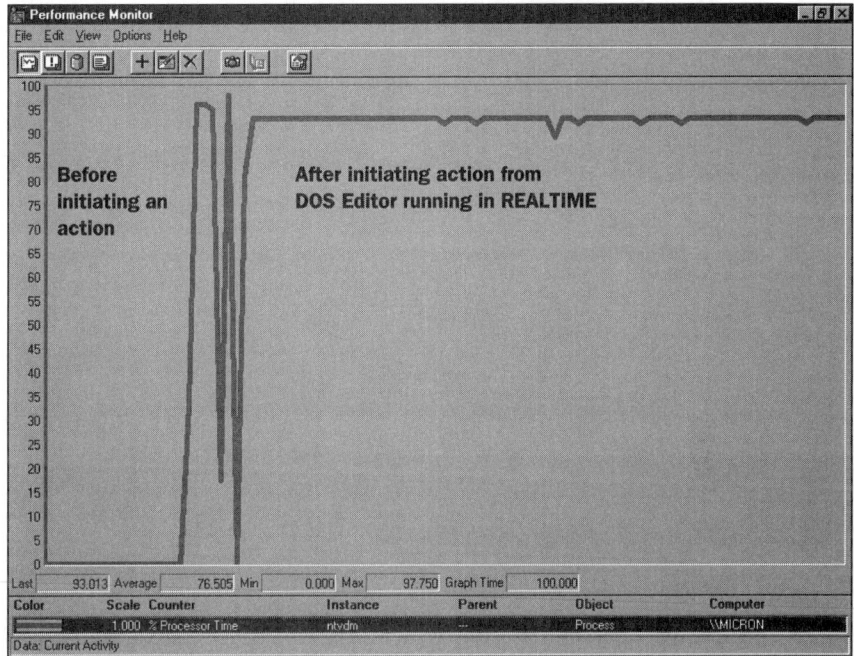

Figure 38.4

The easiest way to close an application that's overtaking system resources is to use Windows NT's Task Manager.

applications. To get a more detailed list of what's running on your system, click on the Processes tab to bring up the screen shown in Figure 38.5. You can use this tab as an alternative to Performance Monitor to see the applications that are running and the resources they're using. Besides getting a list of the available processes followed by a process ID (PID), you'll also see the CPU resources, CPU time, and how much memory is being used by each process. You can stop individual processes by selecting the process you want to kill and clicking End Process.

Figure 38.5

You can measure process use with the Task Manager rather than Performance Monitor for a quick glimpse of what's running on your system and the resources being used.

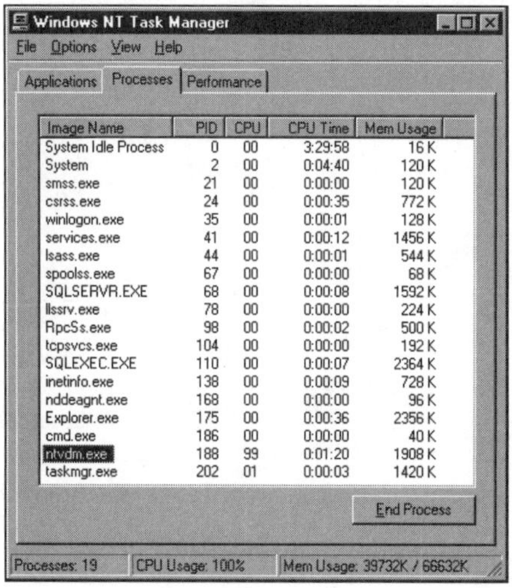

Tune-Up Areas

If you find you need to set the priority of one of your applications, it invites the question: Why? If your system has adequate power and you've not overloaded your system with applications, whether extraneous or essential, you should have enough horsepower to run a fairly large network. The first reason for setting a priority, then, should be to **lower** the priority level for applications you don't want to allocate many resources to—such as Performance Monitor. You may also want to lower the priority of any process that might take away from a critical application, such as Microsoft SQL Server, or any other database server. If you're still running into processor bottlenecks after doing this, you may want to investigate the following areas.

If your Windows NT server is predominantly used as a file server, you probably don't need to adjust your process priorities. File servers in general tax the disk subsystems and network components far more than they use the processor. However, if your system is used as both an application server and a file server, you may want to consider upgrading the bus devices, such as disk controllers or disk drives, and the processor. If you are unable to upgrade your system for any reason, consider scheduling processor-bound applications to hours when the entire network is less busy.

39

How to Optimize and Set Background Performance

WHETHER YOU'RE GOING GROCERY SHOPPING OR TO GRANDMA'S, when you're driving on a highway pushing 75 miles per hour you're probably feeling that you're making good time. You're probably also on the lookout for things that might prove to be a hindrance to getting to where you want to go—mostly police officers but also other cars and highway obstructions. Any one of these would certainly be a bottleneck to your performance, and though you'd rather not let anything get in your way, if something does, you should be prepared to handle it. Such obstacles are really unavoidable because, for the most part, you can't anticipate them soon enough to change your direction.

On your imaginary journey, there are also avoidable problems that can be just as detrimental to your performance as the unavoidable ones. These include things like filling your tank up with gasoline, making sure your spark plugs are in good shape, and keeping your tires inflated properly. It's especially frustrating when something goes wrong that you could have easily taken care of before you hit the road.

Either kind of obstacle demands that you take some action. You can prevent avoidable obstacles by keeping your car in tip-top order. Unavoidable ones also start with keeping your car in good condition—so you can better maneuver around road hazards (and police officers). The other part of the equation is taking the proper reactive stance, such as putting on the brakes when there's a stalled tractor trailer stuck in your lane.

You'll run into similar problems with a network operating system. You'll run into unavoidable hindrances, including the occasionally extraordinary demand for bandwidth on your database server. Even more appropriate is something that fundamentally changes the way your infrastructure operates. This happened with the sudden popularity of the World Wide Web and the Internet. The demand for Internet access opened up individuals to streams of data never before so easily available. But with every luxury, there's a tax, and in this case it was directly on the network operating systems.

We've mentioned that Windows NT is a self-tuning operating system that basically fixes performance problems using whatever physical resources are available to it. But you should also make sure you keep it in top-notch running order to ensure that it can do its job properly. Likewise, you must make sure to take the proper reaction when you hit—and most people will—a performance hitch.

In the previous chapter, we discussed thread and process tuning. We'll take that thought one step further in this chapter and then get into more of Windows NT's architecture including how Windows NT Server schedules tasks. We'll then show you how to ensure that the server is using its virtual memory properly and help you monitor and tune your disk cache to ensure that your operating system is running at peak performance.

■ Five Bottlenecks

There are five major hardware parts that affect system performance. Any one part that's not up to par in your system may result in a major performance bottleneck that slows down your entire network. Using Performance Monitor as outlined in Chapter 37, "How to Monitor Server Performance," you should frequently check these parts to ensure that your system is operating at peak throughput.

Before we get into the five bottlenecks, the first step toward ensuring high-speed and hitchless performance is to make sure you have the right hardware. Many companies think they can get by with an inexpensive system that's barely adequate as a desktop computer. The fact is, systems classified as servers often have important features that separate them from the lower-priced systems. Even if they're equipped with identical processors, for example, a server should provide significantly better performance than a desktop system, and we strongly recommend shelling out the extra bucks for a server-class system.

Servers are usually optimized for multiuser LAN environments and thus have more capacity and perform better than their desktop counterparts. For example, servers usually can be equipped with more memory, they have better disk subsystems, and they even have faster system buses than desktops. They also offer far better fail-safe features than their desktop counterparts. These fault-tolerant capabilities include redundant cooling fans, power supplies, and even motherboards designed to gracefully or even seamlessly operate in the event of a component failure. These features jack up the prices of servers far beyond what you'd expect to pay for a workstation, but they may save money and even your job in the event of a failure.

Bottleneck #1: The Disk Subsystem

One thing that sets servers apart from desktop systems is the disk subsystem, so let's make this the first bottleneck. Servers most likely come with faster disk subsystems than desktops. These subsystems can be configured as RAID devices, which are almost always used in a server environment. (See Chapter 11 for details on setting up RAID.) These subsystems are probably based on the SCSI platform and can transfer data significantly faster than integrated device electronics (IDE) machines, which are common in non-server systems. Additionally, there are a variety of SCSI devices, including SCSI, SCSI-2, Ultra-SCSI, and SCSI-3, that can transfer data up to 40Mbps compared with IDE's 2.5Mbps top throughput.

More importantly, SCSI-based systems can better handle multiple disks, even if they are not set up as RAID devices. IDE devices using the standard driver that ships with Windows NT called the ATDISK device driver usually can only service one I/O request at a time. In a network environment, this can be outrageously slow because of the high number of file requests that occur simultaneously. If your server has an IDE drive, make sure there is a driver available that can handle asynchronous I/O requests.

Also, avoid controllers with programmable input/output (PIO). These cards are flexible and inexpensive, but they consume more CPU cycles than non-PIO controllers (upwards of 40 percent according to a Microsoft technical document).

Instead, opt for cards that support 32-bit direct memory access (DMA), which allows for faster transfers of memory from the system bus to the adapter. Even better are bus-mastering cards, which usually have their own processor to handle memory transfers and therefore don't consume valuable CPU cycles.

Helpful Tip

> *Use Windows NT's high-performance file system (NTFS) on disk volumes above 400MB. It operates more efficiently than the older file allocation table (FAT) model.*

Surprisingly, depending on the environment, a fast disk subsystem can be more important than having a top-performing processor. This means that systems with slower CPUs can outgun systems equipped with faster processors but lesser subsystems. This is especially true if the operating system is used mainly for file and print services and I/O is more important than pure processing power.

Bottleneck #2: RAM

Servers also have increased memory capacity. The average Intel workstation can accommodate 128MB of RAM, but servers can go to 256MB and beyond. Though 128 may seem to be a lot, it's not. In fact, it's about average for handling a moderate network workload because of the increased demands placed on the server, such as multimedia and Internet access. It's also not a lot when considering that 16MB of RAM seemed to be a lot just five or six years ago. The memory bus in many high performance servers is often specially designed by the manufacturer to be faster than the ISA/PSI bus in common desktops.

It's essential to equip your server with a suitable amount of RAM because Windows NT will try to provide a server application with all the RAM it requests at load time. This makes for faster application performance, but if the server is running on limited resources, it will begin using the slower disk subsystem for virtual memory. This will cause an instant bottleneck.

Fortunately, memory is one of the easiest resources to upgrade because you can simply add more. If you suspect that memory is the bottleneck, however, and your system is at maximum capacity, you should either add a new system or eliminate unnecessary applications or services. Some services that aren't necessary include the spooler service, which is only used when a printer is connected to the workstation or server. The spooler uses about 0.5MB of memory—not much, but it adds up. To turn it off, open Control Panel and select Devices. Find the Spooler in the list and select Stop, as shown in Figure 39.1.

Figure 39.1

Turning off services and devices you don't need will save memory and allow for more efficient performance.

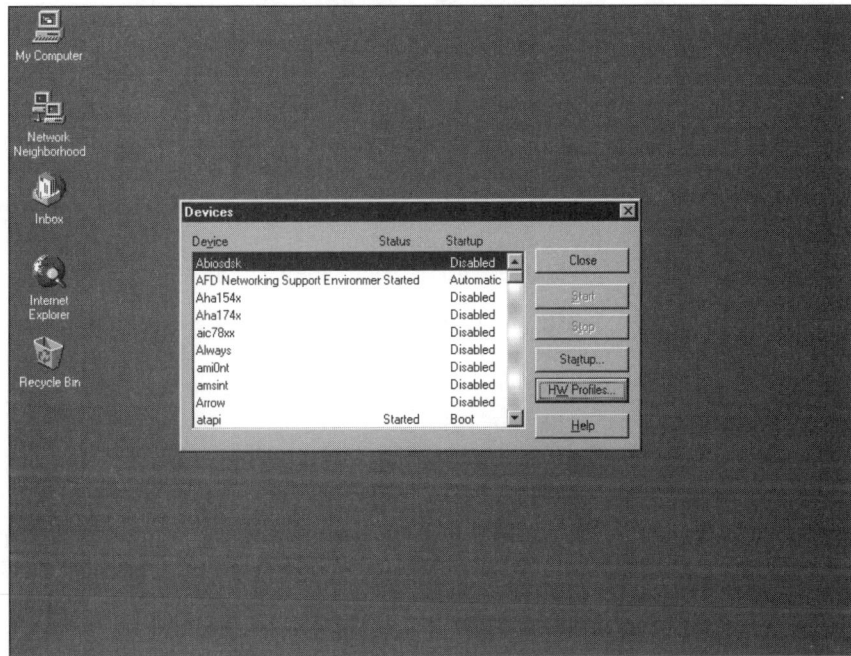

Helpful Tip

A quick way of finding out if you're low on memory is to run the Windows Microsoft Diagnostic program—WINMSD—and click on Memory.

Bottleneck #3: The CPU

Though a CPU is only one part of the performance chain, it's one of the most difficult to upgrade. For example, changes in processor design have made it impossible to upgrade a 486 to a Pentium without also upgrading the motherboard. In general, we recommend that companies purchase a system capable of supporting multiple CPUs, either via daughter cards or through symmetric multiprocessing-capable motherboards.

Also, consider using a RISC-based system. RISC systems are potentially faster than their Intel-based counterparts because they process instructions faster. For example, Intel systems process one instruction in about 2.75 cycles (it takes 2.75 processor cycles or megahertz to complete one instruction). RISC systems, on the other hand, can process instructions in about 2 cycles, making RISC systems with equal megahertz ratings somewhat faster than

Intel systems. Note that design improvements in Pentium Pro systems may have narrowed this gap.

Bottleneck #4: The External Cache

Some of the things that make a server a server are pumped-up secondary caches. These are essential in a server operating system because servers most likely are equipped with more memory than workstations. Secondary caches actually create a virtual map of physical memory, allowing the fast access to the memory. Adding more memory to a system that doesn't have an upgraded secondary cache may actually slow down the system.

NOTE. *Note that some processors have secondary cache built into them, including some Pentium Pro systems. Look for at least a 512K cache in devices designated as server-class systems.*

Bottleneck #5: Network Cards

Network cards installed at the server may seem trivial and commodity oriented, but they can have a significant impact on performance. Older 8-bit cards are slower than 16-bit cards or than counterparts that are PCI-based. They also consume far more processor cycles. This not only makes for poor network throughput, it can actually slow down your entire server's processing power. The best network cards are PCI-based, a standard which goes for any peripheral. PCI cards off-load the processing cycles so that they don't consume extra resources. The PCI bus, which runs at 33Mhz, also can transfer data at 132Mbps—more than adequate for most needs.

■ Boosting Background Performance

Once you've taken care of the hardware, it's time to optimize Windows NT. In the previous chapters, we discussed how Windows NT's threads and processes work and how to set application start-up parameters to give them a small performance boost. We also discussed how to monitor performance using Windows NT's built-in performance monitor utility. In this section, we'll cover three more categories: NT's tasking, page files, and the cache.

Tasking

A task is an item of work to be done in Windows NT. A task can be made up of a single thread or process, but usually it's a sequence of several threads that comprise a task. One of the key components in Windows NT is the task scheduler, which acts almost like a separate operating system and controls how tasks are done. The task scheduler in Windows NT server is optimized for fast network throughput in a file and print server environment. For this to happen, Windows NT is set for long time slices, which allow it to process network requests without interruption. According to Microsoft technical documents, this is especially significant when used with symmetric multiprocessing (SMP) systems; thread and cache synchronization among the processors is essential.

In contrast, desktop operating systems, including Windows NT Workstation, have shorter time slices. This allows users to quickly switch tasks without delay, but causes a subtle performance penalty because the processor and operating system are more frequently interrupted.

Though the task scheduler runs mainly on autopilot, Windows NT includes a few parameters that allow companies to tailor the server to their needs. For instance, we mentioned that Windows NT is an application server just as much as a file and print server. These two types of systems, however, use resources differently. For example, file and print servers use the disk subsystem more than application servers in general because of the numerous file open and close requests that come from users who are running server-based applications and are opening documents located on the server. Application servers, on the other hand, tend to be processor-bound because they typically run a single application. Even database servers, such as Microsoft SQL Server, use processor and memory more than disk because databases are typically stored in a special RAM cache, if the memory is available.

To optimize Windows NT for your environment, follow these steps.

1. Double-click on the Network icon, and then select Control Panel.

2. Click the Services tab.

3. Double-click on Server in the Services window.

4. Check the appropriate setting.

For example, we changed our Windows NT Server setting to optimize it for network applications, as shown in Figure 39.2.

By changing this setting, you're making minor tweaks to how Windows NT schedules tasks. Windows NT will allow for longer time slices when it's set for network performance and shorter time slices when it's set for optimal application server performance. Both the Maximize Throughput for File Sharing and Maximize Throughput for Network Applications are designed for situations when more than 64 users are connected to the Windows NT server. However, the latter setting prioritizes user application access over file cache; the reverse is true for the former setting.

You'll also notice two other settings: Minimize Memory Used and Balance. Minimize Memory Used should only be set if there are ten or fewer users connected to the server. The Balance option should be used for 10–64 users.

Figure 39.2

Choosing the right
optimization setting can
boost your Windows NT
Server performance.

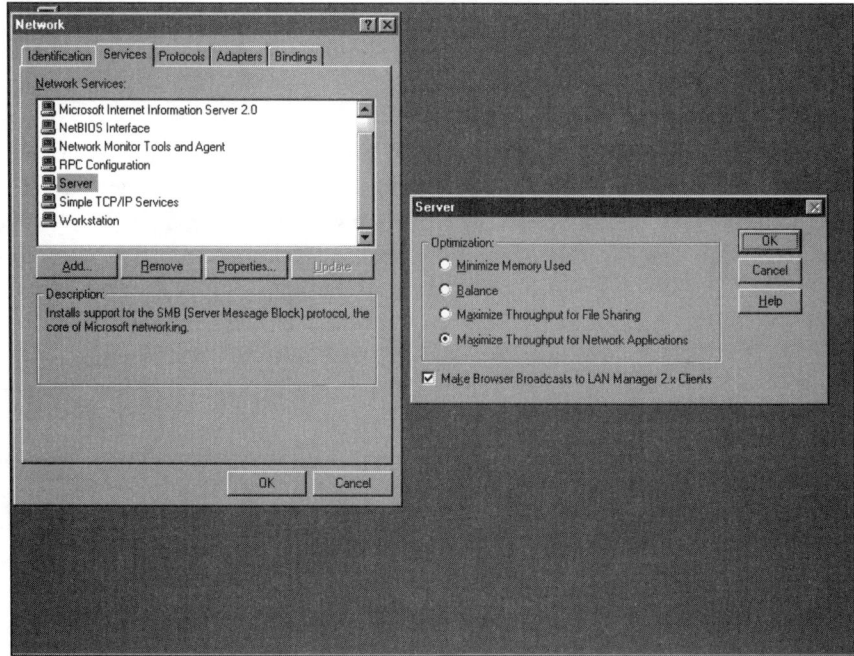

■ Primping your Pagefile

One of the more important adjustments you can make to a Windows NT
Server is the Pagefile setting.

The Pagefile is actually a dynamically changing swap file that Windows NT
uses for virtual memory. When the processes and threads used in applications
deplete memory in Windows NT, the operating system starts to swap out the
data in RAM to disk. This is called paging, and though it is far slower than accessing memory directly, it allows Windows NT to run fairly efficiently if an application requests more than what's currently available. This might be common
at application start-up, when running multiple tasks simultaneously, or when
the operating system is involved in a processor and memory-intensive task.

NOTE. *Windows NT features two kinds of pages: code pages and data pages.*
Code pages are those used to execute programs, while data pages contain data
used by a program. Both code pages and data pages can be swapped to disk.

Since paging is far slower than direct access to memory (hundreds or even thousands of times slower), it makes sense to tune NT's virtual memory settings as much as possible.

Helpful Tip

> *The way to tell if Windows NT has an inadequate amount of memory is to view the Memory: Pages/sec counter in Performance Monitor. If it continuously goes above 20, your system is paging too much.*

To tune virtual memory settings, open Control Panel, click on System, then on Virtual Memory. You'll see three settings, as shown in Figure 39.3. Initial Size is the minimum amount of disk space, in megabytes, set aside for the page file. Windows NT provides a minimum amount that this setting can be. In our case, it's 2MB, but this is an impractical amount because even the smallest network application will certainly take up more than 2MB if any paging has to be done. Windows NT also specifies a recommended size, which can be determined by adding 12 to the physical memory available (27MB in our example).

Figure 39.3

The right mix of virtual memory helps keep systems running at top performance without running low on resources.

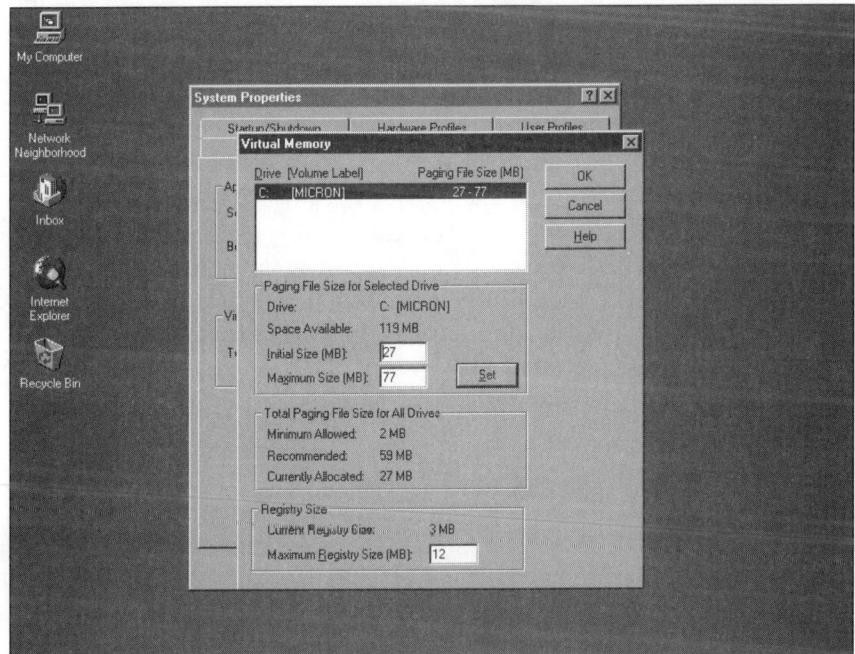

However, if you specify too small a minimum page size, Windows NT will not be able to generate a debugging information file. Windows NT will allow the setting to be made, but it will turn off the debugging log, which will make it difficult to analyze system failures. Figure 39.4 shows this warning.

Figure 39.4

Setting the minimum page file too small will force Windows NT to disable one of it debug information logs.

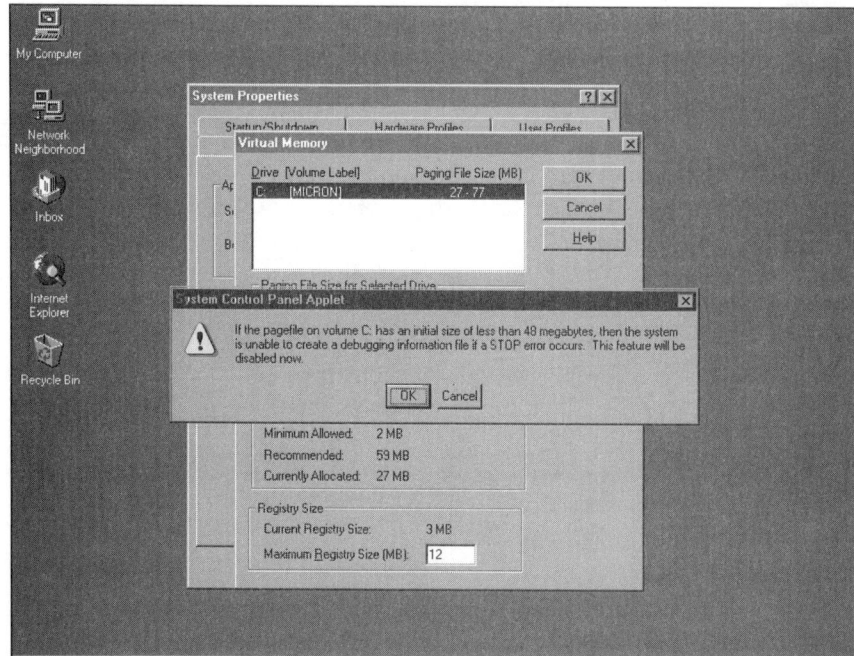

Windows NT also allows you to specify a maximum amount of memory. In general it's not a good idea to exceed its recommended maximum, and we can see no reason you would unless you anticipate adding more RAM to your server or you're running into low memory problems. In these cases, it's essential to add RAM to your system, to distribute some applications running on your server to other servers, or to remove services or devices that are not necessary.

■ Conclusion

There's far more to the nuances of Windows NT tuning than can be provided in this book; in fact, volumes can be written on the subject. The intent of this book was to introduce you to some of the major topics so you can overcome many of the hurdles that might come up during the setup and operation of your Windows NT Server. For more information, you should purchase the Windows NT Resource Kit. At press time, the kit for Windows NT Server 4 wasn't available. The edition for Windows NT Server 3.51, however, includes many extra utilities that will allow you to tune and test your configuration to tweak performance to an even greater level than described in this book.

■ Appendix A

■ Finding Help on the Web

The Web has become more than a place for perusing for extracurricular activities. It's now one of the most important research tools available to companies. Unless an organization is firmly entrenched in its own market or neighborhood, it will need to have a Web site soon. If it doesn't, it will quickly fade away. The companies with the best Web sites offer product information, free trial software, technical documents, and a place where people can post comments and get in contact with members of the sales staff.

There are also thousands of people who create their own Web sites that contain more grass roots information. These sites also lately have become sites of sites. That is, they contain comprehensive listings of other Web sites just like themselves. Because there are so many, it makes the people who make Web search engines very happy: Everyone now has to use a search engine to dig deeper into the Web. You, as a reader of this book, have it a bit easier because we've already searched the Web and picked out some of the better sites.

Microsoft Corporation

This is the biggest and best resource for Windows NT information (and any other Microsoft product) anywhere. The Microsoft site contains free software downloads, links to other sites, technical support, and patches for products you currently own. Watch out, though—maneuvering through the site can be a bear. We recommend that you make full use of the search engine that's available to scan only the Microsoft site for information. You should also make good use of the Microsoft Knowledgebase—a searchable resource that contains solutions to common and not-so-ordinary problems. You'll find Microsoft at http://www.microsoft.com. Get to the Knowledgebase via http://www.microsoft.com/support.

Microsoft's Hardware Quality Lab

The Microsoft Hardware Quality Lab (formerly the Compatibility Lab) contains the specifications for hardware devices that vendors are required to meet to get their products certified. This site also includes all the products that have met the certification. You won't be able to download a list of the products, but you can search for individual products. Find the Lab at http://www.microsoft.com/hwtest.

Microsoft's NT 4.0 Hotfixes

Microsoft frequently updates its operating systems in packages called Service Packs. Before Microsoft gathers enough material for a service pack it posts bug fixes and changes in the form of hot fixes. You can download the latest hot fix from this FTP site, which is ftp://ftp.microsoft.com/bussys/winnt/winnt-public/fixes/usa/nt40/hotfixes-preSP1/.

Jumbo!

Jumbo is a huge site dedicated to personal computing. Unfortunately, the NT site is not that comprehensive. But, we were able to find several programs on the site that made visiting it worthwhile. We expect Jumbo to include more Windows NT software in the near future. Find Jumbo at http://www.jumbo.com/bus/winnt/netutil.

Coast to Coast Software Repository

Coast to Coast is a massive collection of software along the lines of Jumbo. It includes software for DOS, OS/2, Windows 95, and Windows NT. If you're looking for a particular shareware product, this site should be the first place you look. Find Coast to Coast at http://www.coast.net.

WinSite FTP Site

WinSite is another download area for Windows and Windows NT files. Since this is an FTP site, you won't get a slick interface, and you'll have to know at least a little bit about what you're looking for. The address is ftp.winsite.com.

Software.com

Yet another site for software downloads. This one's pretty good, though, and it features good descriptions of the software so you know what you're downloading ahead of time. The address is http://www.software.com/prod/prod.html.

Windows 95 and NT Central

This site is guaranteed to become a hot site. It's graphical and comprehensive, offering Windows NT support as well as a long list of downloadable files. Find them at http://www.hway.net/qube/qube.html.

Sites for Frequently Asked Questions (FAQs)

Name of Site	URL
FAQ for porting UNIX to NT	http://www.nentug.org/unix-to-nt/
Creating Internet sites with NT	http://www.neystadt.org/winnt/site.htm http://www.mcs.net/~thomas/www/ntfaq/
Windows NT administration FAQ	http://www.iftech.com/oltc/admin/admin.stm
Windows NT fax solutions	http://www.mcs.net/~sculptor/NTFAX-FAQ.HTML
Windows NT FAQ resource page	http://129.79.26.167/nt/support/faq.htm

Ziff-Davis Press

Ziff-Davis Press (our publisher) offers a wide variety of high-quality books that make computing easier to do. It's also one of the few companies that produces large-scale four-color computer books. Find Ziff-Davis at http://www.zdpress.com.

Microsoft Press

Here you'll find a bookstore, Hot Off the Press—announcements of new books from Microsoft, contests, exclusive previews of upcoming books, free sample chapters, and other free utilities and help files. Although you can't order online, there's information to help you find a store that carries Microsoft Press books, or order by fax, phone, or mail. Find these resources at http://www.microsoft.com/mspress.

NT Electronic Newsletter

What could be nicer than getting a magazine solely on Windows NT delivered to you via e-mail? That's the gist of the NT Electronic Newsletter, which is comprised of two magazines. They're both free, but to subscribe you'll have to fill out a subscriber survey. A small price for a lot of good information. Find the NT Electronic Newsletter at http://www.bhs.com/microsoft.winntnews/.

NT Advantage e-zine

This monthly electronic news magazine (e-zine) is an excellent resource for keeping up to date on Windows NT. It's fairly biased toward NT as far as we can tell (I guess we can expect that), but it's still an excellent resource. Find e-zine at http://www.ntadvantage.com.

NT!NT!

Another excellent resource, this site is courtesy of the San Diego Windows NT user group. The site offers a monthly magazine that features reviews, technology pieces, and new product announcements. Find NT! NT! at http://www.fbsolutions.com/sdwntug/announce.htm.

Windows NT Magazine

Windows NT magazine's Web site offers a rich selection of technology pieces, news, and links to other sites. Of course, you can also subscribe to the magazine itself—which we think is the ulterior motive behind this site. It's top-notch nonetheless, so check it out for yourself. Find the magazine at http://www.winntmag.com/home/index.dbm.

User Groups

User groups are one of the most important resources for information. There's basically a Windows NT user group for every large community in the United States, so we urge you to investigate and find yours. Some of the more famous ones are listed in Table A.1.

Table A.1

Windows NT user groups

USER GROUP NAME	SITE	NOTES
Advantage System User Group (ASUG)	http://www.asug.org/	This is one spectacularly well-done site.
Bay Area Windows NT User Group	http://wyp.net/users/ntgroup/	This site might be good—eventually. At press time, it was still under construction.
Gotham Windows NT User Group	http://www.ntweb.org/	New York's user group.

USER GROUP NAME	SITE	NOTES
Los Angeles NT User Group	http://www.lantug.org/	LA's user group's site. Nicely done with advisories, surveys, and discussion lists.
Windows Associate of NT User Groups	http://www.wantug.org/	This is a site of user groups. If you're looking for one in your area, refer to this site.

Community ConneXion

We had second thoughts about posting this site. Then we decided it's in everyone's best interest if we do. This site is nothing less than a compendium of security loopholes in Microsoft products. Though this site may give hackers and crackers some ideas, it also allows you to build up your defenses to resist attacks on your computer systems. Find the Community ConneXion at http://www.c2.org/hackmsoft/.

The Intel Secrets Page

This site is dedicated to the X86 architecture. You'll find schematics, motherboard designs, manuals, and, of course, secrets. So why is this interesting to you? It may not be, but if you're a programmer, you'll find a wealth of information on exactly the systems for which you're developing. Find the secrets at http://www.x86.org/.

■ Appendix B

■ More Performance Monitoring Tools

Windows NT's Performance Monitor is a slick utility, but you'll probably find yourself wanting something more. We've scoured the Internet for tools designed to improve Windows NT performance and listed some of the best we've found below. Many of these tools are freeware, which you can download and use without any associated costs. Others are shareware. You can download these for free and use them, but you're expected to pay the nominal fee. It's only fair. Some developer somewhere spent long hours creating this tool, and the profits from the shareware may be the developer's main source of income. Of course, if you try shareware and decide you don't like it enough to continue using it, you're not expected to pay—that's the beauty of it.

Finally, we've listed several products that we've reviewed for PC Week. These are the more traditional tools, which you must pay for before using. We've listed their related sites so you can get more information, and most of the Web sites we list have easy ways to contact the respective vendors.

Microsoft Catapult

This freeware is at http://www.microsoft.com/proxy/. Microsoft has tons of free downloads, many of which work with Windows NT 4. These downloads range from patches and fixes to essential tools. We can't possibly list all of the downloads here, but if you're setting up an Internet with Windows NT 4, you can't go wrong with Catapult—the Microsoft Proxy Server. Catapult is a easy way to bring Internet access to every desktop in an organization. Catapult integrates into Windows NT and works with existing networks. If you're setting up Internet access for your organization, make sure you look at Catapult. Also, be sure to look frequently in the Microsoft downloads section (http://www.microsoft.com/msdownloads) for more free software and operating system fixes.

ServerBench

ServerBench® 3.0 is a tool from Ziff-Davis' Benchmark Operation (ZDBop for short) that measures the performance of application servers in a client/server environment. You basically set up a network with a server running Windows NT, or any other supported server-based operating system. set up as many clients as you'll need and designate one as the controller of the test.

From the controller client, you launch ServerBench, and it automatically tests your system as an application server. This is a good comprehensive tool for measuring performance and it's far easier to set up than running performance monitoring software while in production mode. Currently, Server-Bench 3.0 runs on IBM's OS/2 Warp Server, Microsoft's Windows NT Server for Digital Alpha, MIPS, PowerPC, and x86-compatible processors; Novell's NetWare 4.1 and NetWare 4.1 SMP; and The Santa Cruz Operation's SCO OpenServer Release 5 and SCO UnixWare 2.1. According to ZDBop, Server-Bench uses proprietary server, client, and controller programs that require specific network protocols for each server operating system. The test server must have the correct network protocol to run ServerBench.

ServerBench is freeware, and you can find it at http://www.zdnet.com/zdbop/svrbench/svrbench.html.

NetBench

Another ZDBop tool that measures performance is NetBench® 5.0. This portable benchmark program measures how well a file server handles file I/O requests from as many as four different client types: DOS, 32-bit Windows, 16-bit Windows, and/or Mac OS systems. The clients hammer the server with file and print server requests and then create charts that make it easy for you to compare against a baseline system. To run NetBench, you don't need special network protocol software. All you need is a file server, a PC running Windows 95 or Windows for Workgroups (called the controller) to start and monitor the tests, and clients to actually run the tests. NetBench and Server-bench are excellent programs for performance measurement. In fact, PC Week, PC Magazine, and other Ziff-Davis publications have standardized on the tools. They're also free—which makes them the best possible bargain.

NetBench is freeware, and you can find it at http://www.zdnet.com/zdbop/netbench/netbench.html.

Diskeeper

Everyone knows that disk drives under DOS become fragmented over time, slowing performance. But Windows NT FAT and NTFS drives also can become fragmented, and unlike DOS, Windows 3.x, or Windows 95, Windows NT comes with no disk defragmenter utility. That's where Diskeeper comes in. Though this is a manual utility, it works on all system and user disks, all RAID configurations, and even compressed files. Diskeeper even comes with a feature that detects how fragmented a drive has become so you'll know when to run the program. This is a free "lite" version of Diskeeper, a more feature-rich product.

You'll find Diskeeper at http://www.ans.se/dskkpr/. The filename is
DKLITE_I.zip.

SeNTry

SeNTry monitors WINNT Event Logs and translates them into a common
database format to make it easier for administrators to sort through the
logs—which can grow quite lengthy. The main reason for doing this is so that
administrators can keep an eye on critical conditions; SeNTry sends all of
them to any ODBC database format that an administrator specifies. Administrators then can use powerful third-party reporting tools to get a better idea
of how their server is running. SeNTry is shareware, free to download for a
30-day evaluation. You'll find it at http://www.ntsoftdist.com. The file name is
sentry.zip.

RegSearch

Anyone who's dealt with Windows 95 or Windows NT knows the registry is
extremely difficult to navigate. RegSearch is one of those essential niche
tools whose sole purpose is to make it easier to wade through the Registry.
RegSearch is shareware, and you'll find it at http://oak.oakland.edu. The
file name is regsrc.zip.

Batch Job Server

Batch Job Server is a 32-bit program that manages the scheduling, queuing,
and execution of Windows NT batch files (batch jobs) submitted by users,
programs or other host systems. Administrators submit jobs to Batch Scheduler, and it ensures that all the jobs will run at the specified time. Simple?
Yes, but there's nothing quite like this in Windows NT. This program is free
to download, but it costs $75 to register.
http://www.halcyon.com/camellia/. The file name is BJSA.ZIP.

FireDoor

FireDoor is similar to Catapult—it's made to keep a corporate network
secure from intrusion once a connection to the Internet is made. This free
version is made for a single user. All kinds of connections to the Internet are
supported, from T1 to dial-up, with all major Internet protocols supported.
FireDoor is shareware; you'll find it at http://www.ozemail.com.au/
~equival/.

Guardian

Another firewall system, Guardian also prevents intrusion to a network from the Internet. Guardian is shareware, located at http://www.netguard.com/.

■ Products for Sale

PerformanceWorks

Landmark Systems Corporation specializes in network and client/server performance tools. The company's PerformanceWorks for Windows NT delivers all the tools you'll need to manage and monitor the performance of your Windows NT network. Best of all, you can use the tools while your network is up in production mode—that is, real-time monitoring. This enables you to see exact measurements so that you can pinpoint bottlenecks before they happen. Performance Works is at http://www.landmark.com.

BlueCurve Dynameasure

BlueCurve is a relatively new company, but its Dynameasure product is dynamite! This is by far the easiest total performance management tool we've seen. If there's anything we can ding it on, it's that at press time, it only worked with Windows NT networks and SQL Server 6.x. It's also pricey, at around $25,000. Rumor has it that BlueCurve will start shipping an Oracle version and will make components of the Dynameasure test suite available at more affordable prices. Dynameasure also doesn't measure real-time performance; instead, it's used for capacity planning—a job we think it's best-of-class in. Dynameasure is at http://www.bluecurve.com.

Microsoft Windows NT Resource Kit

The Resource Kit has a wealth of information about Windows NT. It's a set of books (the last set contained three hefty tomes) and software that aims to answer almost every question an administrator might have about Windows NT. The book is expensive and dry, though we consider it a necessity. At press time, the book was not updated to include Windows NT 4. However, many of the free utilities, of which there are several performance measurement tools, will work with Windows NT 4. You'll find the Microsoft Resource Kit at http://www.microsoft.com/mspress.

■ Specialized Testing Tools

The following companies are best known for their graphical user interface testing tools. However, all of them have a product that allows administrators to place a load on a database server and measure performance. This is critical in the Windows NT environment in which the server is often used for application services. These tools allow administrators to stress test their configuration before putting the configuration into production mode. If you plan on installing and running any database server, or if you anticipate developing products for Windows NT, plan on visiting these sites.

- Segue Software Inc. QA Partner—http://www.segue.com

- SQA Inc. SQA Suite—http://www.sqa.com

- Mercury Interactive WinRunner and LoadRunner—
  http://www.merc-int.com

■ Appendix C

■ Certified Backup Software

When backing up a server, you don't want to mess around with third-rate utilities that could fail at the worst possible moments. Most backup programs back up data flawlessly. It's in the restore process that the lesser programs fail. That's why your company needs to invest in the best backup program it can afford. Here's a list of the seven best-known backup programs certified to work with Windows NT.

Cheyenne ArcServe for Windows NT

Cheyenne has not just one product for backing up Windows NT, but a suite of products built around its flagship product, ArcServe. ArcServe was one of the backup programs for Novell NetWare, so the company has a lot of experience with PC server-based systems. Recently—as this book was going to print as a matter of fact—Computer Associates purchased Cheyenne, so you should investigate how Computer Associates views its newly acquired product line and whether ArcServe will be integrated into the company's Computer Associates-Unicenter platform. Arcserve uses a proprietary tape format and is not compatible with any other tape format. So if you're making the transition from one backup system to another, beware.

Cheyenne Software Inc.
3 Expressway Plaza
Roslyn Heights, NY 11577
Phone: 516-484-5110
Fax: 516-484-3446
http://www.cheyenne.com

Palindrome Corporation Backup Director

Palindrome has been around since 1987 with Backup Director. The company was recently purchased by Seagate Software, a division of the huge hard drive manufacturer. Seagate has a reputation for making normally mundane software extremely easy to use. Backup Director is a powerful backup program with a host of features that may win many corporate face-offs. However, the program doesn't have as many disaster recovery features as ArcServe. We think Backup Director's feature set and ease of use more than makes up for its lack of disaster recovery features, making it an excellent choice for all but the pickiest companies.

Palindrome Corp.
600 E. Diehl Road
Naperville, IL 60563
Phone: 708-505-3300
Fax: 708-505-7917
http://www.palindrome.com

Arcada Storage Exec

Storage Exec is another solid backup system that has its roots in the Net-Ware environment. Like other backup programs, Storage Exec has strong management capabilities and supports backup compression and tape spanning. Storage Exec can also read ArcServe tapes, making it possible to switch over from the Cheyenne product gracefully without losing any time or tape investment. Although Storage Exec will win a lot of checklist wars, it can't back up after a primary disk failure, as its competitors can. Before purchasing it, make sure the company has added this feature.

Arcada Software Inc.
37 Skyline Drive
Lake Mary, FL 32746
Phone: 407-333-7500
Fax: 407-333-7770
http://www.arcada.com

Legato Networker

Networker for Windows NT has all the features a company expects from a good backup program, including excellent event notification in the case of a failure (the program can e-mail you or page you). Like many others, Legato works on different operating systems such as OS/2, Windows NT, NetWare 3.x, NetWare 4.x, UNIX, and Vines. The only problem is that Networker requires more system resources and has had performance problems. With today's fast hardware, Networker should allow companies to back up all but the biggest data sets in a single night—the key time frame in a server-class environment.

Legato Systems Inc.
3145 Porter Drive
Palo Alto, CA 94304
Phone: 415-812-6000
Fax: 415-812-6032
http://www.legato.com

In addition to the more traditional software listed above, there are several backup solutions that may suit your company's needs.

Boole and Babbage

Boole and Babbage's Storage Division has software that allows companies to back up files from Microsoft Windows NT to IBM mainframes. Called Stage3, it uses Seagate Technology Inc.'s Arcada Backup Exec, and it appears as an option on the Arcada Backup Exec screen.

Boole & Babbage Corporate Headquarters
3131 Zanker Road
San Jose, California 95134-1933
Phone: 408-526-3484 or 800-544-2152
Fax: 408-526-3053
E-mail: info@boole.com
http://www.catalog.com/boole/Welcome.html

Rimage Televaulting Service

Rimage offers a unique service that we're not sure what to make of yet. The company allows you to back up your company data remotely using high-speed analog or digital ISDN phone lines. Rimage then stores your data onto optical media. The company says it can handle networks with hundreds of users (incremental backups, we assume). To make this happen, Rimage installs software on your network that allows it to become a remote node. They then make a mirror image of all your data, set up passwords, encrypt and compress the data, and transmit it to the Rimage location. Check it out, but be cautious. After all, your corporate data is your second most valuable asset (after your employees, of course).

Televaulting Headquarters
Rimage Central Service Center
7725 Washington Avenue South
Minneapolis, MN 55439
Phone: 612-944-8144
Fax: 612-944-780
http://www.rimage.com

Barratt Edwards International Ultraback

We don't know much about Ultraback, having never reviewed the product. On paper, however, the product looks like a winner that should be evaluated. For more information, contact the company at:

Barratt Edwards International Corporation
14850 Lake Hills Blvd., Suite B-4
Bellevue, Washington 98007
Phone: 206-644-6000
Fax: 206-644-8222
e-mail: info@beicorp.com

■ Appendix D

■ Free Windows NT Utilities

Windows NT is one of the least expensive enterprise-capable operating systems around. But you can still locate utilities and demos you can evaluate for free. All it takes is some time and a connection to the Internet. We've perused the Internet for shareware, freeware, and demo applications designed to run under Windows NT. We can't possibly cover all of the available software—in fact, more software is posted online every day! So we'll just stick to a few entries. If there's any utility we've missed that you'd like to see covered in the next edition of this book, let us know. You can reach us at the e-mail addresses listed in the Introduction.

Microsoft Index Server

Don't brush off this program because it's free. Microsoft Index Server is a powerful program that keeps track of all the files on a Windows NT Server 4. Designed to work with Microsoft's IIS 2.0, which ships with NT 4, the Index Server allows users to query files anywhere on a corporate intranet. Though the Index Server is a separate product now, you'll probably see it included in a future release of Windows NT.

Users can query titles or even the contents of files, including those in Word, Excel, or an HTML page. To allow for this querying, the Index Server provides tools for administrators to create custom forms. Users then simply enter into the form the parameters of their query, and the Index Server returns the results. Even better is that the Index Server can run on autopilot, tracking all new files automatically without administrator intervention. You'll find Index Server at http://www.microsoft.com/msdownload.

The Java Developers Kit

The Java Developers Kit is for developers who want to develop Java applets that can be run from a Java-ready browser, such as Microsoft Internet Explorer or NetScape Navigator. Java has taken the development world by storm making this a must-have product. You'll find the Java Developers Kit at http://java.sun.com/products/JDK/index.html.

The Java Workshop

The Java Workshop is a programming environment for creating Web applications. This environment is written in Java itself and so it's portable, running on any hardware platform or operating system that supports the Java Virtual Machine. Look for the Java Workshop at http://www.sun.com/960325/feature1/index.html.

Liquid Motion Pro

Liquid Motion Pro, from DimensionX Inc., which is available in a free trial copy, is a drag and drop tool that allows developers and power users to create slick applications without coding. It's a hot product, and it's a worthwhile download. Liquid Motion Pro is at http://www.dimensionx.com/products/lm/index.html.

Microsoft ActiveX Software Development Kit

Let's just say that ActiveX is Microsoft's biggest push into Internet development ever—so much so that the company is staking a big chunk of change on making sure ActiveX succeeds. ActiveX is a key set of technologies that allow developers to integrate the Internet into Windows applications. ActiveX consists of component controls for easier developing, a scripting language, and the Java Virtual Machine. There's at least a half dozen books worth of material here, so we'll just point you in the right direction. ActiveX is at http://www.microsoft.com/activex/.

Microsoft Visual J++

Visual J++ is Microsoft's Java development tool complete with a debugger and Wizards that take some of the bite off of programming this relatively new language. Visual J++ seems to be in eternal beta, so check this FTP site often for updates. The address is ftp://ftp.microsoft.com/msdownload/sbn/vj/.

NetCraft

NetCraft from SourceCraft Inc. is a tool for creating multimedia Java applets. You basically use its UI Builder to develop an interface and NetCraft automatically turns all of the objects into Java code. This is a freeware product. Find it at http://www.sourcecraft.com:4800/area/download/.

WinGEN for Java

WinGEN from PRO-C Inc. allows developers to create sophisticated Java applications without having to know Java. Like NetCraft, you use the WinGEN environment to develop applications and magically out comes commented Java code. This is limited free trial version. Find it at http://www.pro-c.com/products/wfj/demo.html.

Cold Fusion

If you need to connect your Web server to a back-end database, Cold Fusion from Allaire Corp. is for you. Cold Fusion somehow manages to tame the complexities involved in this normally arduous task. Allaire offers a 30-day trial version of the software. It's at http://www.allaire.com/.

Fastlane Technologies Incorporated

Fastlane is a development tool and language that lets NT administrators automate their jobs. Find Fastlane at http://www.fastlane.on.ca.

Helpful Tip

> *There are a ton of useful Internet client utilities—most of which are free—on the Internet. For the best of them, check http://www.microsoft.com/msdownload/ and http://www.microsoft.com/ntserver/tools/iclient.htm.*

More Freeware or Shareware

Product name	Site	Filename	Description
Yet Another Time Synchronizer	ftp.winsite.com	yats32.zip	Synchronizes system clock with standard time services on the Internet.
WinBind	http://www.tucows.interlynx.net/server95.html	winbind.zip	DNS name server
War FTP Daemon	http://home.sol.no/jgaa/tftpd.htm	warftpd1.20b.exe	Powerful FTP Daemon
Netproxy	http://www.bitools.com/netproxy/index.html	netprx12.zip	Multiple-protocol proxy server and firewall.
Open Sesame	http://www.csm-usa.com/sesame.htm	sesames.zip	Proxy/Gateway Server. Supports all major internet protocols.

Product name	Site	Filename	Description
WinProxy	http://www.lanprojekt.cz/winproxy	wp1_3b.zip	Proxy server for that accesses the Internet from a local net through only one IP address
BootpdNT	http://rebel.tellurian.com.au/bootpdNT	bootpdnt.zip	Turns Windows NT into a bootp Internet address server
Dstats	ftp.winsite.com	dstats11.zip	Web server log analyzer
4DOS for NT	ftp.csusm.edu	4nt25c.zip	Popular command line processor now for NT
Copyreg	ftp.csusm.edu	copyreg.zip	Copies registry entries between NT systems
Dumpdisk	ftp.csusm.edu	dmpdsk11.zip	Lets you edit NTFS disks
SOMAR Dump Reg	ftp.csusm.edu	dumpreg.zip	Dumps registry values for easier viewing
Editeur	ftp.csusm.edu	ed22nt.zip	Souped up NT text editor

In addition to the files that appear above, check out the following Web sites that contain more Windows NT programs that can be downloaded from within your Web browser:

- http://www.zdnet.com
- http://www.shareware.com
- http://www.bhs.com
- http://www.csusm.edu/NT.html
- http://www.athenaclc.com/html/misc/ntsites.htm
- http://bbs.reproms.si/files/pub/reproms/Windows-NT/Shareware
- http://www.infonetwww.com/sharewnt.htm
- http://www.chancellor.com/ntprog.html
- http://www.koreainterad.com/softw-win_nt.html
- http://bsoftware.com

■ Appendix E

■ Questions and Answers*

The following are real questions asked by participants in the Beverly Hill Software technical forum. Answers are provided by forum members, so we can't take credit (or blame) for the answers. All we did here was put the text into a question and answer format, stripped off private user information, and modified the text slightly for readability.

The Beverly Hills Software site is one of the best Windows NT user groups on the Net, and we check it often. We hope these questions will help you solve some of your own problems. Unfortunately, we couldn't put all the questions and answers into our book, but Beverly Hills Software keeps the threads running all day and night—you can even get on a list server that sends to you via e-mail the questions as they're asked. For those that get too much e-mail anyway, check out the Web site: it's at http://www.bhs.com.

Question: Is there any way to remotely administer an NT 3.51 Server from a Windows 95 workstation?

Answer: There are several NT administrative tools for Windows 95: Server Manager, User Manager for Domains, and Event Viewer among them. Download them from the Microsoft Web page or check update #2 of the Windows NT Resource Kit.

Question: I'm looking for tools that can capture information about NT permissions, server share points, and user data. I want this information for documentation purposes, but would like to automate the task. Any suggestions?

Answer: Software from FastLane (or is it FastTrack) enables you to pull information and to automate jobs. One of their products, FINAL, may be especially helpful. Depending on what you're trying to automate, you may be able to use native NT commands such as NET USER to create users and SETDACL to set directory access control lists.

Question: Does anyone have any experience adding virtual Web servers beyond the five IP addresses that NT imposes? I know how to bypass this limit (go directly to the Registry) but I don't know what to expect in performance.

Answer: Virtual Web servers are quite simple. In the TCP/IP setup for your network adapter card, add the IP addresses you'll be using for the virtual Web sites. Then restart NT so these new IP addresses will be bound to the network adapter card. Start IIS Service Manager (make sure IIS is also running) and double-click on your Web server to open up Properties. Go to the Directories tab and click on New. Then browse to the directory you want as home for the virtual Web site, choose Home-page and Virtual Server, and enter the IP address for that virtual server. Click on OK.

When you return to the Directories tab, you'll notice a new directory at the top with an IP address associated with it. I recently set up a machine with five virtual Web sites on it, and the process went very smoothly. Instructions for adding more than five IP addresses are in the documentation. See the help file under Virtual Server.

Caution

> *FrontPage extensions on virtual Web servers are problematic. Sometimes you must remove all virtual server mappings before you can use FrontPage.*

Question: What performance hits can you expect by having multiple IP addresses on a node? Is it a constant hit per address (say, 5% per IP) or is there a curve, and performance begins to drop radically at some point?

Answer: I have five virtual servers on our Web server and performance is pretty good. Too bad nobody has done a study on this (at least none that we can find).

Question: Assume that the access permissions for all the drives on the computers are for accounts that no longer exist and can't be recreated. Is there any way to get logged onto the NT machine to take back control? None of our logon passwords work any more; as soon as you log on with one of them, the machine just shuts down. On a UNIX machine, I would just restart the machine in single-user mode and put things back to normal. I fear there's no such feature with NT, and that I'm going to have to reformat the drive and reinstall everything. Is that so?

Answer: Your workstation is part of a domain; thus you should be able to set the domain to the local workstation and log on using the administrator account and password you chose during installation. This doesn't change, regardless of the machine's membership in a domain, so it won't depend on finding the domain controller.

This is about as close to single-user mode that NT can get. I had a somewhat similar situation, except our domain controller decided to stop accepting logons from *anywhere*, including the local machine. After three hours on the phone with Microsoft tech support and no solution, we ended up reinstalling. Naturally, we didn't have a backup, either.

So the Golden Rule of NT Server administration is if you have more than one server in a domain, make one a BDC. And do it at installation, not later, since you can't convert a standard server to a BDC without reinstalling NT Server. Anyone else have an NT Golden Rule?

Question: Can a BDC be moved from one domain to another and still remain a BDC? Can it even be moved at all?

Answer: If the BDC you want to move is currently a member of a valid domain, then yes, it can become a BDC in another domain, just as if you were moving an NT Workstation or application server. A domain controller must be reinstalled in order to change domains. Only member servers can change domains without reinstalling. This has to do with the security ID that gets created for the computer account.

Question: I'm having difficulties with a USR Winmodem 28.8 (upgradeable to 33.6). I've contacted USR and all I've received is an e-mail for their fax solutions. Microsoft's update for Windows NT 4 modem.inf file includes entries for USR modems similar to their recommended .inf file, which so far, I've not been able to connect.

Answer: The problems with USR Sportster 28.8 v.34 are well documented. Look at http://www.usr.com/home/2055.html for updated software from USR. Also look at http://www.microsoft.com/kb/bussys/winnt/Q139470.htm, which might be also relevant.

Question: I want to move my Windows NT 4 installation from the primary partition on disk 1 to a partition on disk 0. I have Windows 95 in the primary partition on disk 0 formatted FAT 16. The existing Windows NT partition is NTFS. Can I move everything without re-installing and restoring from tape? Should I format the target partition FAT 16 and then convert to NTFS, or should I format NTFS in the first place?

Answer: Create a bootable floppy that contains the NT boot loader. This disk comes in handy when you want to change the boot drive on multiple disk systems, reload operating systems, or someone accidentally wipes out the root directory of the boot partition. You'll be able to boot NT off this floppy in seconds and fix the problem later without having to use the repair disks.

Assuming you've moved your paging file to somewhere besides C:, what the floppy does is allow you to wipe out the boot partition entirely, which you couldn't do without a floppy because it would contain open files there. Now, for making the floppy:

1. Using NT's command windows, format a new floppy with the command FORMAT A: /FS:FAT /L:BOOTNT /U. This formats the floppy using the FAT filesystem, labels it bootnt and does the format unconditionally. Additional options can be placed on the command line (use format /? to see all options).

2. Using the NT File Manager or Explorer, copy the hidden file C:\ NTLDR onto the A: disk.

3. Using the NT File Manager or Explorer, copy the hidden file C:\NTDETECT.COM onto the A: disk.

4. Using the NT File Manager or Explorer, copy the hidden file C:\ BOOT.INI onto the A: disk.

The floppy should now be bootable.

The NTLDR and NTDETECT.COM files from NT 4 appear to boot the 3.51 operating system, but not visa-versa. If you're installing 3.51 and 4 on the same computer, you'll either need to install 4 after 3.51 or have a backup floppy like this from your 4 system prepared and tested before you install 3.51. Then all you need to do is boot 3.51 and replace the files from the floppy over the ones on the hard disk from 3.51 (but not the newly changed boot.ini file, or you'll lose your entries for the new 3.51 OS).

NOTE. *NTLDR has to be the first file copied to disk or the boot process will fail.*

NTLDR, NTDETECT and BOOT.INI are only startup files. When you look into boot.ini, you'll see that the path points to the NT directory. The next thing executed from _hdd_ is NTOSKRNL and that's—officially or not—the most important part of an operating system.

Helpful Tip

Keep the C:\BOOT.INI file on your floppy disk current; you'll need to recopy it to the floppy if you reinstall NT in a different partition or directory).

Question: I'm looking for tools that can capture information about NT permissions, server share points, and user data. I want this information for documentation purposes, but would like to automate the task. Any suggestions?

Answer: Software from FastLane (or maybe it's FastTrack) allows you to pull information and to automate jobs. A product called FINAL, in particular, may be helpful. Depending on what you're trying to automate, you may be able to use native NT commands, such as NET USER, to create users and SETDACL to set directory ACLs.

Question: I'm having trouble getting RAS to work in NT 4.0b2. I have a triple boot system with MS DOS 6.2, NT 3.51, and NT 4.0b2. I've configured TCP/IP for Windows 95 with instructions from my ISP. The RAS will log on to my provider but when the username and password are being verified, the system just hangs up. Usually it reports ERROR #2, and if I click on More Info, it shows something that appears to be a program variable.

Answer: Deactivate the Enable PPP LCP extensions on the Properties sheet for the RAS phonebook entry. Then select Accept any authentication, including clear text, on the Security sheet.

Question: How can I disable CD autoplay?

Answer: Use Regedit to disable Autorun. This isn't for the faint-of-heart, but the following has worked.

In RegEdit open the following keys:

HKEY_LOCAL_MACHINE\SYSTEM\CONTROLSETxxx\Services\ CDROM

Where xxx is 002 003, and so on.

In each of these keys there'll be an Autorun value, probably set to 1. Change it to 0 and restart NT. The Autorun is no longer active.

Question: I have a ZIP-drive connected to an NT 4 Server, and the server does not appear to know that this is a removable media. It doesn't flush the cache when I try to eject the disk. Anybody know what to do???

Answer: If the zip drive is from IOMEGA, they've posted a patch to make the drive work over the parallel port. We hope this helps.

Question: Is it possible to read and write to my HPFS drive from NT 4? I'd even be willing to pay for a way to do this.

Answer: Copy pinball.sys from 3.51 to your nt40\system32\drivers directory. Edit your registry hkey_local_machine->system->controlset001->services. Create a new key called pinball. Under pinball create:

ErrorControl: REG_DWORD: 0x1

Group: REG_SZ: Boot file system

Start: REG_DWORD: 0x1

Type: REG_DWORD: 0x2

That should do it. Unfortunately chkdsk doesn't seem to work, but you can read and write to your hpfs disks.

Question: I need ideas for how to monitor RAS connection information.

Answer: Use Performance Monitor to view the status of your RAS. Under Performance Monitor you can see stats for all RAS ports and even use the alert log to send network messages if the port drops below 1 bps.

Question: Is there an application that can read DAT tapes recorded on NT. I'd like to migrate some data to DOS, Windows 3.x, and/or Windows 95, but the Cheyenne Software (ARCSOLO) can't read the format type.

Answer: You'll have to find tape software that will read the Microsoft tape format. The NT backup software is a stripped version of backup software from Arcada (now Seagate Software), and it uses the Microsoft tape format. Seagate Backup for Windows 95 should work, although I'd confirm it through them. The older Arcada version of this product should work with

Windows for Workgroups. It's located at http://www.smg.seagatesoftware.com/ds-win95.htm.

Question: What happens when you change the computer name in a domain controller? I've heard that even swapping names between servers can damage the trust domain.

Answer: It shouldn't hurt any trust relationships to change the name of a server since the trust relationship is between the domains, not the servers. Even if it does, it's simple to re-establish a trust relationship.

Question: When I reboot my NT Server PDC, workstation service does not start and I get message in Event Viewer that "Name already exists on network". The server is not the PDC then, of course. I changed the master browser setting in other machines in the area to be "none" but it doesn't help. When I unplug the server cable from the network, reboot it, and then plug it back into network, it all works fine. I have NetBEUI, IPX/SPX, and TCP/IP protocols installed and working. My name server is on an HP-UX machine. Others are Windows 95 and Windows for Workgroups. There are also two HP-UX machines on the same cable. The network is connected with the world by a Cisco router. Behind the router there are other NTs. This didn't change when I created the NT BDC on cable.

Answer: I've encountered this problem when running two network cards in a server on the same wire. This is a NetBEUI problem. It can't be caused by something across a router, because NetBEUI doesn't do routers. I would suggest running nbtstat -n to see if it will give you the network adapter card addresses of the conflicting names. Or, you could remove NetBEUI altogether. You can't have two network adapter cards on the same physical cable segment and run NetBEUI.

Question: I'm a brand new NT 4 user, and I was wondering if I can hook up two computers, one running NT 4 and the other running Windows 95 through 95's direct cable connection settings. I don't know too much about networking, but the person who sold me NT 4 said it should be possible. He also sold me the parallel cable!

Answer: To my knowledge this isn't possible. NT doesn't have any parallel direct connect capabilities. You'll have to install network cards. They're as inexpensive as chips these days. You'll get much more performance from network cards than from the parallel port anyway.

Question: Can I access the WINS database in a server outside of my domain?

Answer: To access the WINS database in a foreign domain, you must use an account that has access to that domain where the WINS data base resides, either explicitly, or via a trust. As you've seen, the local Administrator account of a resource domain has no such authority over Master Account

Domain Resources. I spoke with a WINS expert at Microsoft about this limitation and he agreed it's annoying at best.

Regarding replication, make sure that both the local WINS server and the central WINS server have Pull triggers configured identically for each other. This means the same start time and same interval. Also make sure that each server's clocks are roughly synchronized. Your problem is probably that you don't have PULL configured the same on both sides, and you need to provide some replication interval—leaving it blank won't work. Basically, MS has told me that they don't recommend any replication between two WINS servers other than two-way PUSH-PULL. Hope that helps

Question: We're experiencing a problem with a worldwide Windows NT network and WINS. It employs the master domain model with a BDC in every site and several resource domains sprinkled throughout, with a local domain at each site that trusts the master. The problem is that when we try to pull data down from the central site, it doesn't seem to be updating itself. When we log on to the local domain using the Administrator account, it comes up with a security error when querying the database. However, if we log on as the administrator of the master domain, we can query and see all of its names. The local domain with the WINS server that's having the problem is operating on a WAN over a ISDN line. Is that too slow, or is it possible that there's some sort of security snafu preventing it from synchronizing properly? The central WINS database has less than 2000 names.

Answer: In fact, you definitely want them to be both PUSH and PULL with each other. This ensures that the database is consistent between the two. Make sure you set the PUSH and PULL parameters the same on each side, and run JetPack against the databases on a regular basis. (See the Windows NT Resource Kit for information on this utility.)

Question: I have a primary WINS server setup, and I'm planning to set up a secondary one in order to distribute the load and just have another one available at all times. Can you set them both up as push and pull servers, or must one be a push and the other pull? I would like each of them to update the other when changes take place on one. However, I was concerned that if they're both push/pull, this might trigger a loop of pushing and pulling. Should I be concerned, and is there a better way of doing what I'm attempting to do?

Answer: Use the Schedule service to stop the RAS at a specified time, then restart them. Use the 'at' program to schedule, or if you have the NT Resource Kit, a GUI program will do the same thing.

Question: Is there a way of shutting down a modem link at a specified time? I would like to disconnect my modem at around 6 a.m. Is there an built-in way of doing that? Or does anyone know of a program that will help me do it?

Answer: The file name is NTconfig.pol and is placed in the PDC net-logon share (which is the same place you pointed out in your notes). The fact that the name is NTconfig.pol vs Config.pol means that you can keep both Windows NT and Windows 95 policies in the same directory.

Question: I've been struggling to discover where the config.pol (the file resulting from the policies set by the Windows 95 or Windows NT 4 policy editor) should be placed on a standalone workstation. On NT Server-connected machines, the file resides in winnt/system32/repl/imports/. Where might I place the policy file? The system root and win95\system were not able to enforce my policies for the NT 4 users sharing the machine. Any suggestions for where to place the file to enforce individual user privileges on the system?

Answer: If TCP/IP is your only protocol, you'll want to have a WINS server running to resolve NetBIOS names to IP addresses (or you could manually set up a LMHOSTS file, but this isn't as easy to manage long-term).

Question: I just got a copy of Windows NT 4 and would like to install it. I currently have a Compaq Armada 1120 laptop running Windows 95. For now I'll probably keep both on the machine. I have an 850MB hard drive with about 400 MB left. I don't want to run out of hard drive space. Can I use Drivespace in Windows 95 and then install NT 4? If so, how do I partition the compressed and uncompressed sections? Later I want to have only NT on the machine. Currently I use a Backpack CD-ROM and have installed the 32-bit drivers. However, suppose I reformat the hard drive to start from scratch and then try to install NT 4. The machine will not immediately see the CD-ROM and I need to use it for the NT installation since I have the CD for NT. Is there a way to load the backpack device as part of the NT install?

Answer: As to your first question, sorry. Windows 95 compression is not readable by NT. As to your second one, yes, press F6 when booting and NT will allow you to add a driver.

Question: I'm looking for a third-party Web remote administration tool. I saw something about it a few months ago and lost the address. Unlike the Microsoft tool that comes with NT 4, this tool actually allows you to start and stop services via any Web browser. Can anyone help?

Answer: What you're looking for is a software product from Microsoft. Check out www.microsoft.com/ntserver/webadmin/webadmin.htm.

* Information supplied courtesy of Beverly Hills Software—http://www.BHS.com

■ Glossary

ARAP	AppleTalk Remote Access Protocol
ARC	attached resources computing
ATM	asynchronous transfer mode
BDC	backup domain controller
CHAP	Challenge Handshake Authentication Protocol
COM	component object model
DAT	digital audio tapes
DLC	data link control
DHCP	Dynamic Host Configuration Protocol
DMA	direct memory access
DNS	Domain Naming System
EISA	extended industry standard architecture
FDDI	Fiber Distributed Data Interface
FAT	file attribute table
FQDN	fully qualified domain names
FTP	File Transfer Protocol
FPNW	File and Print Services for NetWare
GSNW	Gateway Services for NetWare
HTML	hypertext markup language
HTTP	Hypertext Transfer Protocol

IDC	Internet database connector
IDE	integrated device electronics
IIS	Internet Information Server
I/O	input/output
IP	Internet Protocol
IPX	Internet Packet Exchange
IRQ	interrupt request line
ISA	industry standard architecture
ISAPI	Internet services application programming interface
ISDN	integrated systems digital network
ISM	Internet Service Manager
ISP	Internet service provider
LAN	local area network
LPD	line printer daemon
LPR	line printer remote
MAC	media access control
MIPS	millions of instructions per second
NetBIOS	network basic input/output system
NetBEUI	NetBIOS Extended User Interface
NDIS	network driver interface specification
NDS	NetWare Directory Services
NFS	network file system

NTFS	NT File System
ODBC	open database connectivity
PAP	Password Authentication Protocol
PCI	peripheral component interconnect
PDC	primary domain controller
PCMIA	Personal Computer Memory Card International Association
PID	process ID
PIO	programmable input/output
PPP	Point-to-Point Protocol
PPTP	Point-to-Point Tunneling Protocol
RAID	redundant array of inexpensive disks
RAS	remote access service
RIP	Routing Information Protocol
RISC	reduced instruction set computing
RPC	remote procedure calls
RPL	remote program load
SAP	Service Advertising Protocol
SCSI	small computer system interface
SNA	systems network architecture
SMB	server message block
SMP	symmetric multiprocessing
SNMP	Simple Network Management Protocol

SPAP	Shiva Password Authentication Protocol
SPX	Sequenced Packet Exchange
SQL	structured query language
SSL	secure sockets layer
TCP/IP	Transmission Control Protocol/Internet Protocol
UART	universal asynchronous receiver/transmitter
UNC	universal naming convention
UPS	uninterruptable power supply
URL	uniform resource locator
VLM	virtual loadable model
WAN	wide area network
WINS	Windows Internet Naming Service
WWW	World Wide Web

■ Index